Scandals and Abstraction

Scandals and Abstraction

FINANCIAL FICTION OF THE LONG 1980S

Leigh Claire La Berge

OXFORD
UNIVERSITY PRESS

OXFORD
UNIVERSITY PRESS

Oxford University Press is a department of the University of Oxford. It furthers
the University's objective of excellence in research, scholarship, and education
by publishing worldwide. Oxford is a registered trade mark of Oxford University
Press in the UK and certain other countries.

Published in the United States of America by Oxford University Press
198 Madison Avenue, New York, NY 10016, United States of America.

© Oxford University Press 2015

First issued as an Oxford University Press paperback, 2020

Library of Congress Cataloging-in-Publication Data
La Berge, Leigh Claire.
Scandals and abstraction : financial fiction of the long 1980s / Leigh Claire La Berge.
pages   cm
Includes index.
ISBN 978-0-19-937287-4 (hardback) | ISBN 978-0-19-084598-8 (paperback) |
ISBN 978-0-19-937288-1 (ebook)
1. American fiction—20th century—History and criticism.   2. Money in literature.
3. Finance in literature.   4. Capitalism and literature.   5. Financial crises in literature.   I. Title.
PS374.M54L3   2014
813.009'3553—dc23   2014033968

To my parents, Ann La Berge, Bernard La Berge,
and Marshall Fishwick; but especially for you, Mom

{ CONTENTS }

{ ACKNOWLEDGMENTS }

This book got its start as a dissertation in the American Studies Program at New York University. Now that I myself have been through the program, and have researched and taught at other universities, I look back on my time at NYU and think: I can't believe how lucky I was. Andrew Ross is as generous and critical an advisor as one could hope for; Kristin Ross is not only a role model intellectually and pedagogically, but also a trusted friend; Mary Poovey is one of the most perspicacious readers I've encountered; Randy Martin continues to provide an example of how to think about value across disciplines and mediums. Outside of my committee, the Marx Reading Group, which morphed into the Dissertation Writing Group, was a place to refine my ideas and learn how to help colleagues refine theirs: Thank you, Maggie Clinton, Michael Palm, John Pat Leary, Quinn Slobodian, Ipek Celic, and Diego Benegas.

At the University of Chicago I found an inspired and inspiring community in the Society of Fellows, including Nitzan Shoshan, Anita Chari, Mara Marin, Emily Steinlight, Reha Kakadal, Ben McKeon, and Dina Gusejnova. Away from the Society, Lauren Berlant and the Affective Publics groups provided a space to work through methodological problems in genuinely new and creative ways. Now at Saint Mary's University, my colleagues in the English department provide intellectual support and a collegial home: Phanuel Antwi, Teresa Heffernan, Steph Morely, and Goran Stanivukovic, I'm thinking of you; outside of the English department Darryl Leroux and John Munro are models of political scholarship. Other scholars such as Andrew Hoberek, Annie McClanahan, Alison Shonkwiler, Alissa Karl, Megan Obourn, Miranda Joseph, Richard Dienst, Aimee Bahng, Joshua Clover, Marcia Kay Klotz, Harry Harootunian, Richard Godden, Maria Farland, Andy Cornell, J. D. Connor, Sarah Brouillette, Doug Henwood, Colleen Lye, Mathias Nilges, Fiona Allon, and Max Haiven, have had large and small conversations with me. Anna Kornbluh is trusted scholar, colleague and friend. Debra Channick helped me with the introduction and the beginning; Doug Barrett helped me with formatting and finishing.

The readers' reports for this book were quite encouraging; one reader in particular took the time to read this manuscript as empathetically and critically as anything of mine has ever been read. I want to thank this person not only for their incisive and generous criticism, but for modeling for me a form of collegiality and collaboration. At Oxford University Press, Brendan O'Neill and Stephen Bradley have been a pleasure to work with. Martha Rosler gave me permission to use her photograph on the cover. My father, Bernard E. La Berge, and my stepfather, Marshall Fishwick, are in these pages in spirit, but no longer here in actual fact. I find it a wonderful historical irony that Marshall taught Tom Wolfe and shared with me their correspondence. Louisa La Berge and Robert, Jack, and Elisabeth Emmett provided a home away from home; Bette Druck provided an actual home. And the Mitten. Finally, two people, both wonderful scholars in their own right, have been my editors, my critics, my soundboards, my encouragement, and my support since, basically, 1999, when I began to think about the relationship between capital and culture in a way that is still recognizable to me today: Ann La Berge and Dehlia Hannah. For Mom, your early morning editing and phone calls have sustained me through many a paper, presentation, application, chapter, and now book; and, for Dehlia, you will always be on my dance card at the predators' ball. To both of you: "Thanks" is a modest return on your investments in me, but it follows the law of compound interest.

Scandals and Abstraction

Introduction

When Marcus Burns, a fictional character important to my book's late twentieth-century archive, articulates his personal philosophy of money, the resulting statement is as ridiculous as it is profound: "Money these days is like water, it's just looking for a place to go." Marcus, who appears in Jane Smiley's *Good Faith*, a novel set during the 1980s savings and loan (S&L) scandals, occupies the recognizable American literary role of a confidence man.[1] He employs a diversity of phrases and idioms to explain in his own vernacular what exists for political economists as a historical fact and for me as a literary one: The United States in the 1980s was beset by a phase of overaccumulation of money capital. Money, Marcus explains, is now "like cockroaches, for every dollar you see there's a hundred more in hiding and it's looking for a home." Indeed money in the 1980s did search for higher profits, as it arrived from abroad through the third-world debt crisis and as money already here was given the freedom to circulate more quickly and expansively as a result of banking deregulation.[2] Surveying the time and space around him, Marcus periodizes the American 1980s as so: "It's like all of a sudden the whole world turned into money…and you can invest in everything and it's all the same." His claims resemble those made by another 1980s confidence man, Ronald Reagan, who, when he signed the 1982 Garn-St Germain Depository Institutions Act that removed interest-rate caps at savings banks, announced that he had penned "the emancipation proclamation of America's savings institutions."[3]

Scandals and Abstraction is a literary history of what happens to narrative form when too much money circulates at once. The particular scene of overaccumulation that the book concentrates on dates in the United States to the late 1970s and 1980s. An event whose effects continue into the present, the fact of too much money was most recently, and spectacularly, represented in the 2007–8 credit crisis. But before that crisis, the presence of overaccumulated money capital had already staked out an impressive archive in literature, film, and the expanse of horizontal, textual space that I call *financial print culture*. When there is too much or too little money—and the condition of possibility of capitalist exchange is that there never is the right amount—finance assumes the difference, as it allocates credits and debts, intentions and expectations, from the present into the future.[4] How this tension and possibility between present and future is represented, I argue, is a crucial part of a financial process that political economy does not theorize but that contemporary American literature does. This book tracks how a surplus of money in the 1980s created new financial devices and logics as well as new channels for the production and contestation of literary meaning and narrative form.[5]

The larger transition that *Scandals and Abstraction* provides through its literary and cultural history is that of how finance came to stand in metonymically for "the economy" in the sense that the representation of the financial sector of economic activity is the closest thing we have to the representation of an economic totality. My contention can be demonstrated empirically, as the *New York Times* did in 2009 when it reported that the bulk of recent economic journalism concerned financial services, but I am more interested in exploring a cultural logic through which economic signification is derived in large part through the representation of finance.[6] My claim is that this metonymic substitution itself is foundational for our contemporary financial society, and I intend to contribute to the growing field of work that some scholars have begun calling "critical finance studies" and others "cultures of finance."[7] Indeed, this process may be considered one possible definition of the process of financialization that has the advantage of uniting the representational and the economic.[8] Furthermore, I suggest that crucial to financialization's efficacy is the moment in which those of us not supported—and in many cases directly burdened—by financial activities nonetheless come to view the data that represent those activities as signs of our economic well-being and as parameters of the economy per se. It helps that those representations are omnipresent: How many times a day can one catch a glimpse of a stock market chart and hear that its value is "up" or "down"?[9] When "the economy" is represented by "the stock market," when access to "the future" is represented by credit and loans, the great majority of us, and almost certainly everyone reading this book, should understand their present as a precarious situation.[10]

Because the ascension of finance to a site of representational dominance frames our contemporary moment, a history of that ascension provides a site for its critique. The literary and cultural analyses that constitute this book reveal that this substitution of finance for the economy transpired on three broad levels. In order to follow its path, I first trace how the very fact of a new economic period in which financial activities were becoming more pervasive and profitable was repeatedly catalogued and disseminated in financial journalism, a limited field of what I more expansively refer to as financial print culture. More than an economic science, in the pages of these publications finance was styled as a manner of knowing and representing, a form of masculinity and aesthetic comportment. Second, I locate political economists and historians who began to discuss a historical moment of financialization as a response to the overaccumulation of money capital in the developed world. They stressed that new financial devices could displace this surplus into the future and could thus maintain the value of money. Third, and most substantially, I analyze contemporary literary texts from the divergent aesthetic modes of realism and postmodernism that represented this explosion of financial themes and logics and used these depictions to craft their narrative forms. Employing contributions from each of these archives of financial print culture, political economy and economic history, and literature, I identify and relate two defining transformations in American literature and culture at the end of the twentieth century as they worked in tandem and in tension: first, the canonization of postmodernism as an aesthetic mode and, with it, the appearance of a revanchist realism; and, second, the transformation of the United States into a financialized, leveraged, and ultimately, neoliberal society.

The Situation

The historical period I demarcate—the "long 1980s," roughly 1979 to the early 2000s—was punctuated by the dissolution of the ostensibly Communist Eastern bloc and the declaration across much academic and popular American culture that there could be no alternative to a market economy. During this period, critical and literary theorists began to reassess what constituted "the economy" and how to analyze it.

They declared an end to the predominantly Marxist use of production and its constituent, labor, as organizing heuristics of economically oriented cultural analysis. In their place, they turned their attention toward economic analytics freshly conceived by the decade's emergent methodologies: cultural-studies notions of consumption, with its focus on agency and empowerment, and new historicist notions of exchange, with its articulations of commensurability across disciplines. While these styles of criticism had the welcome effect of moving economic representation beyond the scope of Marxism, what their methodologies did not render legible, and what *Scandals and Abstraction* organizes and analyzes, is the incredible archive of financial representation that condensed throughout the period. In turn, this archive helped to reconfigure American literary postmodernism so that by the time Fredric Jameson claimed "finance capital sustains and underpins postmodernity as such," it seemed both intuitive and sensible.[11] Finance appeared everywhere in the 1980s: In political economy and cultural production the fact of its increased presence resounded; yet much literary and critical theory seemed curiously deaf to its tone. That lacuna becomes in my book an important site to track the interplay between economic and cultural forms through their emergence and theorization in literary and cultural studies.

I examine the representation of financial narratives, idioms, cultures, and financial organizations of race, class, and gender throughout the 1980s and demonstrate that novelists, journalists, filmmakers, and even bankers themselves began to reimagine the capitalist economy as one that was newly personal, masculine, and anxiety-producing precisely because it was newly financial. Indeed, the discourses produced and exchanged by this disparate group together created the referent for our now-commonplace conception of "finance." There is a surfeit of empirical evidence for the claim that financial revenues have increased and productive ones have decreased from the 1970s onward. Federal Reserve chairman Paul Volcker's comment that the United States' economic policy of the early 1980s would "break unions and empty factories," provides one suggestive if not modest example of why production-based revenues declined.[12] Likewise, Greta Krippner's comment that financial products and profits "do not show up in transparent ways in national economic statistics," insists on the importance of representation to any study of finance's emergence.[13] Nonetheless, the ratio of profit between productive and financial tendencies—and how this is measured is certainly debatable—is less important to my argument than the hegemony of a certain financial identity and the variety of objects and processes that adhere to it across an expanse of cultural production.

During the period that I examine, finance manifested in multigeneric (novel, autobiography, reportage) multimedia (print, film, computer screen) and multimodal (realism, postmodernism) forms. For example, one could view a romantic comedy structured around the surreptitious stock acquisition of one corporation by another, as in Herbert Ross's *The Secret of My Success* (1987); or browse the *New York Times* bestseller list that contained a how-to guide to personal wealth in the form of financial autobiography, as in Donald Trump's *The Art of The Deal* (1987). The day's leading news story might have been about one of the many in a wave of corporate mergers and acquisitions that created some of our largest media companies, including Time Warner, or it might have been about the fraudulent or illegal practices that often accompanied such events, as seen in the news coverage around Ivan Boesky's scandalous involvement in the late 1980s in conjunction with Paramount Communications' leveraged buyout.[14] Furthermore, in this period in which literature and film narrated financial events, financial companies themselves got into the business of selling culture. In the mid-1960s the Diners' Club Credit Card Company had launched its own magazine under the caption, "now you can have culture on credit, too," by which it meant that one could discover culture in the magazine and purchase it with the card.[15] By the early 1980s, the reach of this logic had intensified as finance not only was represented, but began actually to represent: The American Express company made its first foray into cultural production with the launch of MTV in 1981, what would soon become an iconic and prosaic instance of postmodern cultural production.[16]

Engagement with an increased volume of financial activity was particularly prominent in fiction. Throughout this period, writers committed to realist and postmodern aesthetic modes took note of the emergence of finance as a hegemonic economic form and they theorized and debated how it should be represented, both in their texts and in the expanded paratextual world of publicity, advertisements, and interviews that surrounded their texts' publication. I focus on a selection of realist and postmodern novels and, to a lesser degree, visual cultures and financiers' autobiographies, to catalog the aesthetic modes and the visual and narrative tropes of finance that have accompanied this shift into financialization from the late 1970s to our present day as well as on the cultural and organizational logics that have made finance perceptible, representable and, ultimately, I demonstrate, efficacious. In each of these texts, I track how banks, credit cards, automated teller machines, brands, styles of criminality, and organizations of masculinity function as sites of financial representation, and how journalism, the autobiography, and, especially, the novel, generically regulate their delivery. The novel, long noted for its capacious ability to absorb other genres, here assimilates the financial autobiography and financial journalism into its structure while the diverse interplay between financial trope, literary genre, and aesthetic mode reveals the depth and presence of financialization in this period.

In this archive I locate a divergence in narrative form. On the one hand, in its engagement with finance, narrative collapses—evidence of the famous *cri-de-coeur* of 1980s postmodern criticism. Yet on the other hand, there emerges within these texts a new capacity to conceptualize and maintain a relationship between past and future, between abstraction and figuration, and between what I designate as patterns of association and evaluation, of description and transaction. Unlike a narrativized past and future, and unlike an aesthetics of abstraction and figuration, the dichotomies of association and evaluation and of description and transaction will be unfamiliar to readers. I use these dichotomies to navigate some of the structural differences between postmodern and realist texts as they engage finance.[17] For example, realist texts rely on a more conventional plot structure to represent the temporality of a financial deal unfolding than do postmodern texts. Conversely, postmodern texts repeatedly employ the brand name as a structure of association: A character has a seemingly fleeting thought—and evaluation—that "thought" was the result of exposure to some brand name that will now be considered either eventful and emplotted or uneventful and digressive. In such cases, branded representation of a commodity changes that commodity's value in a manner I claim is financial and narrative. Patterns of association and evaluation are more likely found in postmodern texts; those of description and transaction in realist and journalistic ones. As the reader can already ascertain, the analytic vocabulary I deploy throughout this study veers between the narratological and the economic, and is then specified to the local archive and concerns of each particular chapter. What unites these local terms and problems across the book is the central tension between content and information as the first becomes the second during the course of a financial transaction. Content is that which is molded by literary nar-rative; information is what produces value.

Mine is not a claim that this financial period generated postmod-ernism or that postmodernism and finance contain an overdeter-mined ideological or cultural affinity.[18] One could argue, in fact, that a financial logic generates a realist intention.[19] Instead, I pose a series of directed questions that negotiate the space between economic and cultural forms. I trace how certain financial logics were canonized with postmodernism; how still other financial logics were canonized with the realist reaction to postmodernism; and how the manner in which the relationship between these two aesthetic modes, when medi-ated through the representation of finance, offers access to a history of financialization and of contemporary American literature and culture.

Postmodern novelists and realist novelists each turned to the rep-resentation of finance to claim that *theirs* was the properly historical aesthetic of a new economic period and this fact becomes the central problematic of my book. These novelists' engagement with finance marked and rendered possible specific articulations of their respec-tive aesthetic modes, and, I argue, of what finance could be construed to encompass and refer to. Again and again, postmodern texts returned to the representation of financial objects and processes, thereby cre-ating a particular niche of what Mark McGurl has recently dubbed "technomodernism."[20] Yet the period during which 1980s postmod-ernity became canonized, the moment when "*White Noise* replaced *The Crying of Lot 49* on the course syllabus," as one critic neatly put it, saw the emergence of a reactionary, sentimental realism that also turned to finance.[21] "Only realism can penetrate into the reaches of Wall Street," claimed Tom Wolfe, its most ardent and prolific sup-porter.[22] Indeed, soon after Wolfe's claim, realism was given new intellectual purchase in literary studies with the publication of Amy Kaplan's *The Social Construction of American Realism*, which sought to complicate the realist mode and led to a renewed, rigorous en-gagement with its history.[23]

In the work of Bret Easton Ellis and Don DeLillo, I locate a do-mestic postmodernity that broke with its 1970s predecessors including Thomas Pynchon and William Gaddis to become digestible, popular, and recyclable. Indeed, in their representations of finance, post-modern texts followed the banking industry, which had announced in 1982 in the pages of *The Wall Street Journal* that it wanted to "open a branch in your home or office." These postmodern texts framed the advent of what that same industry called "personal banking" and traced the effects and possibilities of institutional finance becoming intimate and domestic, and also disorienting and emasculating.[24] In the work of Tom Wolfe, Oliver Stone, and Jane Smiley I delimit a nostalgic capitalist realism.[25] As that same burgeoning banking industry declared a financial economy of limitless growth and profit through financial mechanisms such as Special Investment Vehicles (SIVs), Leveraged Buyout Offers (LBOs), even formerly staid Savings and Loans institutions, these realist texts presented an informative and pedagogical aesthetic that sought to make legible a now "complex" financial world and to portray the men who would master or succumb to it.[26]

The postmodern sensibility called for the radical newness of finance to effect an aesthetic rupture with the present while the realist sensibility called for the repetition of finance to resuscitate the dominant aesthetic mode that had been used to capture and critique finance capital's early twentieth-century cultural and economic hegemony, from the Gilded Age to the Roaring Twenties to the Great Depression. Each mode made a contradictory appraisal of the economic situation, and both were correct in their assessment. Finance is capitalism's repetition compulsion in times of crisis, yet every repetition is different. Finance in the 1980s was represented as a distinctly private and complicated economic form, a far cry from its early twentieth-century instantiation in "bucket shops," where penny-stocks were traded off ticker tapes, rather like Off Track Betting today.[27] Its 1980s presence was similarly distinct from its the early twentieth-century realistic representation as surreptitious and cartel-like. However, in its new instantiation, finance was conceived of as private in that it delimited a rich psychic interior, and as complicated or complex in that few could understand its exterior representation. Indeed, financial transactions became, in the discourse of the period, too complicated or complex to explain either to lay people or, increasingly, to the financial community in which the transactions originated.[28]

But if these postmodern and realist texts' understanding and construal of finance differed from their predecessors, they were oddly similar to each other. The seemingly antagonistic aesthetic modes of realism and postmodernism employed a quite complementary repertoire of motifs and themes to construct, criticize and represent the financial worlds of their texts. Three theoretical constructions predominate throughout my study, and they traverse and unify my cultural archive; I present them here by the scale in which they structure the book. The first I call "financial masculinity," the second, "financial print culture," and the third, "financial form." Financial masculinity organizes the idioms and logics of interpersonal violence, of white masculine anxiety in the face of a newly global and permeable economy, and of the heterosexual possibility and homosexual intrigue that seems both available and feared wherever financial transactions occur. The second theoretical constant that defines this study is, strictly speaking, not limited to representation: these texts represent and engage with same financial print culture that I have used to introduce and contextualize them, an engagement which ultimately becomes a formal problem.

As the textual space in which this literary history transpires, financial print culture introduces and configures the problem of representation itself.[29] Literally all printed material about finance, from the stock report to the news report to the how-to-guide to personal wealth, financial print culture is part object and part context of my study, and film and other media get subsumed into its frame. To represent finance, both realist and postmodern texts made recourse to financial print culture, and to render finance both real and estranging they extrapolated from the language they found within it, ultimately curating a vernacular of finance that functions as a site of mediation between the literary and the economic. Financial print culture appears as self-reflexive through ekphrastic and multi-media presentations within my archive: the novel about the business newspaper; the newspaper article about the financial novel; the movie about the stock chart; the automated teller screen that narrates a story; the credit card statement that refers to an image; the novel that narrates a bank fraud which had already been chronicled in a true-crime financial exposé. In each example, cultural producers invited their audience to consider the materiality of paper and text in the representation of what were beginning to be understood as gradually more nonmaterial financial transactions.

The writers and cultural producers in my study not only took note of the emergence of finance as a hegemonic economic form, they debated how it should be represented. Some of these debates occurred in the same financial press from which the writers drew their knowledge about finance itself, such as the *New York Times*, *The Wall Street Journal*, and *New York* magazine. Tom Wolfe, for example, claimed in the pages of the *New York Times* that a "period like this" demanded an "economy of realism" as opposed to postmodernism.[30] Meanwhile, *The Wall Street Journal* noted a new genre of "fi-fi," or finance fiction, as one distinctive for its imbrication of international financial markets into its genre-fiction form.[31] The presence of aesthetic debates about finance in business journalism created a site that allowed journalists to recycle literary terminology through their own writing: *Barron's* magazine, for example, described the excess of commercial real estate—one material consequence of monetary overaccumulation—as "post-modernism for rent, 20 dollars a foot, the first year free!"[32]

My interest in retaining and expanding the concept of print culture into financial print culture is twofold. First, financial print culture records different types of capital in communication with each other. An era of financialization requires finance to become a representational dominant, and financial print culture both archives and supports this process. Second, from it I derive a methodology which may be understood as both an expansion and a literalization of what Benedict Anderson once called "print capitalism." Anderson famously used "print capitalism" as an analogue for capitalist modernity and its production of a homogenous, empty, novelistic time.[33] Financial print culture provides more than an analogue for my study; I would suggest a specification of "financial print capitalism" as allowing access to the time/space of financialization. For if financial print culture contains a record, I argue that it also contains an effectivity. Depending on how a financial transaction is delimited, one could claim the transaction does not end until it can be represented. This possibility becomes particularly apparent in my reading of journalism from the S&L scandals in which I argue that the journalist texts about the various transactions are in fact the necessary conclusions to them. Thus while there exists historical documentation of finance in financial print culture, it is my contention that revealed therein is also a logic of the sinews of finance itself, as it stakes out spaces of textual representation and then metabolizes them into sites of profit, loss, and value. My own operation for isolating when and how this process occurs is to place fictional texts in the ambit of financial print culture and isolate the interplay of the formal and the vernacular in the representation of finance.

The result of this interaction is what I call a "financial form," a catalytic mix of language and narrative that delimits the presence of finance

within a text. I explain this concept in depth at the end of the introduction in its own section; for the moment, an example will suffice.
Brand names proliferate throughout my archive. A brand name is a
kind of profitable language. It does not represent profit, but its representation is profitable, as it is through that representation that attention will accrue to the brand itself. The more people who offer their
attention to the brand, the more value accrues to it, ultimately form-
ing what financial analysts call "brand equity" and what I call "association."[34] I subsume the brand under the rubric of the financial because
its moment of profit is an unstable mix of language and temporality.
When a brand name appears in a fictional text, it may be an actual
accrual of value, or it may be disarticulated from this economic process, transformed into only a sign, and instead used to organize narrative movement, particularly the manipulation of time.

A brand name, then, may instantiate a financial form. We will see
that automated teller machines, bonds, and real estate transactions
all organize narrative time in a similar, and what I claim is a potentially financial, manner. It does not have to be, though, which introduces some element of risk. I apply the method of locating financial
form equally to all the cultural objects in my study, but the results are
distinct. Again, the example of the brand as it takes a financial form
is elucidating. The realist texts I read, *The Bonfire of the Vanities* and
Good Faith, for example, fictionalize brands a large extent and deploy actually existing branded commodities only rarely. Why? Theirs
is an attempt to represent and not to instantiate an economic transaction, thereby separating clearly representation and accumulation.
Whether this separation is possible in a financial era will be one of
my guiding questions. Their postmodern counterparts, *White Noise*
and *American Psycho*, by contrast, remain committed to what might
seem a kind of branded mimetic representation—both texts are well
known for their deployment of brand names—and they use actual
brands as narrative devices in order to turn psychic association into
narrative time. The postmodern texts have internalized the logic of
finance formally: the temporal breaks and recreations, the circularity
and lack the tension between the abstract and figurative. Yet it is the
realist texts that define and propagate the very categories we continue to use for cultural analysis of finance: its complexity, its scandalous
circulation, and its inability to be represented. Jameson is correct, then,
finance capital does sustain postmodernity, but the relationship is
less deterministic, more mutual, and, centrally, more mediated than

he allows. Likewise, readers may well recognize their own understandings and interpretive categories of finance in nascent form in 1980s
literature and journalism.

One could reasonably conjecture that print culture is too anti-
quated a heuristic to investigate the relatively contemporary financial transactions I analyze herein, with their requirements of satellite
communications, instantaneous data transfer through a global network infrastructure, mathematical dimensionality, and so forth.[35]
But one could also rejoin that the conceptual divide between digital
and print has been too exaggerated, as, for example, Lisa Gitelman
has done.[36] Likewise, it is *still* the case that much of our cultural sense
of actually existing business "common sense" derives from the stories and analyses found circulating in financial newspapers and the
companies that own them, such as the Dow Jones Company.[37] Scholars
of contemporary literature and culture repeatedly cite *The Wall Street
Journal* and the *Financial Times* without an articulated methodology
for doing so, and this is a lacuna my project seeks to amend.

I argue that as descriptions and representations of finance circulated through financial print culture, and as financial print culture
was represented in different aesthetic modes and remediated back
into itself through reviews, author/director features, investigations
of mergers and acquisition culture, and so on, both finance and the
spaces of its representation were transformed. For literary scholars
this claim is of particular interest as it was through the representation of finance that realism was rendered more postmodern; that
postmodernism became more canonical; and that finance appeared
more clearly as a distinct economic and literary object. Realism, in
this process, was given over to the dictates of circulation, mimicry,
externality and fragmentation. Postmodernism followed its Modernist
predecessor as its own avant-garde became generic. And cumulatively, finance metamorphosed from an economic subspecialty into
a describable social science phenomenon and finally into a recognizable aesthetic form.

My title, *Scandals and Abstraction: Financial Fiction of the Long
1980s*, makes reference to the two financial problematics that bookend
this archive and organize its representations: the scandal with its
dramatic presence and personality and the abstraction with its re-
fraction of temporality and refusal of representation. Both producers
and critics of financial cultures and texts turn to these devices repeatedly to frame their financial object and to convey the incitements

and anxieties of financialization. The scandal has an immediacy to it; it is highly narrativized and conclusive.[38] An abstraction is just the opposite, of course: It cannot be located either temporally or spatially, it refracts matter and refuses any kind of sensuousness. In the fictional, historical and theoretical texts I draw on here, the scandal and the abstraction work together to give finance its sense of identity and possibility. The financial scandal provides a narrative organization; the financial abstraction offers an interruption of narrative. The scandal isolates fixtures and figures of financial culture and provides them a manageable form in which to circulate. Several of the texts I read herein, Tom Wolfe's *The Bonfire of the Vanities*, for example, plot a financial scandal; another of the texts, *American Psycho*, itself became a financial scandal; another still, Jane Smiley's *Good Faith*, allegorizes the oddly unresolved S&L scandals that dragged on from their emergence in 1984 until their disappearance in the mid-1990s.

Nonetheless, when critics of varying disciplines read financial texts and analyze cultures of finance, they are more likely to seek out and to record the abstractions or the abstraction, as the case may be. Benjamin LiPuma and Edward Lee argue, for example, that "there is no way to represent the abstract violence of finance."[39] In a different register, Fredric Jameson suggests that in the moment of financialization "we have reached the limit of representability," and thus need a "new account of abstraction," to make sense of its transformative scope.[40] Is finance uniquely abstract in a manner that differentiates it from the abstractions of capital?[41] Is capitalism, or life, more abstract now than it was thirty years ago? In the criticism I engage, the assumption of more abstraction is prevalent but never adequately explained, probably because abstraction, by its very nature, is not quantifiable; if it were, it would hardly be abstract.[42] Abstraction is not a property of finance. The diversity of opinion on how exactly finance engages with capital's abstract and concrete dimensions is an important economic and aesthetic question, and my archive allows access to and reframing of the contemporary assumption of finance as abstract. Throughout the chapters, I maintain a concern with the interplay of abstraction as a denominator of both an aesthetic style in which it indicates nonfigurative media and as a conceptual heuristic that indicates something not fully realizable by a particular. I argue that without proper specification, the problem of "abstraction" has the effect of rendering intangible and invisible an economic literary/

textual form that has in fact produced an incredible archive of modes, genres and media, and has been doing so for some time.

The Economy, Finance, and Literary Criticism

In situating my book in relationship to current scholarship, I track the three fields of political economy, critical theory, and (to a lesser degree) financial journalism as each debated throughout the 1980s and 1990s what the referent of "the economy" should encompass and when it should be expanded or delimited. I then examine more contemporary work in literary studies to see how this field has inherited and answered the debates I trace herein. All literature reviews produce arguments of course, but mine may do so a bit more manifestly as I ascertain a concept, finance, that emerged and disappeared in the different frames and fields that compose my historical situation. To arrive at a definition of finance that allows for its use as a literary and cultural heuristic and maintains some sense of fidelity to its economic functionality is effectively to begin by asking: What has happened to Marxism in literary studies? I argue that weaving together a certain history of political economy, critical theory, and literary criticism allows us to inquire into the state of literary studies now and suggests how finance, as both an object and a process, can and should be articulated in our own historical present.

Political economy, critical theory, and literary criticism are distinct fields and each has its own genealogy. Yet they once coalesced together in what used to be known as economically oriented cultural criticism. Works such as Kristin Ross's *Fast Cars, Clean Bodies* or Anne McClintock's *Imperial Leather*, for example, sought to negotiate the disciplinary divide around commodities and cultures/texts in a manner that retained the integrity of the commodity form while expanding its analytic capacity for critique into representational space.[43] This field of criticism has changed dramatically in the last thirty years, with perhaps the most substantial transformation being the gradual disavowal of political economy that began in the 1980s. And that intellectual history is itself part of the unwritten story of finance and the financialization of the United States. This was the moment of confrontation and negotiation between Marx-inspired cultural studies and the twin poststructuralist camps of Foucault-inspired new historicism and Derridian deconstruction that in many ways defined critically the period under consideration here. The result of this period of intellectual ferment continues to structure our critical world such that, until very recently anyway, economically oriented criticism could be reduced to this simple question: are economic structures homologous to representational structures or do economic structures over-determine representational structures?[44]

If we return to the beginning of this moment, we see that Marxism began to lose its theoretical hold in critical theory because the economy was correctly perceived to be changing in a manner that challenged central Marxist categories. Once primary, "production" began to lose its legitimacy as an orienting concept.[45] Jean Baudrillard, for example, claimed in *The Mirror of Production* that in Marxist criticism "production [had been] elevated to a total abstraction...to the power of a code, which no longer even [risked] being called into question by an abolished referent."[46] Production had become, in this vocabulary, a signifier without a signified. Derrida continued this line, claiming in *Given Time* that value itself had been "extracted from production."[47] Ernesto Laclau and Chantal Mouffe were more direct in their criticism. They argued that "[during this period] there was an increasing gap in the realities of contemporary capitalism and what Marxism could legitimately subsume under its categories. It is enough to remember the desperate contortions which took place around notions such as 'determination in the last instance' and 'relative autonomy.'"[48] According to this logic, Marxism no longer possessed the conceptual apparatus to criticize capitalism and, what's worse, it may in fact have been further obfuscating its object of critique.[49] Foucault, of course, provided a different genealogy altogether—once famously comparing the difference between Ricardo and Marx's political economies as measurable by "storms in a children's splashing pool"—and I examine his contribution toward the end of my introduction.[50] Meanwhile, Jameson examined the economic and theoretical situation shortly after the publication of his "Postmodernism" essay in 1984 and conjectured that "the apparent return to some finance capitalism with dizzying edifices of credit and paper no longer reposing on the infrastructure or ground of real production offers some peculiar analogies to current [poststructuralist] theory itself."[51] Jameson's comment provides a historical perspective and anticipates his own "Culture and Finance Capital" essay of some years later, in which he would attempt to present finance as a categorical form that is uniquely abstract and that comes oddly close to his excoriation here. Right now, it is sufficient to note his prescience; the problem of abstraction I return to throughout this study.[52]

To summarize the "desperate contortions" of these theoretical debates now is to realize that the changing conceptual world of economically oriented criticism was structured around a rather contradictory historical logic. On the one hand, economically oriented criticism underwent a transformation, as the economy itself changed. On the other hand, the conceptual demand of the new historicism and its derivative school that eventually came to be called the "new economic criticism" was precisely that such criticism should not be determined by the economy.[53] Texts such as Walter Benn Michaels's *The Gold Standard and the Logic of American Naturalism,* Marc Shell's *Poetry, Money, Thought* and Jean-Joseph Goux's *Symbolic Economies* stressed the exchangeability between systems of value without linking value to the economy per se.[54] Shell, whose "enormous impact on economic criticism can scarcely be over-emphasized," in the words of one critic, argues that "money, which refers to a system of tropes, is also an 'internal' participant in the logical or semiological organization of language, which itself refers to a system of tropes."[55] By the time Martha Woodmanse and Mark Osteen's *The New Economic Criticism* was published in 1999, the standard in economically oriented criticism stressed precisely that there was nothing uniquely economic about "the economy," however it was figured. Rather "the economy" was one more arbitrary system of difference that could be positioned aside other such systems; the economy, in Brain Rotman's term, could rely on significations of "nothing."[56]

Whether the totality of "the economy" existed and how it could best be described was a central problem not limited to critical theory per se. In each of the archives I use herein—political economy, critical theory, journalism and literary and filmic texts—a similar tension appears. In a *Time* magazine cover from September 1982, for example, "Wall Street" is presented as separate from "the economy," as though the two had only tangential relationships to each other and were not bound by any deterministic identity. In a strange prefiguration of NAFTA, the title includes idiomatic English and Spanish—*"The economy? Eh. Wall Street: Olé!"*—to explain the early 1980s' discrepancy between economic growth and financial gain. In the image, an easily recognizable Wall Street bull breaks through what first appears to be some kind of constraint. On closer inspection, its constraint is revealed to be the very paper of a financial transaction: the famed stock

ticker-tape of so many parades. This cover could be read as an allegory to explore the relationship among finance, "the economy," and
the stability of paper-based representation. It suggests that finance is
a discrete object that cannot be contained by representation and that
"the economy" does not refer to "Wall Street." A similar sentiment
emerged from Mexican financial print culture, which reflected the
country's own financial turmoil produced by the 1982 Mexican Peso
crisis: "Financially things are going very well, but economically things
are going very badly," ventured a Mexican economist.[57] "The economy,"
a term Timothy Mitchell insists is its own recent abstraction, refers
here to industrial production and commodity consumption; finance
refers to something that instigates a break, both visually and concep-
tually, something profitable but not yet defined.[58]

Simultaneously, a tension played out in political economy over
whether production was the appropriate term for economic analysis,
much as it had played out in critical and literary theory and as it had
been evinced in popular writing.[59] The stakes were high. If production were to lose its economic and thus social hegemony, if a new
economic order were to appear, Marxism would necessarily forfeit
some of its exegetical and analytic power because it is production
that stabilizes the central, analytical categories of "commodity" and
"class." When Marx claimed that only an epistemic move that carried
the critic "behind the door of production" was able to reveal the content of the social relations of capitalism, he was describing more than
a method. He was also describing the benefits of "production," as an
indexical site of analysis.[60] Production can, through proper dialectical study, be rendered visible as a social, even an aesthetic relation.[61]
(Indeed, some contemporary Marxists such as Andrew Kliman continue to hew to this concept and reject finance or financialization
as an orienting analytic.[62]) Conversely, to make the claim that the
economy had become postproductive was to begin to move beyond
the scope of a Marxist analysis. And during the period that this book
covers, the 1980s and concomitant moments of financialization, this
is precisely what happened, as Marxists debated how much fidelity to
maintain to the trope of production and its associated social and historical world of industrial, albeit monopoly, capitalism.

For Marx, and for Marxism, production is a period of historical development (as in "mode of production"), a social relation, and an epistemic form. Writing in the early 1970s, Ernest Mandel, for example,
claimed that "late capitalism, far from representing a postindustrial

society, thus appears as the period in which all branches of the economy are fully industrialized for the first time."[63] Mandel makes two claims with this statement: rhetorically, he makes an argument for the continued use of the optic of production; empirically, he reads changes in economic content through the "organic composition of capital," the term Marx gives for ratios of value within the capitalist mode of production.[64] Financialization did begin to appear as an emergent logic, but one that David Harvey, for example, could still claim constituted a "secondary circuit of exploitation" in his 1982 *Limits to Capital*.[65]

While the *Monthly Review* crowd of John Bellamy Foster, Paul Baran, Fred Madgoff, et al. diagnosed the overaccumulation of money capital in the late 1980s as an empirical fact and suggested that something like financialization would be required to siphon and distribute its excesses, the transformation of that scene into a heuristic for economic history transpired through Giovanni Arrighi, who rendered a conception of money-cum-finance as primary to his conceptual apparatus.[66] Writing from a world-systems perspective in the 1990s, Arrighi locates the precise moment of Mandel's text—the early '70s dissolution of the Bretton Woods accords and the end of the international gold standard—in order to fortify a different rhetorical approach and subsequently to indicate a different empirical field. "Over the last quarter of a century something fundamental seems to have changed in the way in which capitalism works," Arrighi argues.[67] In his tremendously influential *The Long Twentieth Century*, Arrighi claims that "by the mid-1970s the volume of purely monetary transactions carried out in offshore money markets already exceeded the value of world trade many times over. From then on the financial expansion became unstoppable. These changes [constitute] the global financial revolution."[68] Mandel attempts to organize economic facts so that they may be read through a model of production; Arrighi attempts to buttress his larger claim that "world capitalism was thus born of a divorce from rather than a marriage with industry."[69]

Whether these claims are mutually exclusive is less important than the fact that their economic referents are entirely different. Much as, for Walter Benjamin, the commodity form provides both an optic for seeing and an object to see, finance provides Arrighi with an object of investigation and a method for investigating.[70] For Benjamin, the field is culture; for Arrighi, it is national and international economic history.[71] Arrighi's break within political economy is that his is a Marxism stripped of its central protagonist, labor as commodity, and replaced with a new one, money as a sign, which then has two functions, each in tension with the other: measure of value and medium of exchange. That contradiction becomes for Arrighi the basis of finance, and, as a result, finance remains a concept for which Arrighi does not need to appeal to a logic of independent abstraction for support, as for example Jameson does when he employs Arrighi's argument.[72]

More recently, outside of political economy proper, finance has become a newly observable object and practice in the field of economic sociology and anthropology, where it has had the similar rhetorical effect of allowing opportunity to reconfigure or abandon aspects of Marxist critique. According to these readings—Alex Preda's recent *Framing Finance* might be the example par excellence as it renarrates the history of political economy itself through a financial optic—the heuristic centrality of finance offers a way outside of Marx's conceptual apparatus.[73] Donald MacKenzie's *An Engine Not a Camera* provides the most in-depth historical account of the emergence of the epistemic object of finance through his description of the habits, practices, and daily rituals of the economics profession. He surveys the emergence of academic financial economics as it produced discrete technologies, including the Black-Scholes-Merton model and the Capital Asset Pricing Model, for predicting financial markets but also, and this is MacKenzie's intervention, as the models themselves became more accurate through their instantiation.[74]

From the varied sites and methodologies of its investigation, finance has emerged from political economy and sociology as a more distinct economic object; it has become observable, describable, and *representable*, and it has provided economically oriented literary and cultural studies scholars with a different grounding for their analytic frames. Of course, part of the larger argument of this book is that it was precisely the representation in the literary and cultural fields that allowed for this conceptual differentiation of finance, but, for the moment, I want to suspend that line of investigation in order to speculate on the theoretical labor that "finance" can accomplish as a heuristic. It was the industrially produced commodity that was made by wage labor and sold on the market that grounded the commodity form. And it was the commodity form that grounded the kind of economically oriented criticism that I have cited as both incisive and as one genuinely invested in mediation as opposed to homology or determination. A robust concept of finance in place of the "commodity," then,

has the potential to refigure models of interpretation such as surface/
depth, homology/determination, translation between different fields
and disciplines, and, most notably, the problem of "value" itself.

In a range of works that inform my study, value, far from being a
concept in need of elaboration and definition, becomes the axis of
translation between different realms without being clearly defined.
Arrighi's text may provide the model here: It does not construct a
theory of value beyond that of money itself. "Labor," for example, is
absent from his history. Value is a stand-in: sometimes for money, as
in Arrighi's book; sometimes for knowledge, as in Mary Poovey's
Genres of the Credit Economy, where value allows for movement between economic and literary writing; sometimes for canonicity, as in
John Guillory's *Cultural Capital*. However, unlike in Gayatri Spivak's
"Scattered Speculations on the Question of Value," and unlike in
Marx's oeuvre, value is no longer derived from labor, nor is it clearly
related to exploitation.[75] Similarly, "abstract" no longer is paired with
"concrete." Rather, these terms become deracinated and some mani-
festation of value becomes a placeholder. But for what? Value is a
placeholder for another placeholder, and this deferral, belatedness,
and ultimately stabilization, organizes many of the homologies that
themselves structure histories of value, however broadly defined
value is.[76] Thus Arrighi as well as Preda and the now-called "Social
Studies of Finance School" have proven a popular source for cultural
critics who seek to write about finance as a form of value without the
accompanying Marxist epistemology even while employing some of
its key terminology.[77] The point is not to accuse these critics of some
sort of heresy or to claim that Marxists are entitled to a monopoly on
economic criticism; I too have plenty of problems with the intellectual traditions of Marxism, many of which are reactionary and scle-
rotic, full of what Benjamin himself so accurately diagnosed as "leftist
melancholy." But it is to point out that perhaps Marx's strongest argument—that value is social, exploitative and imminently transform-
able—is itself abandoned in many of these critiques.

Beyond Homology or Determination:
Contemporary Literary Scholarship

The question that has been repeatedly asked in the development of an
economic criticism in a moment of financialization is "what does the

economy represent?" and the answer has just as often been "something that is similar to something else." This homological approach continues to define the field, and only within the last few years does the approach show signs of change. So, for example, a text such as Michael Tratner's *Deficits and Desires* is organized around the claim that in the early twentieth century, "a strange parallelism [exists] between attitudes about debt and about sexuality."[78] Critics have been problematizing homology for as long as it has been a practiced logic of economic criticism. Where, for example, do homologies derive the stability of their own meaning? The ultimate source of any pair of shared logics would seem to be a shared historical present. But, as James Chandler has shown us in a different context, the line between homology and tautology is a fine one indeed. After all, how do we delimit what constitutes a shared historical present? Usually by locating a certain group of texts that share a similar logic and are produced in some temporal proximity to each other, proximity being an axis of textual consistency, and so on. Chandler's title, *England in 1819*, is itself an argument and it draws an interesting comparison to the longue durée that has been appended to many recent, periodized studies, including mine.[79]

By contrast Richard Godden's work on twentieth-century American literature is exemplary of a determinist approach whereby whatever constitutes the economy stands as a theoretical buttress outside literary texts themselves. In his *Fictions of Labor* and *Fictions of Capital* and, more recently, in *William Faulkner, an Economy of Complex Words*, he makes an explicit contradistinction between his own methodology and that of the new economic criticism, which he groups under the logic of "analogy" (what I have called homology). For example, he states that "economic structures are the generative source of fictional forms," and he thus rejects what he labels a Sausserian tradition of splitting and difference. In its place, he registers of series of Jamesonian contradictions and sites of unevenness lodged deep within the texts themselves as they record history.[80]

Only recently does this divide between homology and determination show signs of evolving, and it is precisely the continuation of this trend that I hope to contribute to herein. Michael Clune offers a sort of Heideggerian aesthetic approach in his *American Literature and the Free Market,* a work whose central categories of "money" and "free-market" remain evenly suspended between their economic and aesthetic referents in his investigation of what he calls "the economic

novel." Money, for example, "becomes a means of shaping action distinct from both society and individual" while the market is understood to be "a matter of generating desire and perception."[81] Clune
moves beyond homology, but also beyond political economy itself
and it is this insistence that constitutes his central methodological insistence. Christopher Nealon also attempts to reconfigure economically oriented criticism in his *The Matter of Capital* by asking us to
refuse the very distinction between form and content in literary studies and—by extension—in Marxism itself. Joshua Clover's recent article, "Autumn of the System: Poetry and Finance Capital" offers a
similar approach through the destabilization of any kind of a priori
time/space matrix.[82] Time and space are "constantly being mistaken
for each other," he writes of Thomas Pynchon's novel, *Against the Day*,
but that's the point to be taken from his essay, too, and it is encouraging as it points beyond discrete scenes of representation. Instead,
Clover demonstrates how categories created by capital may be disaggregated in social spaces of capital, and how once disaggregated textually, their initial appearance in "reality" seems less reified and more
elastic.

   Another trend of existing literary scholarship might be called, borrowing from art history and visual arts, institutional critique, in that it
selects an institution and narrates a multimodal literary history through
it. Andrew Hoberek and Mark McGurl have done so quite convincingly
in looking at the midcentury capitalist "organization" and the commodity logic of the Master of Fine Arts program and its "creative writing" technology, respectively.[83] Stephen Schryer's *Fantasies of the New
Class* follows a similar methodological trajectory as it navigates the pro-
fessionalization and politicization (or lack thereof) of literary criticism
in the wake of infrastructural growth of higher education in the postwar
United States.[84] In film studies, Jerome Christensen considers the abso-
lute immanence of the corporate structure as an aesthetic form in his
*America's Corporate Art: The Studio Authorship of Hollywood Motion
Pictures* where movie plots double as corporate organizational plots,
and vice versa. These works leave latent the description of the larger
structure—contemporary capitalism—that animates the local contexts
that they examine, and it is precisely this theoretical space that my
project seeks to fill. In reference to McGurl's book, for example, it is
certainly   important,   but   unacknowledged,   that   the   cost   of
obtaining   a   Master   of   Fine   Arts   is   between $50,000   and
$100,000. Students either enter these programs very rich or leave

very poor, and in both scenarios the logic of indebtedness and accumulation (in addition to that of commodification) is crucial for students to be able to "write what [they] know."

Some of the most trenchant work on finance as a problem of literary history has been completed in fields other than American literature and culture, and I hope to be in dialogue with those texts as well. Texts such as the already-cited work of Baucom or Poovey, or Anna Kornbluh's *Realizing Capital* seek to frame something called finance as a literary object—one that demands a specific methodology and thus transcends national or historical categories.[85] All three of these works rely heavily on the kind of archival research I employ here—indeed they each consider what I have called "financial print culture" to be a fundamental component of literary analysis. Perhaps because of the assumed contemporaneity, scholarship in contemporary American literature and culture treats news archives with an assumption of transparency that these 18th- and 19th-century-oriented works do not. It will become clear, then, that I am engaging with two bodies of work: contemporary American literary and cultural studies and economically oriented criticism itself, whether of the time/space of Victorian England or of the 18th-century Black Atlantic.

I begin with a concept of finance derived from political economy, from Marx through the its self-defined practitioners in the present, and I locate something similar to that concept that has repeatedly manifest in contemporary American fictional texts, non-fictional texts and films, be they realist or postmodern, popular or professional. What I have located there has made me realize that such representational narratives are fundamental to the efficaciousness of finance itself in a manner that differentiates it from other forms of value. This unique property of finance has not been fully accounted for in political economy. Jonathan Beller has probably come closest to the form of value I attempt to capture here. Beller's work accounts for representation as process and value in his *The Cinematic Mode of Production*. Crucially, in his argument representation does more than represent, it constitutes the value that it is supposedly representing.[86] While Beller does not name this as a specifically financial operation, I do. And because representation is part of finance, the study of its representation has the potential to reveal something about the object itself. At the same time, the repeated claim from critics such as Shell that money, like language, is a system of signs is as true as it is in need of refinement. David Graeber has suggested that money's lack of a stable referent, its imaginary qualities, are themselves a kind of property distributed by class so that the question one should ask is not whether finance contains literary-like fictions, but: For whom and how do these fictitious values become real?[87] Each side of my archive is haunted by the other: Within the literary archive of novels, journalism, and autobiography remains the question: is not all representation of the economy a metaphorical elaboration of some quality, in finance, particularly, the elaboration of violence? Conversely, political economy remains haunted by the poststructuralist question: what if value itself is fundamentally a discursive problem? Such fundamental questions, problematics really, cannot be answered but only negotiated anew.

Financial Form

The literary and cultural archive I provide here presents a diversity of interpretive problems that result from and enjoin finance to its representation and that appear in the theoretical construction and representation of value that I label a *financial form*. This is simultaneously a narrative and economic construction. From its representation in vernacular speech to its textual presence in conceptual art, everything written about finance may be configured as part of its process. *Finance* may be an instrument, a device, a plan, or method, any of which allocate a relationship between present and future. This is why Robert Guttman suggests that financial devices "bridge the real temporal disjuncture between intention, production and consumption."[88] But whereas for political economists such as Guttman or Arrighi, finance happens *within* historical time, my concept of financial form argues that financial transactions produce time. Those transactions almost always involve money as a site of mediation in the texts I use herein and, indeed, in the modern economic world.

If I take out a loan for ten years, both the description of that loan and the time and space between now and the ultimate repayment of that loan constitute finance. These are some of the oldest institutional arrangements of human society.[89] Nonetheless, they are also some of the newest. To give credit, for example, is a millennia-old practice. But it is distinctly contemporary in that credit is now given in money form from transnational conglomerates such as Citibank or Chase as opposed to the local suzerain or neighborhood grocery store. In my study, various subjects and objects delimit and reconfigure the social potentiality and anxiety of this financial relationship that dwells for most of its duration in a state of becoming, a movement toward realization. When that process is complete, when it has been realized, its potentiality has been objectified as either money or a commodity and, most likely, it has been routed through a text where something about it has been recorded and will now be remembered as it had been previously anticipated. Finance's description at the level of the text enables its transaction at the level of the economic, and vice versa. In my account, it is this temporal and discursive projection and rehabilitation of time and text that distinguishes finance from a conception of "money" as a static site of translation between literary and economic value, as, for example, is found in an approach such as Shell's.

Finance is an orientation and a contestation over futurity, and because it navigates both the textual and the economic either through or in opposition to temporality, I will pair it with narrative throughout this study.[90] That does not mean finance always manifests through narrative forms; indeed sometimes its value-producing operation requires the avoidance of narrative, as, for example, in the case of arbitrage. Either way, finance palpates a future: when to access it, how to avoid it, and what to profit off of.[91] Unsurprisingly, financial vocabulary itself retains some concept of temporal unfolding. The etymology of the word "finance" derives from the Latin noun *finis* (the end) and French verb *finir* (to end); the idea of a "futures market" is eponymous; and the term "mortgage," literally and figuratively translates as "death measure." In political economy, finance is what you do when you have too much or too little money in the present. In literary studies, narrative, for its part, is an experience of meaning over time and a guarantee of more meaning to come when comprehension between the immediate and the conclusion is expected, but not yet possible. Why am I reading about this character/event now? To what end? Both finance and realist narrative promise their participants that an end will come. Yet in a postmodern mode, the refusal of an ending and the elevation of circularity and fragmentation is the narrative dominant. Both finance and postmodernism ask their participants to risk that the ending may not be recognized as such, that the ending may not come last. Just as it navigates immediacy and durée, finance may represent and be represented in realist and postmodern modes.

To finance is to have a narrative about how the future will unfold, and to narrate finance is to introduce a distinct temporal dynamic into the narrative form. In bringing these two constructions together, I explore what happens when finance, a kind of value that demands the mediation of the present by the future, is represented by narrative, an aesthetic construction that itself is always a mix of past, present and the anticipation that something will follow. No person or institution gives credit without the anticipation of a specific future. The converse, of course, is true, too: who wouldn't be willing to take out a debt were they assured that there was no future, that whatever social order validated their debts would end imminently?[92] But to know about the future, or to assume one knows, is to live in a world of uncertain representations. That world of interested and committed representation has traditionally been explored through studies of ideology, an area I largely avoid. In place of that term, I employ what Marx called, in a different context, "the expenses of representation," literally the cost of making the world appear amenable to certain transactions.[93] I prefer the latter because it reminds us that representation is a space of transaction, whereas, ideology has traditionally been understood as separate from the economic, even as it reflects the economic.

In my study, this ceaseless tension between the economic and the representational in finance requires multiple theoretical orientations for its analysis. My theoretical tracing of a financial form might be seen as an answer to the question: How does one reconcile Marxist and poststructuralist conceptions of value, with the former's focus on labor-generated accumulation and the latter's focus on discursivity, subjectivity and now, we can add, affectivity?[94] And that question itself could serve as an allegory for the transformations of literary theory in a period of financialization: how does economically oriented criticism change when the economy changes? The theoretical frame through which I articulate finance transpires somewhere between these two conceptions of value, for which I will let Marx and Foucault serve as representatives. Kevin Floyd has already begun this process in his *The Reification of Desire: Toward a Queer Marxism*, which stakes out a similar tension between Marxist and Foucauldian heritage and I follow his lead here.

Marx claims that finance constitutes "capital elaborated into pure form."[95] Yet finance still requires some content for that formal elaboration.[96] Finance, I will show, is more sutured to a scene of representation than other forms of value and it becomes efficacious through this property; yet it nonetheless requires a material, laboring world for its operations. There is no financial device or practice that does not refer to something.[97] If I take out a mortgage for a house, and that mortgage is combined with other mortgages, and that tranche is then spun off into the future through its acquisition by a Norwegian pension fund through a sale by a New York bank, all of this still refers in some very real sense to my house. Indeed, it is indexed to my house. When it *appears* as though I can afford the house, these transactions may continue unabated; if it begins to *appear* as though I cannot afford it, interruptions in accumulation are imminent. It scarcely matters if some of these transactions are fraudulent or even fictitious as long as they secure a present and plan a future. As such, finance is an excitable and impressionistic form. This is a fact of which Marx was aware and for which he was full of contempt. He writes that:

> In interest-bearing capital, the capital relationship reaches its most superficial and fetishized form. Here we have M–M′, money that produces more money, self-valorizing value, without the process that mediates the two extremes. In commercial capital, M–C–M′, at least the general form of the capitalist movement is present... [at least] it presents itself as the product of a social *relation* not the product of a mere *thing*... in M–M′ we have the irrational form of capital, the misrepresentation and objectification of the relations of production in its highest power.[98]

What seems so interesting about this passage now is that, first, it orients us toward representation and perception (even misrepresentation is a form of representation, after all); and, second, that one could argue that our current experience of finance has transformed into precisely the opposite. Because finance is a superficial form it becomes more able to reveal and represent social relations than other forms of value. David Harvey, for example, quite literally calls interest rates a "representation of value."[99] Harvey's claim suggests that capitalism requires financial representation for its coordination and, furthermore, that while finance is dependent on representation for its execution, it also represents. Were the Obama administration to announce tomorrow the complete privatization of social security, "the market" would rightly cheer. Were it to announce a plan of universal healthcare or free higher education, the market would rightly depress, as limited commodification produces limited opportunities for financialization.

Despite the fact that they are sometimes used as loosely inter-changeable, commodification and financialization are two separate though complementary practices. Indeed, Robert Meister has argued that perhaps the central question, and tension, of *Capital* is found in the initial outlay of credit in the form of the worker forgoing her wage until after her labor is completed. In positing that central bifurcation, Meister poses the question: What if the cycle of credit were reversed? What if the worker demanded his wage before he undertook his labor? From this, Meister hypothesizes two logics at work in *Capital* and capitalism: a "commodity logic" and an "asset logic." One might propose an "asset model" of reading in which this delayed and pro-ductive temporality creates the horizon for all value, a reading strategy that would complement the commodity model of reading which so much of Western Marxist derived work on culture has been devoted to explicating.[100] Or one might reconfigure "labor" so that the advanc-ing of the wage is itself a labor process.

What I mean by "financial form" is likewise a way to discern these complementary but differing organizations of accumulation. Com-modification primarily refers to a condition of human labor itself, and I like the succinct definition of commodity as "made by waged labor and sold on the market" that Dan Schiller has offered.[101] If the commodity is an object permanently formed by past-labors, and money is a representation of all labors embodied in the present, then finance is the promise of a revaluation of those labors linked to the future. "Money with a guaranteed rate of return," is how Dick Bryan, Randy Martin and Mike Rafferty define finance.[102] Marx had already said something similar: "The fiscal system contains within itself the germ of automatic progression," he writes.[103]

Borrowing from these understandings, I define finance as the rep-resentational present of that promised future, and, accordingly, an era of financialization is defined by the assumption of finance to a site of representational dominance. The utopian hope of finance is the moment when all representation can become value producing, and my book is structured so as to unfold toward that realization. However, even in their hegemony, finance and financialization con-tain a certain element of risk. Finance does not necessarily produce a return, even if it is guaranteed to do so; and it does not progress automatically without an incredible infrastructure of state support. Yet the assumption of that support produces discrete forms of writ-ing such as "mark to market" accounting (made both famous and infamous by Enron), whereby profits are recorded as if they had already been made. An investment of present money in such a company may very well be guaranteed—until it isn't.[104] A whole laboring world of contest, representation and open-endedness separates the now and then of finance.

What we can take from Marx's and Marxist analysis is this temporal and formal structure of finance and the relationship of finance to other capitals. But where this analysis must be supplemented is within the more poststructuralist field of writing, representation, and subjectification.[105] Foucault, for example, writing in *The Order of Things*, offers a conception of value that moves away from the rubric of commodification, yet, in this older text, he is not yet engaged in the development of a concept of biopower.[106] In his attempt to historicize the development of the field of political economy and the basic epistemic transition from wealth to value, Foucault repeatedly returns to the scene of representation to argue that any conception of value cannot be prior to language itself. The crux of his argument is that: "In order that one thing can represent another in exchange, they must both exist as bearers of value; and yet value exists only within representation (actual or possible), that is within the exchange of the exchangeability."[107] For any form of value to be valued, it must enter into a network of representations; but for it to enter that network, it must be valued. Foucault does not resolve this tautology theoretically within this text, where it is given its clearest explication—although he certainly does resolve it in his own oeuvre. By the time of the repressive hypothesis it becomes clear that all representation is value producing, and that is the logic I want to preserve in my analysis of finance.[108]

What I want to suggest is that a financial form includes qualities that are positioned as alternatives by the discourses of Marxism and poststructuralism and therefore must be analyzed by the orientations of both traditions. Value, for Marx, is additive since it requires a commitment of labor. Machines, computers, derivative trades, and so on do not produce value. Value, for Foucault, is repetitive, since it requires mirroring in discourse and since it must always refer to itself before it can refer to something else. Indeed, when Marx does address interest-bearing capital, his concern is that it is too much orientated toward this logic of doubling (M–M´) whereas for Foucault value is possible only because of this operation. It may be objected that the tension I have isolated is a rehearsal of the basic axis that defines, and thus, separates Marxism and poststructuralism: externality versus internality, durée versus spatiality, production versus exchange, class versus subject, immanent versus transcendent, and so on. If literary scholars accept the first set of alternatives, then they see texts as *determined by* the economy; if they accept the second, then texts have a homological structure that is *like* the economy.

Rather than accept that dichotomy, throughout this book I demonstrate that a financial form is an organization in which the field of representation is simultaneously indexical and value producing—the indexing is itself a form of evaluation. Finance depends, by way of the reiterative, citational, and illocutionary force with which it pervades our literary and filmic culture, on a causal connection between its signs and their referents, and on an ability to profit therein.[109] Financial practices draw attention to the process of recording, writing, and describing; they contain what I will label in chapter four a "descriptive imperative." But they only do so on the chance that description cedes into something more through a value-producing transaction. For my purposes in this literary study, the logic of finance is sutured between a description (which is repetitive) and a transaction (which is additive). A thing, or person, has to be described and a time period delimited based on that description. It is between these two operations that a time/space matrix of finance foments. Unlike poststructuralist accounts of value as belated, desiring, or purely linguistic, I want to introduce a more causal logic for the relationship between value and index. At least since the modern era, the link between describing and transacting has been impressive, a relationship preserved in the phrase "mark to market" and between the verb "to tell" and its noun form of "teller." James Scott, in fact, has argued that writing and the codification and standardization of language are themselves requirements for and products of early capitalist state formation. Indeed, there is no more of an Althusserian example than the one that Scott provides in *Seeing Like a State*, in which surname regularity is understood as a project of early taxation schemes—what Scott calls fiscal legibility.[110] David Graeber explains that the term "indentured," as in the servant, quite literally came from the dents in the tally sticks used to measure debt.[111] In both examples, for the transaction to proceed, there has to be an index to a subject or object, whether verbal as in Scott's example, or simply semantic as in Graeber's. I suggest that the reverse is true, too: there is only an indexing with the hope that it will become value-producing.

In my understanding, writing appears as content, with the expectation and possibility that it can be transformed into profit or loss. For there to be finance, there must exist some bounded transaction that initiates this process and delimits a time-space which reproduces some economic and representational content; when that transaction ends, the content is monetized, as it were. When Christian Marazzi claims that "language [is a] means of production," or that "capital itself has become linguistic," it's not that his assertions are incorrect. Rather, without a temporal component that is additive and labor-based, they are incomplete.[112] That temporal component is found in the deployment or avoidance of narrative itself. A financial form, connate with a narrative form, is both additive and repetitive. And a narrative form, connate with a financial form, "requires motion and change."[113] In addition to relying on a similar structural process of development through consistency and change, narrative offers a crucial element through which to engage financialization: narrative mitigates abstraction.

In each chapter of this book, I locate how the descriptive imperatives of finance and temporal logics of the transaction intersect so that they may metabolize each other to produce value and/or narrative. That this process happens through such different figurations of narrative structure, both postmodern and realist, invites us to reconceptualize what precisely we mean to delimit with those terms. It is through the twin processes of association and evaluation, and description and transaction, that all of the objects/subjects located herein maintain some sort of financial identity: the brand name in *White Noise*; information in the film, *Wall Street*; the automated teller machine in *American Psycho*; retrospection and tautology in *Good Faith*—all of these devices create a texture and possibility for description to cede into transaction, for all writing to create value.

Chapter Summaries

The first chapter, "Personal Banking and Depersonalization in Don DeLillo's *White Noise*," is structured around a profound financial event that hardly seems worthy of the claim: the introduction of the technique of "personal banking," as termed by *American Banker* magazine in 1981. "Banks want to open a branch in your home," further cheered *The Wall Street Journal* in 1982. I use the case of *White Noise* to explore how the early material practices of personal banking and the discursive formations of financial print culture and postmodernism became increasingly entwined throughout the decade. I argue that the novel's emphasis on the familial and domestic is the site of the first sustained critique of personal banking and the decommodified labor that it requires. *White Noise*'s most distinct narrative devices are in fact the very financial devices of personal banking: the automated teller machine; receipts from accounts payable; the expansion and deracination of the corporate brand name, and credit cards. But if *White Noise* is historical because of its engagements with personal banking, what has made it so readable and teachable is its presentation of an easy, domestic postmodern form: its looping narrative structure, its "automated" narration—moments where its first person narrator is seemingly absent—its use of list-form, indeed all of the trappings of postmodern narrative realized in a white, heterosexual domestic space that is both academic and financial. Its narrator, Jack Gladney, is a subject of "financial masculinity," a construction that repeats throughout every text in my study and denotes a new global, postindustrial subjectivity in the form of patriarchal whiteness that *White Noise* both ironizes and propagates. What has been canonized with *White Noise*, then, is the expansion of finance into the deep recesses of the psyche as a recognizable postmodern habit of narration.

My second chapter moves from the quotidian world of personal banking to the dramatic, even melodramatic, world of investment banking and high finance. "Capitalist Realism: The 1987 Stock Market Crash and the New Proprietary of Tom Wolfe and Oliver Stone," examines the 1987 stock market crash, perhaps the codified financial event of the period, alongside the codified financial narratives of the same moment: Tom Wolfe's novel *The Bonfire of the Vanities* and Oliver Stone's film, *Wall Street*. By virtue of their timing and their channels of distribution, Wolfe's novel and Stone's film were transformed into prescient and perspicacious cultural objects in the pages of financial print culture. "Life Imitates Art in a City of Wealth and Welfare," explained the *New York Times* in an article describing the crash. Even as finance developed a kind of representational monopoly on economic knowledge, I argue, these fictional works developed a different kind of narrative monopoly on the representation of an emergent financial era. I focus on the twin questions that are repeated in financial print culture: what is a financial age, and what is a financial aesthetic mode? Wolfe and Stone serendipitously became spokesmen for what they understood as a radical new realism that could uniquely capture finance. They represent financial print culture in their fictional works in order to make finance seem real; conversely, that same financial print culture bestows on them as cultural producers the accolade of "financial realist." I designate the result of this interplay as "capitalist realism" to denote how realism is transformed by the same economic processes it intends to record. I observe two important legacies that the novel and film bequeathed to financial representation: first, a highly masculinized professional financial subject whose idiomatic, violent language echoes through financial print culture; and, second, a realist description of finance that is formally nonidentical to itself: in Wolfe's novel, finance is described as complex through a narrative mode that is simple; in Stone's film, information that is "inside" and "illegal" and that should be subject to an economy of scarcity actually exists in surplus.

Chapter three, "The Men Who Make the Killings: *American Psycho*, Financial Masculinity and the Genre of the Financial Autobiography," examines the destabilization of the masculine, financial subject, as well as its linguistic, particularly its metaphorical, and its narrative, particularly its generic, consequences. I argue that *American Psycho*'s primary historical engagement is less with its postmodern contemporaries than with 1980s financial narratives in fiction, autobiography, and economic journalism. Indeed, I claim that *American Psycho* renders legible a logic of 1980s financial writing through its intertextual connections in different genres including the novel *The Bonfire of the Vanities*; a series of memoirs by financiers such as Ivan Boesky's 1985 *Merger Mania*, Donald Trump's 1987 *The Art of the Deal*, and T. Boone Pickens's 1987 *Boone*; and, finally, 1980s economic journalism. First reporting in 1982 on "corporate raiders," the *New York Times* noted that "they have even developed their own language." Interestingly, soon after, periodicals quit analyzing this language and began to employ it, regularly referring to financiers as murderers, rapists and cannibals. I argue that Ellis's text mirrors these concerns and, in doing so, appropriates financial, journalistic language to synthesize the content of *The Bonfire of the Vanities*—the story of a financier who becomes known as a murderer—and the form of the financial autobiography—first-person, masculine grandiosity based on successful financial deals—into a fictional autobiography, a novel whose manifest violence caused its circulation to become as scandalous as the 1980s financial world it represented. *American Psycho*, then, provides a collection of realist and autobiographical tropes of financial representation.

Thus it introduces the problem of generic possibility and indeed of the genre of the financial text. Ellis borrows from each mode and appends his own text alongside of these others and, in doing so, he pulls together a series of seemingly incommensurable texts into a common representational and discursive space whose object is finance. If *White Noise* is a canonical postmodern text that elaborates the interiorization of personal banking, then *American Psycho* is the postmodern sequel that refuses such an operation by making all interiority external and by revealing that in transforming narration one can transform financial transactions as such.

Like its object, the S&L scandals, the fourth chapter begins with a series of scandals and ends with an abstraction. "Realism and Unreal Estate: The Savings and Loan Scandals and The Epistemologies of American Finance," charts the history of how these two tropes have become our limit and possibility for thinking finance as such and what the implications of this dichotomy are for the study of narrative. It is the most methodologically distinct of the chapters as I make an argument within the journalism and economic history itself, and use a fictional text as critique. One of the first academic histories of the S&L crisis, this chapter draws on archival work in *Barron's* and *The Dallas Morning News*, academic criminology, and Jane Smiley's novel *Good Faith*. I argue that what the S&L crisis contributed to American finance is the curious model and mode of writing about finance that I designate as "the descriptive imperative," or the need to record and obscure financial transactions simultaneously. The descriptive imperative reveals a kind of literary and economic realism that is based on, in the memorable words of one of Smiley's characters, "unreal estate." Here, it renders the S&L crisis both value producing and unable to be represented in narrative form. In this chapter, the descriptive imperative of finance encounters the retrospective logic of narration and the result is another articulation of my financial form. This particular instantiation contains a crucial new addition to the epistemology of finance: through the S&L crisis, finance becomes knowable and articulable on the condition that it be considered not economic knowledge but rather criminal knowledge, a transition made possible by academic theories of white-collar crime; and it becomes narrative on the condition that it is not an economic narrative but rather a sexual narrative, a transition made possible by the construction of the scandal itself.

Personal Banking and Depersonalization in Don DeLillo's *White Noise*

Personal Banking

Don DeLillo's 1985 *White Noise* can be read as a novel that records the saturation of everyday life by a new economic structure, one that the financial industry began to designate as "personal banking" in the early 1980s. The representation of credit cards, monetary transactions, and bills is necessary for the protagonist's sense of white, masculine self while the presence of the automated teller machine and the use of branded language offer crucial insight into the novel's narrative organization. Perhaps the most canonical postmodern novel of the period, *White Noise* has consistently been used by literary scholars to investigate how economic changes in the 1980s, particularly the rise of what has been called an "information economy" or a "consumer society," are represented in American literary postmodernism.[1] Yet the presence and necessity of finance in the novel, and in the functioning of a consumer society, have garnered less critical attention in literary studies. In this chapter, I use the case of *White Noise* to explore how the material practices of finance capital and the discursive formations of both postmodernism and financial print culture became increasingly entwined throughout the decade via a proliferation of automated teller machines, brand names, and the expansion of a personal credit apparatus.

The surprising result of this entwining is that with the canonization of *White Noise* as *the* postmodern text of 1980s, an unrecognized set of financial tropes and logics was canonized as part of that aesthetic mode. Called an "overread" and "overhistoricized" text, *White Noise* is one of what are surely the select few novels to provoke a scholarly plea against their continued interpretation.[2] That suggestion is made in jest, but it is not without a point. The problem of "overreading"

reminds us as scholars that to study any canonical text is necessarily
to study the process of canonization itself. *White Noise* captured and
historicized some of the most pervasive and intimate financial logics
that we have—personal banking and credit, branding, and automated telling, all of which I discuss and define herein. Yet the text
itself has been canonized as part of a moment in American literary
postmodernism in which the overfamiliar presence of commodification and consumption were employed in the service of literary defa-
miliarization. That the setting of this process in DeLillo's novel is
within a heterosexual family unit whose male partner is a professor
is surely important to its endurance, although Jack Gladney's labor is
rarely academic. Rather, he spends much of his time paying bills, visiting his branch bank, and tracking the corporate speech that flows
through his domicile. These acts compose the precise content that
has been understood by critics such as Frank Lentricchia as part of
the text's engagement with the economic realm.[3] In resituating the
economic of the text away from the rubrics of consumption and
commodification and toward that of finance and financialization, I
use the novel to rethink the specificity of economic categories in a
literary field. And because it is the economic which subtends the
text's other crucial categories of gender and periodization, these too
become newly available for review.

Delimiting the financial content in *White Noise* necessarily delimits a style of masculinity that the novel inaugurates and that it sutures
to both a changing global economy and to an expanding readership.
DeLillo himself commented, "I don't think women had been reading
my work before *White Noise*."[4] If that's true, then the novel increased
DeLillo's readership by a considerable amount. Perhaps this increase
came through what the author explained as *White Noise*'s "around-
the-house-and-backyard" aesthetic, a style that he had previously
avoided.[5] What drew "women" to his work or, more specifically, what
placed *White Noise* in the realm of what Lauren Berlant has called a
women's public, was a domestic and feminized masculinity that is
unique to the kind of service economy this era of financialization
produces.[6]

What I introduce as the text's "financial masculinity" reveals a transformation of personal forms of labor and service work in an age of
financialization, and these economic forms correspond to a changed
masculine subject position in a newly global era.[7] To the world of
high finance, often represented by gleaming skyscrapers and the suited

men who populate them, we can add the world of domestic service. And to the hypermasculine regime of investment banking, we must add the compromised regime of personal banking. The service economy of personal banking is distinct in that it involves one doing the service work for oneself. Jack Gladney, as we will see, has become his own bank teller; he goes to the bank and tells for himself. This relationship between finance and self-service marks the period of financialization that this book covers and introduces a connection between the economic and the aesthetic that I will articulate throughout this chapter. Just as Jack does the self-service work of being his own banker, one of the narrative habits of postmodernism is the conscious sense that the reader must do some of the narrative labor herself. For this style of postmodernism, the representation and historicization of finance and its gendering of the masculine subject, it is crucial that all banking is personal banking.

Under the rubric of personal banking, we may include the nagging, prosaic tasks of bill paying, checking-account balancing, and credit-card charging—all of which the banking industry began to qualify as such in 1982. Personal banking is perhaps the first discursive category of what Randy Martin has called the "financialization of daily life," and it is through its representation that I locate *White Noise's* financial forms.[8] I use personal banking to interrogate the distinction between what we have come to know as "high" and "low" finance as well as the distinction between abstract and concrete labor, and I use series of representations of personal banking to question how, exactly, banking became category of personhood, masculinity in particular. Moving between the high finance of global capital flows and low finance of personal banking introduces the problem of scale, but also of identity. In affirming the financial character of objects like the automated teller machine and practices like corporate branding, this chapter establishes an archive that will be deployed throughout the book. When banking is made personal, as it was throughout the 1980s, it is the personal that seems to be "abstract." But, I argue, the personal has rather been *depersonalized.* This is a term I borrow from psychoanalytic thought to indicate a seeming cognitive divorce from reality, one not associated with the unconscious processes of repression and eruption but rather with the formation of a psychic space from which an individual can make sense of her world, however idiosyncratic it may be.[9]

In our contemporary moment, after the Great Recession and after the inauguration of finance as an object of study in social science and literary studies, postmodernism has become newly available for periodization. Critical texts such as Andrew Hoberek's "After Postmodernism," Rachel Adams's "The Ends of America, The Ends of Postmodernism" and Mark McGurl's *The Program Era* have all begun this conversation by asking not what is but what was postmodernism.[10] And as a consequence of the work of Fredric Jameson, it has become literary-critical common sense to accept a linkage between postmodernism and finance capital in the sense that they share a disposition of nonfiguration, fragmentation, and abstraction.[11] In order to analyze this connection, it is important to specify the level and scale of abstraction.[12] The representation of personal banking in *White Noise* may be seen to critique what Marx meant by "abstract labor." And it offers an occasion to rethink the discourse of abstraction as it relates to finance and representation itself. To make the argument that abstraction contains its own economic specificity, I track finance-related practices and objects that might well have been described as abstract but have never achieved that status, corporate branding for instance. I consider objects that could be described as key components of a virtuosic, deracinated economic world-system, but that instead remain quotidian and boring, the automated teller machine, for example. *White Noise* does not present finance as an abstraction; rather, it uses the discursive and material practices of finance in its instantiation as personal banking to shape its postmodern narrative form. In doing so, the novel offers us a chance to specify what we as critics mean by finance, by abstraction, and perhaps by postmodernism as well. On a larger historical level, then, I use *White Noise* to explore how the representation of the nascent technologies in financial print culture might enable critics to think about the historical relationship between financialization and postmodernism before their discrete periodization.

I. Postmodernism, Finance Capital, and the Automated Teller Machine

New and still-canonical theorizations of postmodernity proliferated in the academy in the 1980s; outside of the academy, similarly new and some similarly canonical narratives about finance began to appear in financial print culture.[13] Financial scandals dominated mid-1980s news coverage, with some attached to particular financiers, such as

Michael Milken, and others more notable for their lack of eventfulness or personas, such as the many bank failures that composed the
S&L scandals. Financiers including Ivan Boesky, Donald Trump, Lee
Iacocca, and T. Boone Pickens began publishing best-selling autobiographies and "how to" books on their craft. Romantic comedy films
such as *Working Girl* and *The Secret of My Success* used the corporate
"hostile takeover" as a plot device, while the nonfiction *Barbarians at
the Gate* transformed the leveraged buyout offer into a scene of high
drama.[14]

In this particular convergence between postmodern aesthetic mode
and financial economic form, the former has come to be understood
by literary critics as increasingly dated while the latter has been understood to be increasingly present. In returning to the early moments
of this transmogrification, I want to leave open a space to resignify
the economic and to include more recent, and more nuanced, theories
of what constitutes a stage of finance capital. Saskia Sassen, whose
work was some of the earliest to popularize globalization as a discourses, remembers the 1980s as a time when "everyone was talking
about postmodernism, but I wanted to talk about finance and the
service economy."[15] While mention of service-work is a common-
enough claim to make within sociological and historical studies of
financialization, it is rarely what literary critics think of when they
conceptualize of an age of finance capital or of postmodernity. But as
Sassen's work as well as the more recent work of Randy Martin and
Bethany Moreton have shown, the links between service work and
finance capital are definitional.[16] The site where postmodernism,
finance capital, and the service economy are articulated as one is at
the center of the problematic of personal banking.

The 1980s have been historicized as a time of the high finance of
investment banking, but they were also a time of the low finance of
"personal banking"—the industry's own term for all the picayune technologies and tasks that accompanied the more narrated, and perhaps
more narratable, financial events, such as frauds and scandals, market crashes, and corporate mergers and acquisitions. Indeed, it is a
curious fact of academic work on the abstract qualities of finance that
the ostensibly nonrepresentable forms of high finance have a robust
scholarly archive while the quotidian objects of personal banking
seem to have eluded academic attention. Throughout the decade, newspapers such as the *New York Times* and *The Wall Street Journal's* front
pages were dominated by stories of high finance, but their business

and technology sections were filled with reports on changes and developments in personal banking. In a similar fashion to that of the recently founded *Money* (1972) magazine and other investment periodicals, newspapers focused on changes in technology and on the introduction of new banking services that were targeted toward another novel discursive formation, that of "the individual investor." Most professional observers agreed that personal computers and technological change would revolutionize banking, and those revolutionary aspects were divided into the personal and institutional financial worlds.[17]

Periodicals and newspapers covered all of these technologies discretely, but few of them sought to represent *en toto* the event of personal banking, which I take to be the decision of the banking industry to move into the most intimate domains of private life and to ask customers to undertake the self-service labor required for it to remain there. The term "personal finance" has been in use since the 1920s, but the early 1980s witnessed a new articulation and specification of it when "personal banking" began to circulate in professional banking publications such as *American Banker*.[18] For the banking industry, personal banking was a reference to a planned expansion of the consumer-banking sector: it included the proliferation of credit cards and individual saving and checking accounts, as well the introduction of self-managed retirement accounts in the form of the 401k, and, finally, the popularization of new banking technologies that could make each of the foregoing as facile as possible. The logic behind the decision to expand personal banking services is well captured by Joseph Nocera, who explains that, by the end of the 1970s, Citibank, for example, realized that "Third World loans weren't going to take [the bank] where [its leadership] wanted it to go, nor would commercial lending, only the consumer could take [it] there."[19] But it was *The Wall Street Journal* which most fully articulated the hopes of personal banking: "Banks want to open a branch in your home or office," relayed the paper in 1982.[20] If the banks' move into personal banking was a result of lagging profit in global economic sectors, the representation of personal banking in texts throughout the 1980s may be understood as a site to connect these larger historical trends that have today been periodized somewhat separately as globalization and financialization. As Sassen's previous comment suggests, globalization and financialization are irreducibly linked.[21] Indeed, the recording of this interstitial economic space in fictional texts throughout my study offers a glimpse into a yet to be written history of personal banking as both an intimate and global situation. This is a history that *White Noise* first articulates as a literary problem.[22]

As a result of their expansion into the consumer sector, banks' profits increased dramatically. By the mid-1990s, the personal banking industry, particularly its credit card business, had become the most profitable sector of banking and one of the most profitable sectors of all American business (as it still is today).[23] And as they began to reorient their service practices, banks modified their own productive geographies. In poor neighborhoods, particularly black and Latino neighborhoods, banks began to close and check-cashing operations replaced them; in upper-middle-class neighborhoods banking services expanded, and in high-end urban dwellings banks indeed succeeded in moving self-service branches into buildings' lobbies, just as *The Wall Street Journal* had encouraged. Bankers and technicians considered the phone and television the most likely avenues into customers' homes and persons. In financial print culture, however, it was the automated teller machine that became the dominant visual and textual icon of personal banking. The automated teller machine became a popular symbol of the transition to a computerized, information society, what is now recognized as a financial society. The machine had been invented in the late 1960s (in 1971 one was installed in a Chemical Bank in New York) but it was not until the early 1980s that automated teller machines were common enough to produce sustained journalistic engagement in editorial pages, lifestyle columns, business pages, and national news.[24] *The Boston Globe*, in a story on the city's first outdoor stand of ATMs—what the bank had designated as a "personal banking center"—recorded the event with the self-consciously narratological headline: "No Telling What This Means."[25]

One thing it did mean, however, was that customers would soon become their own bankers through assuming the service work tellers had once been paid to perform. Technology and banking columns explained that customers were now free to engage in their own banking activities twenty-four hours a day, seven days a week; they noted that customers now controlled their own banking transactions.[26] Exciting as this may have been for banks—what better way to increase profits than have customers do for free the very work that paid employees once did?—the automated teller machine was greeted by customers as a site of uncertainty, possibility, and anxiety. Nocera claims that Chemical Bank had to resort to "shoving ATMs down the throats of their reluctant customers."[27] A computerized steel casing that ejects cash to a single, expectant customer, soon the ATM was also figured as a place to be robbed, raped, or even bombed. By the time Mary Harron released her film adaptation of Bret Easton Ellis's *American Psycho* in 2000, the ATM could be assumed metonymically to stand in for all that was terrifying about personal banking. But if the ATM was terrifying, then it also held the potential for sublimity. It was a deracinated technology, free from the local constraints of time and space. It was a computerized technology with an individual computer interface before the popularization of the personal computer. It connected its users to an amorphous global financial network and it disconnected them from their immediate environs.

Modernity has been understood by fiction writers and social theorists alike to foster the proliferation of objectifying institutions. Postmodernity might be said designate the process by which those same institutions become personalized and internalized, by which people are rendered not subjects of so much as subjectivized by those institutions.[28] This logic holds true for forms of daily banking no less than for forms of capital and governance. One bank manager, in describing her customers' reaction to a new "personal banking center," explained that "people look at it and wonder where the bank is."[29] To that geographical question of "where" may be added to the more ontological question of "*what* the bank is" or, more precisely, what kind of referent is "bank" in an era in which the bank itself is becoming despatialized and internalized?

This reconfiguration of the bank from place to person is a productive displacement in more ways than one. And it makes money for the bank, as the customer and worker are now a singular entity. Likewise, this displacement introduces a new logic of capital into the home, but this is a logic of finance capital and decommodification rather than commodity capital and commodification. The internalization of banking extracts labor, but it is a domestic labor of self-service; and it creates a new subject, that of financial masculinity, but he is feminized by the very service economy that subjectivized him as such. Personal banking is a postmodern institution that finds its aesthetic expression in the kind domestic postmodernity *White Noise* that has been canonized as offering. In *White Noise*, Jack Gladney's first-person narration is influenced, interrupted, and, at times, coopted by his personal banking experiences, particularly his visits to the ATM and his home-based self-service work. His disaffected, canonically postmodern, narration relies on personal banking and its consequent subjectivization for its tone and structure.

In an article that is similar in scope and methodology to this chapter, Ivan Kreilkamp argues that the problem of "voice" in modernism—*Heart of Darkness* is his object—is made possible by the "phonographic logic" that saturated late Victorian England.[30] What, after all, is the disembodied, repeatable sound that haunts Conrad's text other than phonographic? "The horror, the horror," famously cries Kurtz; "his words will remain," explains Marlow. From a device that records a voice, to a mode that reconfigures literary point of view through voice, the phonograph saturates this particular modernist novel. The automated teller is a device comparable to the phonograph in that it is both mechanical and literary. It is dissimilar, however, in that the automated teller is firmly connected to global political economy.[31] And yet the distance from voice to voice seems more easily traversed than the distance from the automated teller machine to what I want to designate in *White Noise* a form of narration called the "automated teller." True, the phonograph records a voice, while the automated teller emits money. But *White Noise* prompts its reader to rethink the link between telling and telling, and it asks: If we have all become our own tellers, what is it that we actually say, how do we say it, who profits from our speech and how should this constellation of meaning and value be represented?

Indeed, *White Noise* offers one of the more substantial histories of a machine that has otherwise gone unnoticed. And that machine itself offers a site to consider some of the problems of narratology in a financial era. Jack makes a visit to what he refers to as "the automated teller machine" (no abbreviation to "ATM") and reports, toward the end of his transaction, that:

> I sensed that something of deep personal value, but not money, not that at all, had been authenticated and confirmed. A deranged person was escorted from the bank by two armed guards. The system was invisible, which made it all the more impressive, all the more disquieting to deal with. But we were in accord, at least for now. The networks, the circuits, the streams, the harmonies. (*WN*, 46)[32]

Jack Gladney, narrator of the domestic postmodern, has chosen perhaps the first public postmodern technology to introduce some of the larger structuring themes and forms of the novel. These include

the sense of comfortable dissociation between Jack and his immediate physical world, which will become one of the most reliable aspects
of his narration; and the tension between excitement and anxiety,
between autonomy and entrapment, which accord with the teller's
representation throughout the novel. Finally, there is an intimation
of random violence, which will disrupt the novel the way it here disrupts Jack's easy rapport with the machine. Much as Jack is somehow
disconnected, he disconnects representations of value and one of its
most common instantiations, money, in his pursuit of an ironic if
not sublime excitement which he cannot fully narrate but rather that
he renders as a feeling of correspondence between his object world
and his subjective state. Formally, the novel's use of an idiosyncratic
listlike structure ends the paragraph and will become a recurring feature in suspending or altering the narrative form. These lists usually
appear as a collection of nouns delimited only by serial commas. They
have some identity together as a group, but no clear meaning or order
and they interrupt momentarily the narrative.

At one point in *White Noise*, the narrator records the radio announcing "it's the rainbow hologram that gives this credit card its marketing intrigue" (*WN*, 122). The credit card is intriguing, and in recent
years it has become an object of some interdisciplinary, academic
investigation.[33] By contrast, nothing seems to give the automated teller
intrigue, marketing or otherwise. Its entrance into the everyday was
as pervasive as it was unextraordinary, and it remains part of the unbranded infrastructure of financialization, a fact that will also be important in *White Noise*'s historicization of the machine via its own
narrative construction.[34] Unsurprisingly, the automated teller received the most journalistic coverage from *The Wall Street Journal* in
the 1980s and, once it became pervasive, the coverage devoted to it
in financial print culture began to fade. By the 1990s, the automated
teller could be assumed. These various bits of automated teller history present an object that is boring and violent, everywhere and
nowhere, a burden and an opportunity, personal and impersonal. The
teller is an ambivalent object, one that is simultaneously familiar and
disorienting, surely another reason Jack finds it so engaging.

White Noise is one of the first fictional texts to engage with the automated teller and although the machine itself only makes one appearance in *White Noise*, its importance is assured by both the rhetorical
and plot-based effects it produces in the text. The automated teller
migrates from quotidian object to trope and ultimately takes its place

in the center of what critics have found so compelling about this novel. Jack himself is particularly conflicted about what it means to be a narrator, to participate in or construct a plot, or to face the morbid temporality that, for him, all plotting necessarily entails. "All plots move deathward," he incants to himself and others, "this is the nature of plots," as though not to plot might be a way to evade that futurity. He searches for a way to move forward and generate meaning without plotting, and what I want to assign as a function of "telling" may be understood as a compromise formation between futurity and stasis.

In my study, this sort of tension is almost always a site of financial form. The problem of being a "teller" is a trope that structures the novel and the automated teller is one instantiation of this larger question of how to tell during the novel's historical moment, which, throughout *White Noise*, is sutured to the representation of the financial and is periodized as a time of personal banking. Telling, then, is more expansive than the automated teller, although their relationship does provoke the necessary question of why the first would be signified by the second. Aside from an ironic play on words, why is the teller necessarily a teller? In this first passage, the automated teller does not yet have a narrative presence. But in the novel Jack is not the only narrator. Through a tropic turning of signification, the teller ramifies into something more and becomes a critique of narration and historicization and a site to distinguish the various narrators at work in the text.

White Noise's tropic use of the automated teller is a reminder that while the credit card has a richer and more exciting literary and material history—it was "invented" in Edward Bellamy's 1888 *Looking Backward* and had its own feature length film by 1961—the automated teller has a properly narrative etymology.[35] The automated teller machine is a machine that automates the function of telling. As with so many financial and monetary terms, including finance itself, the word "teller" originated in Old English. It was a feudal term of interpersonal relation whose meaning changed as it described, and was described by, institutions of modern and late capitalism. The verb "to tell" refers to a narrated production of meaning, while a "teller" is a person or thing "that makes known or announces" and also "one who counts money."[36] Public announcing and public counting begin to be woven together in the etymology of "teller." An automated teller is a machine that takes over the functions of the teller who counts or exchanges money. But an automated teller is also a narrator whose function seems automated. Jack himself struggles with and against being his own, and the novel's, "teller." He is once removed from the affective charge of his own narration. He is a recalcitrant narrator who provides an account of a machine that automates telling and, in the process, he becomes a transformed teller.

Without the usual academic and domestic distraction surrounding him, Jack alone interacts with the machine. The paragraph is offset from the rest of the text, suspended as if an afterthought to the rest of the chapter's kitchen-based familial interactions.

> In the morning I walked to the bank. I went to the automated teller machine to check my balance. I inserted my card, entered my secret code, tapped out my request. The figure on the screen roughly corresponded to my independent estimate, feebly arrived at after long searches through documents, tormented arithmetic. (WN, 46)

Like all of *White Noise*'s representations of personal banking, this one is unique to Jack; it removes him from his local context and provides him energy, excitement and awareness—balance doubles between its accounting and psychic referents. He uses an exterior representation to confirm an interior state, and he seeks to correlate the subjective and impressionistic with the objective and institutional. Such a cycle of projection and introjection is an intersubjective operation, though, and one of which a machine is technically incapable. Jack, then, is interacting with himself. His colleague, Murray, his children, or his current or former wives, are not present, nor does he relate to these interlocutors his interactions with the machine as he does the many other events of his life. The teller is his alone. In his rhythmic description of personal banking (inserted, entered, tapped), phenomenology and tactile experience are emphasized, as is the fact that Jack already knew the likely result of his trip: that his own feeble estimation would prove correct. His feeling of serenity in response to that alignment is momentarily interrupted by "two armed guards" and a "deranged person" (in the previous quote) but just as easily reinstated. The final verbless sentence returns the text to a mode of sequential listing that categorizes the ephemeral world that becomes accessible through the machine called the teller.

Ultimately, Jack's interaction with the machine might be seen as a kind of exchange: He does a certain amount of work before his visit and he is compensated with a certain affective stability after his visit. The work he must do is precisely the work of a banker, and, more specifically that of a teller, which calls into question whether "automated" is the most accurate description of the device and, if it is, who or what is being automated? Where a teller once served him, he now engages in self-service at the teller. He does this labor on his own time, in his own house: "tormented" arithmetic, "feeble" estimating and long searching. Once at the bank, he receives confirmation of his skill and encouragement that his work was not at all feeble. His representation of the exchange ends with a listlike, verbless sentence that appears as a paratactic collection of nouns. Some of the most transformative narrative moments of *White Noise* suggest a structural link between the work of telling as it relates to personal banking and the work of telling as it relates to novelistic, in this case postmodern, narration. One question the text provokes is whether one can do the labor of a banker and a narrative teller simultaneously.

In his study of the relationship between the rise of the professional managerial class and the modern, midcentury-American novel, Andrew Hoberek offers a suggestive, Jamesonian addendum on postmodernity. "The postmodern turn comes about when artists abandon [trying to differentiate themselves from alienated laborers] and instead self-consciously reimagine themselves as laboring within and through the mass cultural forms and formulas against which their predecessors had struggled."[37] Hoberek's example par excellence is Andy Warhol, who performed similar (if not the same) labor first in the context of advertising and later in the context of artistic production. This compromise, if not celebratory inversion, between autonomous and alienated labor in postmodern aesthetic production is indicative of a larger transition of labor within an age of financialization, one that is seemingly at odds with an understanding of postmodernism as a result of limitless yet total commodification. Commodification means "produced by wage labor within and for a market," writes Dan Schiller.[38] But the logic of personal banking is quite the reverse, in fact: It is that of the decommodifying of tasks, of skills, of actions, and jobs. Most of us have pejorative enough connotations to the problem of "commodification" that we rarely stop to wonder whether decommodification might actually be a more problematic state of affairs. When the commodification of labor allows for social reproduction, its decommodification must signal a transformation of that process.

At least commodified labor pays it workers to work. But decommodification has no need for the wage. Service becomes self-service;

workers begin to volunteer as, for instance, Babette does throughout *White Noise*. Of course certain people do commodified work in *White Noise*, but rarely are those white people—an important racial logic that will be addressed toward the end of the chapter—and certainly Jack is not doing it at the automated teller. Jack Gladney, then, may be moving in the reverse direction from Warhol as he transforms from a narrator who delights in witticisms and ironies—he claims his daughter Bee "liked me best when I was dry, derisive and cutting" (*WN*, 96)—to one who demonstrates a depersonalized affective presence, a refusal to narrate, when personal labor is required of him at the automated teller.

Jack substitutes the work of a teller for that of a narrator, both literally and figuratively, in a manner that has larger implications for the relationship between labor as value production and postmodern narrative production. One possible reading of the late postmodern novel, from *White Noise* though its more recent issues such as David Foster Wallace's *Infinite Jest*, is that it renders visible the labor of narration. In Wallace's novel, the reader must return again and again to the cumbersome footnotes that compose the last hundred pages of the text. This strategy has been broadly understood by critics as recursive and fragmentary, and certainly this assessment is correct. But such recursivity additionally displays the work of narrative construction and borrows from a literary style, the academic monograph, which has rarely been considered an expressive form, but rather a form of work.[39] Modernism was hard; postmodernism shows how much work it is to be hard, and how much that work costs. In Dave Eggers's memoir, *A Heartbreaking Work of Staggering Genius,* the introductory paratext (or is it paratext? one has to ask) includes a list of dominant objects and their symbolic and material value within the memoir. Eggers draws the reader's attention to the semantic and infrastructural material he has purchased and thus to the price of his labor within his text.

Wallace's novel, Eggers's memoir, and *White Noise* ask the reader to assume a joint responsibility with the narrator for completing the tasks of narration. Any successful narrative act requires labor from both narrator and narratee. The postmodern difference is that the process itself has become aestheticized and celebrated. *White Noise* asks its reader to become conscious of the labor of the narrator through the difference it stages between the work of telling and the much more elusive construction of plotting. Such demands on the reader come through Jack's repeated engagements with the world of personal banking. The teller, then, links the labor of telling with labor as a form of value in a historical moment in which labor is being both revaluated and resignified. Jack himself distinguishes between money and value, but that will only be one of many varieties of value that the text addresses. There is a discourse of commodification in *White Noise* but it comes as a refusal to link all value with commodities or with the process of commodification itself. Read in such a fashion, the novel calls into question the remarkable consistency of the critical literature in interpreting the text's economic representation as reducible to consumption, on the one hand, or commodification on the other.

Jack Gladney is like an automated teller in his narrative tone and in his own narrative analysis. When lecturing to his Hitler-Studies students on the nature and direction of plots, he concludes by thinking to himself, "is this true? Why did I say it? What does it mean?" (*WN*, 26). Jack is much more of a teller than he is a plotter. Indeed, the latter is a function that he abhors since he believes that "all plots move deathward." His narration is flat and without affect, but he does narrate, as if automatically. He is "the false character who follows [his] name around" (*WN*, 17). Yet all narrators, even the most passive, are active agents, and Jack himself manages the text's transitions between story and discourse, or the addenda of non-narrative material into the text, to borrow a useful distinction from Dorrit Cohn.[40] The context in which such transitions are made would seem of crucial importance then, and yet Jack makes it very difficult to trust his own evaluation of context. For example, he himself describes an erection during a lovemaking scene with Babette as "stupid and out of context," but it is difficult to think of a more appropriate context.

At other times he cedes his narrative authority to what appears to be another narrator, a kind of literal "automated teller" who inserts discourses of capital into the text. These include brand names, bills, and messages from his bank. They may or may not be out of context, but as the first person cedes into a kind of institutional second person—"please note, in several days your automated teller card will arrive in the mail"—the text itself becomes recontextualized. Jack and the "automated teller" occupy two distinct narrative positions within the text. Personal banking requires, among other things, a personal relationship with the bank, and when Jack is in such a space, the effect on him is a depersonalizing one. His narration assumes a form of automaticity. He displays narratively an inability to correlate past, present, and future. At some points in the text, the first person seems to recede entirely.

This depersonalized financial subjectivity is made more specific in *White Noise* as it becomes central to Jack's sense of masculinity, which is itself deeply relevant to his ability and desire to tell a story. Of the discomfort he felt with one of his former wives, Dana Breedlove, Jack simply says, "she liked to plot" (*WN*, 48). The ATM performs a calming function for Jack unlike, for example, his experience with another former, this one, entrepreneurial, wife, Janet Savory, with whom he became involved in a "complex investment scheme with a bunch of multilingual people." Their investment scheme was financially successful but psychically unsettling. "We made vast sums. I was entangled, enmeshed. She was always maneuvering. My security was threatened. My sense of a long and uneventful life. She wanted to incorporate us" (*WN*, 87–8). "Incorporation" refers to the establishment of a legal entity as well as the process of taking something into one's own body or being taken into someone else's body. As with the checking of his "balance" at the ATM, here "incorporation" doubles between its financial and subjective referents; Jack is suspended between the two. Both of these matrimonial memories are contrasted to Jack's experience at the ATM. Instead of a bounded legal entity, he describes "streams" and invisibility; instead of feminized merging, he describes autonomy.[41] Jack, as a narrator, refuses to construct a plot: "To plot is to die," he says, and to die is to end a first person narration. But to tell from a depersonalized site is to continue without the risk. "The men consult lists, the women do not," (326) he explains, after having provided a series of lists that may or may not be traceable to him.

To tell is to avoid the risk of plotting, but the teller itself is a risky, violent site. The annals of 1980s financial print culture are filled with tales of teller terror. *The Wall Street Journal*, for example, noted a wave of "rising crime against cash machine users."[42] In another newspaper story on teller violence, a customer, one who was robbed and assaulted during an ATM transaction, asks "why can't the bank protect customers outside like money inside?" Indeed, the teller itself might stand in as a representation of the transfer of risk, like that of labor, from institution to individual in an era of financialization. The teller represents the new precarity of a decommodified life. Robin Blackburn explains that in a financial era "the individual is encouraged to think of himself or herself as a two-legged cost and profit center, with financial concerns anxious to help them manage their income and outgoings, their debts and credits...."[43] This transfer means, however, that the customer assumes the risk of being her own banker, only without the state to protect her as it does the bank.

The most salient way to explore the distinction between teller and plotting and to locate the "I" around whom the text is constructed is to examine the many statements in *White Noise* that do not seem to be narrated by Jack. The most dramatic of these in terms of the novel's narrative construction and denouement is from his bank and related to Jack's automated teller experience. It occurs after the realization of Babette's infidelity but before Jack's decision to take revenge. Jack's sense of a secure and "uneventful" life has unraveled with the news of Babette's affair. He has been cuckolded, he is furious, and he begins to plot self-consciously in order to transform himself from a "dier" into a "killer." Jack wonders if this transformation from dier into killer "adds to a person's store of credit, like a bank transaction" (*WN*, 291). Whether or not the transformation is *like* a bank transaction, before Jack undertakes his attempted assassination of his wife's lover, Willie Mink (a.k.a. Dr. Gray), there appears in the text instructions for a bank transaction, another incidence of personal banking that temporarily suspends Jack's own narrative voice.

> PLEASE NOTE: In several days, your new automated banking card will arrive in the mail. If it is a red card with a silver stripe, your secret code will be the same as now. If it is a green card with a gray stripe, your must appear at your branch, with your card, to devise a new secret code. Codes based on birthdays are popular. WARNING: Do not write down your code. Do not carry your code on your person. REMEMBER: you cannot access your account unless your code is entered properly. Know your code. Reveal your code to no one. Only your code allows you to enter the system. (WN, 295, capitals in original)

At the moment he attempts to transform telling into plotting, an automated teller card—what previously gave him access to the violent, invisible "system"—returns and offers him advice. Crucially, the teller is made manifest and present here as it delimits the narrative organization of telling and plotting. In trying to move from the first to the second, Jack must confront the device and the text it omits provides access to a different narrative and psychic space. The familiar intimacy that the bank assumes with him contrasts to the ruptured intimacy of his life with Babette. To her he says, "I thought we told each other everything." In contrast, the bank says to him, "reveal your code to no one." The opposition between the surety of personal banking and the capriciousness of feminine comportment is crucial to Jack's ability to undertake a plot. He begins to plot, to act furtively, and he engages in an act of retributive violence, an attempted assassination of his wife's lover. Why does Jack choose personal banking as a site for these experiences of alienation, alterity, sublimity, and, ultimately, for plotting itself? He doesn't, of course. Like anyone who has ever received an unsolicited credit card, preferably one with her name already on it, personal banking chooses him. Jack does, however, accept its invitation.

At the automated teller, Jack was sublimely removed from his immediate surroundings. In this moment, he is as well and again it is domesticity from which he breaks free. The gendered logic of sexual jealously accentuates financial masculinity for Jack. It is a masculinity that fails him in his attempted assassination, but it does enable him to do now what before he could not: To plot. Financial masculinity is an important historical construct in *White Noise*; it is a newly available masculinity because the type of finance—that of personal banking—is itself new. Unlike the institutional finance represented, for example, in the "Trusts" of American naturalism, the scene of personal banking is domestic, intimate and private. It is indeed feminized. This is where Jack constructs his masculinity, and it is precisely the financial that allows him to be separate from the domestic even while he is surrounded by it. As postmodernism leveled divisions between traditionally masculinized high modernism and traditionally feminized mass culture, the new prominence of finance in the 1980s confused distinctions between the primarily masculine place of production and the primarily feminized act of consumption.[44] Like telling, financial masculinity is a compromise formation that negotiates the style of the narrator and the subject position he occupies.

Chapter 31 begins with what appears to be a complete transcription—again, how would we know if something was omitted?—of a cable bill payment form.

DID YOU REMEMBER: 1) to make out your check to Waveform Dynamics? 2) to write your account number on your check? 3) to sign your check? 4) to send payment in full, as we do not accept partial payment? 5) to enclose your original payment document, not a reproduced copy?

6) to enclose your document in such a way that the address appears on the window? 7) to detach the green portion of your document along the dotted line and retain it for your records? ... [The instructions continue for 12 steps]

CABLE HEALTH, CABLE WEATHER, CABLE NEWS, CABLE NATURE. (*WN*, 231, capitals in original)

After this paragraph, the chapter begins its local narrative of the family's take-out dinner at a strip mall. Because Jack does not comment on the bill, and because it is nongermane to the structure of the text, it has also received scant critical commentary. Indeed, like any bill that one receives, this one invites being ignored, seems burdensome to read, and is easy to skip over. In one sense, these are jarring textual intrusions into *White Noise*'s diegesis; conversely, because they are not commented on, they are not intrusive at all. This passage could be read as a satire of naturalist form in which newspaper clippings have been replaced by bills, one whose satirical nature would lie in the fact that it provides no informational value to the novel and presents no possibility of a moral discourse. There are in fact many such "tellings" spread throughout the text, these two are unique in their length and their second-person directive. It remains unclear, however, whether Jack or the reader is the subject of this second-person address.

Like the automated teller instructions, the cable bill appears to be a complete transcription with no commentary either before or after the paragraph. And it too presents a series of instructions that concern personal banking, namely the transformation of customers into their own service agents. Here one learns to become an account manager through a series of controlling and patronizing Taylorist disaggregations of motion. But they are not time-motion studies so much as institutional narratives of them; anticipating every potential lapse in the logistics of payment, the directions manage the customer's behavior. Again, the customer does the work of account coordination, and that much less labor is left to do for the clerical worker who receives the bill. The paragraph does, however, end with a verbless collection of nouns delimited by serial commas. Since this is one of Jack's familiar narrative constructions, the passage suggests this is part of his narration, however depersonal it may be.

Because they are delimited from the rest of the text by their tone, formatting, structure and function, N. Katherine Hayles has referred to such paragraphs as a key component of *White Noise*'s "postmodern

paratactic" form. In a reading that gives these odd passages more
attention than most critics do, Hayles claims that "parataxis does not
necessarily mean that there is no relation between the terms put into
juxtaposition. Rather the relation, unspecified except for proximity, is
polysemous and unstable."[45] For Hayles, this paratactic form recapitulates a "postmodern information" society in which one is so deluged
with information that deciphering it becomes a matter of happen-
stance rather than a reaction or relation to certain conditions or texts.
The specific qualification Hayles gives such content in *White Noise* is
"weightless information," because it is seemingly random and connected to the narrative only by proximity.

A problem that has long occupied the attention of narratologists,
the question of what content is necessary to and what content is extraneous from a text's structure is given new shape in *White Noise*.
One remembers Georg Lukács's excoriation of Zola for his too technical description of a horse race: "Mere filler for the novel" he scolds
in "Narrate or Describe?"[46] A realistic, indeed approaching an identical, representation of a bill or banking instruction document would
seem to take the problem of "mere filler" to a new formal level and
into a new historical period. Lukács, of course, does not use the word
"information," but Hayles's use of it to critique a paratactic text suggests that she could be hinting at an example of what Brian Richardson
calls "denarration." Richardson delimits this effect as a moment when
the text appears to turn on itself. It ceases to possess a narrator and
instead appears to have an "arranger." " 'The arranger' designate[s] the
sensibility responsible for the many different voices and effects beyond those of the primary narrator," Richardson explains.[47] An arranger of a "denarrated" sequence seems an appropriate qualification
of these passages in *White Noise*. Yet *weightless* seems too dismissive
a word, even as I agree with Hayles's assessment of the text's structure
as paratactic. To conclude that the bill offers only useless information
is to efface the bill's manifest content, and even the formal fact that it
is a bill, as opposed to a parking ticket, recipe, tax form, and so on.
Indeed, I want to consider the substantial gravitas that this discourse
has within the text and take note of the specificity of its personal-
banking content as it relates to information.

One of DeLillo's most astute critics, Frank Lentricchia, labels these
two passages part of the text's "unconscious epistemology of consumption."[48] Since Jack is a first-person narrator, the bill must have
been recorded by him without his awareness of the process. Lentricchia

concludes that at such moments Jack is possessed and becomes "a mere medium who speaks the discourse of consumption."[49] I want to follow Hayles and Lentricchia and think about information and narration, and those forms' seemingly unconscious relations to the economic within the text, but I also want to modify their criticisms. For certain information to be weightless, other information must be focalized, an opposition that *White Noise* does not necessarily support. After all, the novel contains such memorable exchanges as an extended discussion of whether "outer space is hot or cold," which ends with twelve-year-old Steffie's recognition of the sun's "Corolla," a brand of car by which she means to refer to a "corona," or a hotspot on the sun (also, appropriately, a brand of beer). The family may be a "cradle of the world's misinformation" (*WN*, 81), but it is not clear that the correct information acquired outside the family has any more value to either the family or the reader. Indeed, it is not clear what distinguishes correct information from incorrect information or for whom that distinction matters.

A consumer society produces the contradictory effect of producing heretofore unimaginable quantities of content, some of which will be valorized into information and thus become profitable and some of which will be rendered useless.[50] At the level of plot organization, *White Noise* conveys this socioeconomic condition by overinterpreting random, daily banalities, a specialty of both Heinrich and Murray, and refusing to interpret others. Which is Jack doing here? To answer this requires an understanding of what is content and what is information within the novel, and within the larger scheme I proposed in the introduction in which content is that which is molded by literary narrative; information is what produces value. In the novel, we find a correlation between what forms remain within Jack's voice and what must be ceded to the automated teller. Commodities can be interpreted, as we will see in the next section. The bill appears to be information, and it appears to be outside of Jack's own voice. Jack could be *speaking* the discourse of consumption, but the capital letters and the placement of numbers suggest written transcription as distinguished from speech. This is one aspect that differentiates the bill payment from *White Noise*'s many random lists of commodities— which do appear to be spoken and which I will discuss in the following section. A bill or a brand name, however, may not necessarily correlate to "consumption," as Lentricchia and Hayles both suggest. To understand the text as such requires reducing representations of money and value, of commodities and decommodified labor to the trope of "consumption." This is a reduction that the text itself does not make, and, indeed, actively rejects by repeatedly distinguishing and identifying forms of value. The text invites its critics to be sensitive to a similar separation through its narration of personal banking and its suturing of that narration to the subject of financial masculinity.

As with the visit to the automated teller, the emphasis in the cable bill is not on money. We never learn the amount of payment. Rather, the emphasis of the bill is on the coordination between customer and company via an account. The bill instructs its recipient how to pay, not how much to pay. Jack, by not interrupting, transforms momentarily the text's narrative structure: He lets the cable company itself speak directly to the reader. Yet even in his own narrative absence he assures a recognition of his presence through listing, his habit of telling, his refuge in sequencing, and his refusal to plot. Personal banking provides the context in which to manage the transition between the two narrative forms of telling and plotting. In representing the decommodified labor of being his own account manager, Jack temporarily suspends the more active labor of being the text's narrator. The reader is invited to perform a similar task herself through having to analyze who, in fact, is speaking.

At the most crucial moment of his plotting—his attempted assassination of Mink—Jack himself turns to the language of telling and to the self-conscious analysis of his own narrative. "It was time to tell him who I was. This was part of my plan. My plan was this. Tell him who I am, let him know the reason for his slow and agonizing death. I revealed my name...."(312). A narrative declaration of sorts, Jack loops, repeats, frustrates, and comments on his own bifurcated narrative tendencies. The chiastic structure of his language, "this was part of my plan/ my plan was this" is a kind of suspension, a refusal to distinguish between his own forms of narration even as he undertakes a plotted action.

II. Know Logo

What is the better setting for an advertisement: a place where they already proliferate, perhaps Times Square, or a place that does not yet have them, imagine that stretch of geographical space now known as "nature," a peopleless and billboardless expanse? Neither seems to be perfectly suited to a new advertisement and, indeed, the best place for another one would seem to be a place that already has them, but does not have too many of them. Could that place be the postmodern novel? *White Noise* asks its reader to consider that possibility through its transformation of branded language into novelistic discourse and its refusal to place that discourse within Jack Gladney's narrative frame. The fact that the ATM and the cable bill are not branded (and that the ATM continues not to be branded) in fact serves as segue into the realization that brands are a site of multifaceted historicization in the novel. They are both a representation and an effect of the process of financialization that is the historical context of my study.[51] Brands occupy a peculiar position in the larger interest I have in this book of examining how realist texts and postmodern texts responded to and were transformed by the financialization they recorded. In a society organized around access to cheap credit in order to enable bountiful consumption, few words or images could be more "real" than the ubiquitous brand names that remind subjects to consume. And no realistic representation of any public space in the United States could neglect the icons and words that "sponsor" that space itself. Yet as we will see throughout this study, the reality of the brand saturates post-modern novels as much as it is avoided by realist ones.[52]

In the case of *White Noise* the brand form extends to the author himself. Don DeLillo, through its publication, became one of the United States' most branded authors at the same time he became one of its most canonized, a result not necessarily of his own designs but of changes in the publishing industry throughout the 1980s. That he worked as a copywriter before beginning his career as a novelist is fit-ting. Indeed, *White Noise* is advertised on its cover as a novel that "navigat[es] the usual rocky passages of family life to the background babble of brand-name consumerism." Branding authors may be new to the decade, but branding itself is new too, with the *Oxford English Dictionary* first recording the gerund of the verb "to brand" in the mid-1980s. It is a word whose variations have expanded considerably since then.[53] To talk of branding is already to enter a nonacademic world. "Value," "labor," "capital," "commodity"—all of these terms have a kind of critical cache and bibliographic reach that the brand lacks. The brand is a popular economic term; it is lowbrow economics much like the ATM is a lowbrow economic device. It is an imperial term as well, now used to describe whole processes of the dissemina-tion and reification of meaning from politics to education, from to particular athletes to particular cities. The brand in all of its noun and verb forms may be the most conversational economic term in circulation today. Yet it does not make it into the study of political economy proper, where the brand, more than anything, is understood as "added on" value. The brand name has an "added-on" structure in *White Noise*, too. It dwells nonnarratively in the text and its words are frequently untraceable to any speaker, much as the automated teller machine provides a non–plot-based form of narration.

One of the few critical studies of the brand as its own economic device is found in Naomi Klein's appropriately titled, *No Logo*, an international bestseller whose distinctly branded cover seems both to further and parody the object that it critiques. Klein refers to what she calls "brand-equity mania of the eighties" and isolates a single event to frame this historical problem: the Philip Morris purchase of Kraft for "six times what the company was worth on paper. The price difference, apparently, was the cost of the word "Kraft." "[This] huge dollar value had been assigned to something that had previously been abstract and unquantifiable—a brand name."[54] In a manner quite different from mine, Klein seeks to materialize and historicize a specific process of financialization that occurs within language and representation itself. She isolates branding as able to reveal the process whereby "advertising spending [becomes] more than just a sales strategy: it [becomes] an investment in cold hard equity. The more you spend, the more your company is worth." Klein offers an instructive distinction between branding and advertising: the latter concerns buying a product; the former concerns cathecting to a product, an act which may lead to its purchase, but by a more circuitous and associative route.

Branding, then, is an investment in future earnings mediated through contemporaneous representation wherein the representation itself should be understood as both associative and evaluative. The associative is transformed into the evaluative and, retroactively, the associative becomes the evaluative. An example may render this process, in which most of us engage daily, a bit less opaque. I need a new computer and I immediately imagine an Apple. Whether I buy it or not, the fact of my association from desire to branded commodity is already an evaluation, one which is a value-producing operation for Apple, although that value may not be realized immanently (perhaps I buy the computer next year; perhaps I do not buy it). As these two operations of association and evaluation merge together and retroactively come to constitute each other, they participate in the financial form that I outlined in the book's introduction whereby representation itself becomes value producing, or has the potential to do so under certain conditions.

White Noise manipulates this tension between financial futurity and present, branded representation to disjoint its narrative structure and further its critique of decommodified labor. As the novel's back-cover advertisement correctly states, branded language forms a kind of background babble throughout *White Noise*, in which a common occurrence is a tripartite list of branded items. This babble is clearly spoken and set in quotes. It is given its own paragraph structure but it is unattributed to any speaker: "Master Card, Visa, American Express" (*WN,* 100); "The Airport Marriot, The Downtown Travelodge, The Sheraton Inn and Conference Center" (15); "Krylon, Rust Oleum, Red Devil" (153); "Clorets, Velamints, Freedent" (229). Unlike the tran-scribed paragraphs of personal banking instructions, the content of these lists has received some amount of critical attention. Lentricchia goes so far as to label them *White Noise*'s "most astonishing formal feature."[55] As the representation of personal banking reframed the in-teriority of the subject of narration, the brand transforms the "public space" of the novel's diegesis into corporate tableaux. *White Noise* represents this process as a psychic one filtered through Jack's denar-ration and his depersonalization, where it appears not to be within his own speech. Yet the uncertain narration of this speech is not, in the language of narratology, akin to "unreliability" because few construc-tions could be more reliable than a brand. In the text, brands may also be related to the decommodified labor of personal banking. It may not be concrete or abstract "labor," in the classical sense of the terms that you have completed when you ask for an item with which to blow your nose and you say "Kleenex." But it is, I argue, an evaluative finan-cial operation that functions narratively in *White Noise*.

A brand represents a commodity and, if it is successful in its representation, it will come to efface linguistically the object that it represents. Think, for example, of a Q-tip or a Kleenex. Perhaps this transformation might be even better represented by analyzing those branding operations that failed, since the ones that have succeeded now seem second nature. When it was not tracking the expansion of banking deep into the psyche, 1980s financial print culture was re-cording another territorial rush into personal space. This one was into language itself as corporations sought out the liminal conscious space between signifier and signified. The ever-reliable *Wall Street Journal* reported that the coffee-pot manufacturer Mr. Coffee was attempting to draw an associative link between its own signifier, "Mr. Coffee," and a new signified, coffee.

> IT SOUNDS LIKE a natural: Mr. Coffee coffee. Just now hitting the shelves in Cleveland, Chicago and St. Louis, the new product is an attempt to cash in on positive consumer feelings toward the top selling brand of coffee maker.[56]

Actually, "it sounds like" something Heinrich might utter in the Gladney kitchen. The doubling here of the word "coffee," serves as an odd reminder that the referent and the object to which is refers are already one. Coffee coffee would be a better trademark and the best branding operation would be to own the noun "coffee" itself, a move attempted by many agricultural conglomerates in the selling of basic foodstuffs. *The Journal* also reported that:

> Several companies are planning to put their brand names on fresh food, and many of their initial forays will be in produce. Aided by advances in biotechnology, which companies claim will make produce taste better and last longer, the quest to develop fresh, branded food is one of the highest priorities in the industry.[57]

This apparently did not happen (at least as far as I am aware). But one thinks of Murray's forays through the generic isle in the supermarket or his acquisition of irregular peanuts with a new historical appreciation. This *Journal* article describes companies trying to negotiate a semantic space whereby a branded tomato would signify the taste "vine-ripened"; a branded ear of corn would be associated with an "on-the-cob taste." That is, the linguistic operation in which a signifier refers to a signified would now become a value-producing one. Branding offered a site not dissimilar to personal banking in that it explicitly called on a refiguration of the psychic space of the consumer as a value-producing operation. This operation is quite similar to what Jonathan Beller has called "the attention theory of value," in which all forms of sentience offer the chance of profit.[58] *White Noise* distinguishes formally between the spoken, effortless presence of branded language and the laborious written transcriptions of personal banking, but both of the constructions are financial forms that mold the novel's narrative.

Jack himself explains the brand in the readerly terms of surface and depth. After hearing his child incant brand names in her sleep, he notes that branded speech emanates from "substatic regions too deep to probe" and that it is "familiar and elusive at the same time" (*WN*, 155). His own narration, however, follows a different pattern. Indeed, the colonizing nature of brands within the domain of language would seem to make literature an ideal site to historicize and critique their representation. When Murray argues that "even Tibet is not Tibet anymore" this is no mere tautology. And when Heinrich claims that "everything is a car" he is not in the throes of his adolescent obstructionism. Rather both of these claims locate a doubling and parodying of the branded logic that structures the text, as does the epidemic of déjà vu that sweeps through Blacksmith.

Anne McClintock first drew our attention to how brands have historically been crucial in recontextualizing the domestic as capitalistic, a problem not unrelated to financial masculinity in *White Noise*.[59] In McClintock's nineteenth-century historical narrative, soap is branded with names such as "Pears," whose ads present images of imperial conquest in the process of transition from industrial to monopoly capital. "Soap" becomes "Pears' soap." But the linguistic power of branding changes in different historical moments. If one were to follow the branding process later into its historical development "Pears' soap" would simply become "Pears," the apostrophe vanishes as surely as the object referent. The closest thing that literary or cultural studies have to a brand may be the genre, and particularly genre as defined by Lauren Berlant as giving the reader the pleasure of encountering what she expected. Berlant's psychoanalytic qualification of pleasure—neither evaluated as good or bad but rather identifiably repetitive—is the operative logic of the brand, too.[60] Both offer the similar reassurance of valueless familiarity: McDonald's doesn't necessarily taste good, but it does necessarily taste like McDonald's. The structuring difference between the two can be located in the genre's nonproprietary openness to anyone or thing willing to follow enough of its rules to allow for legibility. Anyone can have a brand, but they may not adopt as their brand what has already been branded.

In one of the novel's early domestic, kitchen-based scenes, Jack reports on the banter of his children and discusses his former wives with his current wife. His narration is interrupted by a phone call. When he answers, he hears a "computer-generated voice" offer him a "high-performance hello." Jack has been contacted by yet another type of automated teller, a recorded voice that calls phone numbers at random to record levels of "consumer desire." Jack hands the phone to his daughter, Steffie, and when he realizes she is "occupied" with the "synthesized voice," he turns to Babette and they continue their conversation. Indeed, it is this scene in which Jack furtively explains to Babette that his former wife "liked to plot," a clear contrast to the random productions of "tellings" around him. The last thing Jack reports about Steffie's phone conversation before the scene ends is that Steffie "twisted around, used her free hand to pull her sweater away from her body, [which enabled] her to read the label. 'Virgin acrylic' she said into the phone" (*WN*, 49). The comment seems humorous and ridiculous in itself: How can a synthetic fabric be "virgin"? Steffie has been asked what fabric she is wearing and she has supplied a technical but generic answer.

Several pages later, as Jack is walking home with Babette, the words "Dacron, Orlon, Lycra, Spandex" appear in the text (*WN*, 52). This list is presented as a stand-alone paragraph, not integrated into the description or dialogue around it and not surrounded by quotation marks. It leads one to wonder if these words are spoken by Jack or by someone else, if they are heard by Jack only, or if Jack and Babette listen to them together. Or is someone or something speaking to the narratee and bypassing the narrator? Whatever the origin of the words, what is stated is a list of patented, branded, and synthetic fabrics. This list, then, is related to Steffie's answer, "virgin acrylic." Each item in the list is a branded variation of some branded, synthetic fiber. The list is part of the answer to the computer's phone call into the Gladney home, but it is not narrated in the context of that phone call. But, then, what was the context of that phone call? The brand is the context that has no context and the part of the answer that is branded replicates this form. The brand is permanently out of context and yet it subsequently creates its own context through its articulation. When this occurs in the novel, brands transform momentarily the narrative structure of the text. They provide for a sense of randomness and discontinuity even though they are hardly random or discontinuous.

This narrative separation between commodity and brand and between experience and brand loops through *White Noise*. The novel provides the narrative of experience before the branded interaction that has caused experience itself. Once one has had the pre-prepared

narrative experience, the actual encounter with the branded commodity only serves as a reminder, but a reminder of something that
had never been experienced. The text's distribution of brands metabolizes strands of narrative and its requisite consistency of meaning
for Jack and for the reader. These transactions, this branded series of
if/thens, are separated in narrative space and time because they are
separated from the narrator himself. The déjà vu that residents of
Blacksmith and that Jack's own daughter Steffie begin to experience
after the Airborne Toxic Event might be said to allegorize the logic of
the brand that structures the text. When one arrives at the commodity to which the brand refers, is one not experiencing a kind of
already-been-there-but-not-exactly effect? The distance between the
two is both traversed and confused in *White Noise*, as it is in capitalist space and speech.

More troubling, however, is the question of whether the brand is
a commodity referent or an actual commodity. Have we just read,
comprehended, and analyzed an advertisement for Dupont? Lee
Konstantinou believes so and he has introduced the provocative
thesis that brands are not available for novelistic representation.
"Tommy Hilfiger and Google and Starbucks cannot be read as allegorical figures. They do not *stand in for* or *refer to* the world system
or consumerism or even late capitalism, but rather are its *real products*, pieces of intellectual property, reproducing themselves again in
textual form" (italics in original).[61] Certainly, Konstantinou is on
some level correct. (Even though one can debate whether the brand
is reducible to the word unit without the appropriate colors, fonts,
copyright tag, and so on). Every iteration of a brand name might be
an accrual of value of some sort, at some future point, to the company that owns said brand, and this is the sense in which the brand
most adheres to my concept of financial form. All publicity is good
publicity, and the novel is open for business.[62] But if that is true, then
literature, not to mention historical criticism, is bounded in the representation of history by certain forms of value. The brand does not
inherently limit such criticism as much as it provides an opportunity
to update what kinds of critical operations are efficacious in a period
of financialization and how different aesthetic modes respond to different economic forms. Thus it is unclear to me, for example, how
Konstantinou's concern about brands is different than the age-old
charge against realism itself, namely that any kind of verisimilitude
is immanent to its object in a manner that limits the ability of that

representation to produce genuinely critical alternative aesthetic or epistemological organizations.

Yet even within the understood strictures of verisimilitude, brands seem less worthy of critical respect. To talk of branding, even without the mention of a particular brand, seems an endorsement of its logic. To criticize the brand, without replicating it, one has to mimic its form without its content while simultaneously indicating that the brand reconfigures the relationship between form and content. And this problem does seem unique to late twentieth-century capitalism. For example, in the realist and naturalist economic novels of the early twentieth century, representations of industrial and financial value were important narrative structures. And in interpreting Theodore Dreiser's representation of harsh industrial conditions in the Brooklyn rail yards, critics have not said that Dreiser somehow replicated those conditions. Likewise, one does not reproduce a factory or meat-packing plant when one describes it. This freedom may derive from the fact that a sweatshop is not a brand, much as Andrew Carnegie's steel corporation produced a commodity called "steel" and not a commodity called "Carnegie."

DeLillo's text accomplishes its critique of branded capital at a formal level in a way that, for example, Haruki Murakami's brand-saturated *Sputnik Sweetheart* does not.[63] *White Noise* offers one possibility of such critical representation when Jack and his family go on a consumerist binge at the local mall. The passage begins with a colleague casually insulting Jack's masculine comportment when the two encounter each other "at the cash terminals" (*WN*, 82). The colleague notes something different about Jack and asks him to promise "not to take offense" if he reveals what the difference is. He says: "You look so harmless, Jack. A big, harmless, aging, indistinct sort of guy" (*WN*, 83). This slight launches Jack into the feminized world of consumption, but only so far. He provides rambling lists of things he buys, might buy, and could buy. He catalogues lists of foods available for purchase at the food court and offers a detailed description of the architecture of the mall. At a certain point, however, the narrative changes from lists that categorize the objects around him, to a discussion of the effect (or affects) that this object world has on him:

> I began to grow in value and self-regard. I filled myself out, found new aspects of myself, located a person I'd forgotten existed. Brightness settled around me.... I traded money for goods. The more money I spent, the less

important it seemed. I was bigger than these sums. These sums poured off
my skin like so much rain. These sums in fact came back to me in the
form of existential credit.…(*WN*, 84)

This passage is interesting for two reasons. First, it is transformed
into another denarrated, seemingly automated telling: one with
credit as its object. The mall scene ends and the family returns home,
each self-sequestered in his or her own room. The narrative then
advances in the form of a new chapter and the arrival of Jack's
daughter by a former marriage. Yet the branded representation of
this experience returns as Jack and Babette discuss their fear of death
and express their mutual wish to die before the other one. Babette
confides her worries of aloneness, which Jack represents as "the emptiness, the sense of cosmic darkness." Then this standalone paragraph appears, without quotation marks or attribution:

MasterCard, Visa, American Express.

The tripartite list receives no comment and Jack responds to Babette
that "I want to die first" (*WN*, 100).

   This list of branded credit is an effect of the shopping scene at the
mall. It is not the return of the repressed, but the acknowledgement of
the external. In this sense, it is similar to the depersonalized textual
productions of personal banking. While paying for his goods, Jack
explained that the value of money had lost any meaning for him and
that "these sums poured off my skin like so much rain," and "came
back to me in the form of existential credit." In the branded list of
three, the sums come back not as existential credit, but as the brands
of monetary credit that Jack probably used for his purchases. The list
completes the shopping scene much as the list of branded fabrics
completed the computerized phone survey. While shopping, Jack
claimed that he had "filled myself out," and that "brightness [had]
settled around" him. Here is the closing of that scene: to the brightness of having credit extended is the "cosmic darkness" of having his
"existential credit" expire; to the expansive fullness now comes the
"emptiness." The transaction has been completed. The brand, then,
serves as a site of displacement and recuperation in a variety of contexts. It introduces and discloses that which cannot be integrated at a
given time, but no one can predict when that time may be. Jack
describes his family's speech thusly: "This is the level of our discourse.

The relative size of holes, abysses and gaps" (*WN*, 101). Brands are one way that those disparate dialogues and interactions are connected in the narrative structure. Brands disjoint time, space, and its narrative representation; they become lodged into a consciousness that is not fully presented or fully absent—but rather external to its subject, much as the brand is external to its object. This is not an unconscious, however. Instead, it is an effect of a reorganization of interior space. Brands are ideal sites of meaning for those who would rather not plot, and Jack steps outside of branded language when he does finally undertake a plot.

It is credit that mediates between branded and unbranded content. At the mall, it is access to credit that puts him in the position of patriarch and benefactor—credit becomes crucial to his financial masculinity. That credit it is not branded when it is used, but is retroactively branded. When his colleague insults him, he turns to credit ("existential credit"). When his sense of self is challenged by Babette's disclosure of her affair, she seeks to comfort him and minimize the damage she might have inflicted on their marriage by referring to it only as "a capitalist transaction." Jack responds to her: "You call this an indiscretion, as if we haven't had a revolution in frank and bold language. Call it what it was, describe it honestly, give it the credit it deserves" (*WN*, 194). Here Jack refers to unbranded credit. Finally, Jack seems to accept Murray's reasoning that "to kill [someone] is to gain life-credit. The more people you kill, the more credit you store up" (*WN*, 290). Indeed, Jack's credibility as an academic comes from his institutionalization of "Hitler Studies." It is his "Socratic" exchange with Murray about the nature of credit and his receipt of automated teller instructions from a bank—both events are nonbranded—that motivate Jack's shooting of Mink. During that shooting, Jack fantasizes about how Mink sees him and wonders whether he [Jack] appears as "looming, dominant, gaining life-power, storing up life-credit" (*WN*, 312).

Unsurprisingly, then, when examining the gun that he will use to execute his murder plot, Jack notes that the bullets are "bullet-shaped" and that the gun itself is "gun-shaped." These descriptions are in a contrast to the distance and decontextualization produced by branded language. The gun is outside this morass of confused meaning precisely because it is not mediated through a recognizable brand for either Jack or the reader. Of the immediacy and power of the gun, Jack concludes that "I guess I thought new names and shapes had been given to just about everything in the decades since I first became aware of objects and their functions" (*WN*, 297). Unlike the language of his children, "supranational names, computer-generated, more or less universally pronounceable. Part of every child's brain noise" (*WN*, 155) the language of violence, whether at the behest of a gun or at the ATM, is unbranded.[64]

While acts of violence offer the possibility of credit, Jack is unable to complete the necessary transaction. He heads into the underworld of Iron City in a stolen car. He disregards the road's tolls, exclaiming "what's a quarter to a state that's billions in debt?" (*WN*, 302). When he finally locates Mink, who is presented as a kind of global, nationless specter, Jack falters.[65] He shoots Mink once, then shoots himself for purposes of exculpation, then conveys both of them to the nearest hospital. In contrast to his earlier expressed fears of "incorporation" with Janet Savory, Jack now has an increased sense of comfort with others. In attending to Mink's wounds, he explains that: "I felt I did honor to both of us, to all of us, by merging our fortunes..." (*WN*, 314–15).

Despite his claims, however, new names and shapes have not been assigned to everything in Jack's life. The naming of geographical space in the text is itself a commentary on the associations of branding. As we read *White Noise*, we tour through locales such as Blacksmith, Iron City, Mechanicsville, and Glassboro. With each of the towns' names, the raw materials of industrial capitalism are transposed onto an emptying space that ultimately, like the bank, becomes despatialized. The names serve only to highlight the obsolescence of their nominal function. We never learn where the town of Blacksmith is located. We only learn its location relative to Iron City, Glassboro, and Mechanicsville. Murray asks, "Who could be unhappy in a town called Blacksmith?" And Jack suggests "these things don't happen in places like Blacksmith" and reports that Iron City is "a large town sunk in confusion, a center of abandonment and broken glass rather than a place of fully realized urban decay" (*WN*, 85). The towns' names no longer refer to the nominally correct things: There are no blacksmiths in Blacksmith, and there is no industry in Iron City. Both names produce an already-expired associative train that leads back to a moment of industrial capital. In the moment of the text's present, industrial capitalism has become little more than a name. Blacksmith might provoke images of blacksmiths working, or it might highlight the anachronism of the term, the fact that blacksmiths no longer work. Both of these associations, however, are outside the structure of linguistic commodification that the brand provides. They produce an unbranded associative train.

Finally, there exists in the text another group of referents that must also be considered "not quite of this world," to borrow Jack's description of branded language (155). These would be the text's periodic references to the second and third world and to hierarchies of global development, all of which have been oddly reassembled in Blacksmith. Casual references to third-worldness are peppered throughout *White Noise*. Iron City is a place of permanent "third-world decay." Jack's medical assistants, including his family physician, Dr. Chakravarty, are "the finest technicians the third-world has to offer." Another of those skilled workers is "Dr. Shiv Chatterjee" whom Babette imitates in a "warm and mellow Indian-accented English" (*WN*, 143–44). A neighbor's child continues to be understood as "adopted" and "everyone refer[s] to the baby by name: Chun Duc," Jack explains" (39). Dakar is either the name of the neighbor's dog or the capital of a country called Lagos. A "middle-aged Iranian man delivers the paper in a Nissan Sentra," and his nationality is as noteworthy as the brand of his car. To relate brand identity and racial or ethnic identity is to return to the remedial natural of branding as an economic logic. It seems an insulting comparison. But in his argument about "the possessive investment in whiteness," George Lipsitz suggests that whiteness accumulates very much like branded identity.[66] Both are sites of aggregated value wherein a representation of symbolic exteriority confirms an evaluation of interiority. In both, future profit and past investment come to stabilize and justify each other, and association between them becomes a site of value. These two logics are more similar than they first appear. If *White Noise* can be read as a novel that records the saturation of everyday life by personal banking, then this claim not distinct from Tim Engles's claim that "novel [is] about the noise that white people make."[67]

White Noise could be read as a novel about the noise that white people make while undertaking the tasks of a decommodified present. While the novel is dramatically postindustrial, much of what get recognized as commodified "labor" in the text adheres to its third-world origin, from building construction to technical knowledge. The others' labor is in stark contrast with Jack and Murray's academic employment, Jack's personal banking self-service, and Babette's volunteer teaching at the community center—all of which is presented as effete and foppish, a comic imitation of the work once done by the middle class. Much of the labor that the Gladneys and their cohort do is self-service labor and volunteer labor. Even Orest Mercator, Heinrich's "snake-handling" buddy is working for another's value, executing decommodified labor in pursuit of a *Guinness Book of World Records'* entry. This doesn't mean that the Gladneys don't work. They do, but they work in a different register of value.

In the opening lines of *White Noise's* chapter ten Jack explains that tuition at the College-on-the-Hill is fourteen thousand dollars a year. He goes on to wonder about the relationship between that number and the physical reality of the students, how they compose them-selves in groups and what their lives express. In one of his common narrative constructions, Jack presents a series of free associative images that become continually more removed from their referent, each one building on the next, until the free association is ended with a declaration of common sense. The most far-reaching of these associations, the one most removed from Jack's immediate reality, is an orientializing reference to depersonalization: "Sometimes I feel I've wandered into a Far Eastern dream, too remote to be inter-preted." From the most exotic to the most banal, Jack then concludes "but it is only the language of economic class they are speaking, in one of its allowable outward forms, like the convocation of station wagons at the start of the year" (*WN*, 41).

Conclusion

The historical and conceptual space between personal banking, brand-ing, and globalization is what the text poses as a series of structural problems and then attempts to ameliorate through its deployment of financial form. *White Noise* presents several possibilities for narrating, not narrating, and for maintaining ambivalence between the two. Narrate; list; let the ATM card do the telling. Record a brand, refuse a brand; do both at once by transforming branded space into narrative time. With each possibility, *White Noise* domesticates new forms of finance within a tone and ambit of the postmodern novel. Its easy re-lationship between finance and postmodernity has allowed it to be canonized and taught in a manner that, for example, a text such as William Gaddis's *JR* has not accomplished (no doubt due its lack of teachability). Mine will necessarily remain an unproven claim, but I do want to make the suggestion that by bringing personal banking into the home as a postmodern narrative device, when personal banking was coming into the home as a capitalist profit device, *White Noise* began the periodization of finance as postmodern, and vice versa. Correspondingly, in canonizing its domestic postmodernity, critics have also canonized these financial logics as postmodern logics.

When Citibank claimed that profits from Third World Loans and corporate lending would cede into the new space of the customer, it was probably not imagining Jack Gladney. But could it have asked for a better spokesman? As *White Noise* records this history, it also records those moments in any history that cannot yet be narrated, cannot yet be transformed into historical time, but rather dwell beside it, as it were, in the personal space I have labeled a depersonal one. And much as DeLillo's novel became a success, so did personal banking. Citibank, currently the world's tenth largest financial company, was correct: the customer could take it there.

Capitalist Realism

THE 1987 STOCK MARKET CRASH
AND THE NEW PROPRIETARY OF TOM WOLFE
AND OLIVER STONE

Realist Subsumption

The stock market crash of October 19, 1987 was almost the end of an era. On that day, the Dow Jones Industrial Average dropped 22.6 percent, still the largest daily percentage drop in history. The event of the crash, Black Monday it would soon be called, suspended the incredible bull-market run that had begun with the Volcker shock of 1981 and continued until 1987.[1] From the depths of a blistering recession in the late 1970s, the American economy had been restructured to devalue production and revalue financial activities. The decommodification of certain labors through personal banking and the transformation of the masculine subject who performs them, as recorded in a domestic postmodern mode, is part of that story. The masculine manipulation of institutional, financial information and the introduction of a new realism that could express and critique such content is another aspect of 1980s economic and aesthetic transformation. A literary history of financialization must consider both realist and postmodern modes and their imbrication in financial print culture.

I define financialization as the assumption of finance to a site of representational dominance because, I argue, it is at the level of representation that finance becomes efficacious.[2] Representation in this case encompasses both social historical and literary processes. In 1975, only 20 percent of Americans were invested in the stock market. By 2000, that number had reached 55 percent; today it is at 62 percent.[3] As the commodified labor market was depressed throughout the 1980s, stock indices rose and profit was decoupled from productive investment. As wages began their long stagnancy and as unemployment increased,

Americans began going into debt at heretofore unimagined levels. Those who still had retirement plans found them in the form of self-managed retirement accounts tied to the stock market. Each of these discrete facts reveals an aspect of finance as the basic epistemic unit of analysis, and the continual measurement and dispersion of such facts in financial print culture has led to a situation where financial indicators function as the most oft-cited, if not accurate, measures of the economy itself.

In the introduction I suggested that to represent finance is to represent "the economy." How that development has been intimately connected to the circulation of certain canonical realist cultural objects is the subject of this chapter. As finance developed a kind of representational monopoly on economic knowledge, Tom Wolfe's novel *The Bonfire of the Vanities* and Oliver Stone's film *Wall Street* were transformed into cultural objects that, by virtue of their timing, their channels of distribution, and their announcement of a radical new realism, claimed a narrative monopoly on representing an emergent financial era. One of the effects of such representational dominance of finance in literature, film, and social history is that finance has become a metonymic stand-in for "the economy" as such.

Black Monday produced the first public, discursive space to consider this recent economic, literary, and filmic history. In financial print culture, but particularly in *The Wall Street Journal*, the *New York Times,* and *Business Week*, evaluative features and articles about the crash appeared in almost every issue for the months that followed. Features, editorials, and news stories questioned whether a new recession would emerge, if the age of mergers and acquisitions was over, and if 1987 was the end of a renaissance financial period. The *New York Times* considered the event historic enough that the paper solicited comments not only from the newly named "supply-siders" and institutional economists of the day, such as the regularly quoted Arthur Laffer, but from a range of self-identified Marxist economists including the Chairman of the Communist Party USA, Victor Perlo. In one "From the Left" column that ran in the paper's national section, Perlo explained that "like all speculative booms—which discount not only the future but the hereafter—this one had to end."[4] That the *Times* was running this column and soliciting such opinions in the late 1980s demonstrates that in this historical moment, the meaning and implications of financialization were elastic and open-ended in a way that is unimaginable today.

Wolfe's novel was released just days before Black Monday. Six weeks after the crash, Stone's film arrived in theaters. Together these three objects—the novel, the film, and the event itself—ground an emerging aesthetic and understanding of finance. In this condensed historical moment, both producers and critics of culture began to ask: What is a financial period, what is a financial text and, most crucially, what is a financial aesthetic mode? I argue that *The Bonfire of the Vanities* and *Wall Street* were central, cementing an aesthetic mode that captured the way a new financial class was beginning to identify itself and its economic object.[5] Both author Wolfe and director Stone agreed that a new financial age required a new attention to realism. After the "illusions" of fictitious capital have "become real," as Oliver Stone's character Gordon Gekko will say, we must ask: What kind of realism have they produced?

My answer is: a capitalist one.[6] Since the publication of Mark Fisher's eponymous *Capitalist Realism* in 2009 this term has gained currency in literary and cultural studies. I use it here with some caveats but also with the sense that there is no better term. For Fisher, "capitalist realism is not a particular type of realism; it is more like realism in itself."[7] I use the term differently. In this book, capitalist realism refers to a prescient realism that demarcates a particular literary-historical period. What Fisher presents as an omnipresent condition appears in my archive as an aesthetic aspiration. My use of the term bridges different "reals" with different "capitals." Mine is a realism that is conversant with Marx's "real subsumption," in which a previously noncapitalist organization cedes into a capitalized one.[8] In contrast to Marx, however, what interests me is not capital producing a new labor process but a new aesthetic mode.[9] I use capitalist realism to indicate the realistic representation of the commodification of realism. I pay particular attention to how Wolfe's novel and Stone's film circulated in financial print culture and show how their circulation became part of their heavily mediated and advertised aesthetic form. In the capitalist realist mode, historical context and a kind of expanded paratext run together.[10] They do so in my archive as well, as I freely borrow from multiple reviews in the *New York Times*, intimate features in *The Wall Street Journal*, profiles in *Business Week*, the second edition of Wolfe's book, the collector's edition of Stone's film, and so on. These are key archival documents for capitalist realism.

Capitalist realism reimagines the economy while maintaining that the economy cannot be imagined because "that's the way it is." Declarative claims are always normative, of course, and this one is no exception. The *New York Times* may have included opinions from those for whom neoliberal financialization was not a foregone conclusion, but Wolfe's and Stone's new aesthetic did not. The economy comes to signify all that is organizing, objective, and historical, all that changes but cannot be changed. It is that from which there can be no outside. In his genealogy of the word realism, Raymond Williams notes that variations on the term function in two rather contradictory fashions. Realism is famously a site of "social extension," a mode which can integrate all the worlds and actors who have been heretofore excluded from codified narrativization. But in its adjectival form "realistic" signifies social contraction. Williams cites the phrase "let's be realistic" as an idiom of limitation and suggests that it is particularly germane to economic situations where it more often means "let's accept the limits of the situation," as they relate to money and distributions of social power.[11] The capitalist realist's realism is realistic in both senses.

For its purveyors, capitalist realism and finance develop a symbiotic relationship that distinguishes such realism from postmodernism. For Wolfe, finance is complicated and therefore difficult to represent; for Stone, finance is exclusive and therefore difficult to represent. For both, the capture of finance, its representation, signals a success of the realist mode. The capitalist realist narrates from a position of identification; sources confide in him and he is trusted to represent those sites and individuals who hold title deeds to the representable world. In exchange for access, he is charged with providing to his subject a mirroring-back, a kind of psychic holding and narrativizing, which necessarily judges the good and bad. The judgment that he renders in the late 1980s is that finance is unequivocally bad— but in a good way. Linda Williams has suggested that it is necessary to maintain a certain amount of skepticism toward Hollywood realism's disavowal of its own melodramatic tendencies, and those twin tendencies (both the melodrama and its disavowal) are present here.[12] At the point when Stone's and Wolfe's texts would seem to be able to subsume all content into their frames, their realism devolves into a kind of generic melodrama.[13]

In keeping with an older realist tradition, from the radical objectivity of a financial economy and its realistic representation comes the radical subjectivity of the financier himself. He is a new kind of white, postindustrial man who is able to locate information, a concept that will itself be re-theorized throughout the decade as a mode of financial content and form. But his is a different financial masculinity than the one introduced in the previous chapter in the form of *White Noise's* Jack Gladney. Financiers do not work for free. Everything they narrate has the potential to become valuable and they are affectively attuned to sites of financial possibility. The characters that populate this chapter may be found in prison, but they will never be found at an automated teller machine. They avoid personal banking and its intersubjective worlds.

In the previous chapter, personal banking offered a site of marked narrative transition and indicated the reorganization of plot. In this chapter, the high finance of the investment bank is sutured to plot. Indeed, high finance is the plot, and it has two dominant and intimately related narrative constructions: the scandal and the crash. *The Bonfire of the Vanities* and *Wall Street* are narratives about personal scandals that just happened to be released at the moment of one of contemporary capitalism's most important narrated events, a stock-market crash. The scandal is a discourse centered on an individual while the crash finds its representation in an aggregate, but as narratives they have certain structural features in common. Both scandal and crash are sites of embedded contradiction that erupt at the moment in which the contradiction can no longer be suspended. In a scandal, the affair becomes public or the insider-trading ring is revealed. In a crash, some novel bit of information reconfigures the horizon of value, causing anticipated profit to collide with present evaluation. Thus both scandal and crash are moments of impasse that are fundamentally narrative: The past is recollected and a new future is tentatively conceived. If narrative form is one manner in which social contradiction is represented and imaginarily resolved, then it is not surprising that after the 1987 stock market crash admirers and critics of finance alike sought an understanding of the past and present of this event through narrative.[14] Perhaps there's no such thing as historical coincidence, but the narratives had just arrived.

The Economy of Realism

Tom Wolfe's *The Bonfire of the Vanities* was not supposed to be about finance. It was serialized in *Rolling Stone* from July 1984 through August 1985 and in its first circulation its protagonist was a wealthy, Park-Avenue dwelling writer. But Wolfe quite self-consciously attempted to produce the canonical novel of the 1980s. Thus, for the publication of his book two years later, he transformed his protagonist, Sherman McCoy, into a bond salesman.[15] Even in this short time period between serialization and novelistic publication, a public culture of finance represented by a select group of male financiers had manifested itself in the United States. This was particularly evident in financial print culture, where financiers were lauded for their deeds and misdeeds and where their best-selling books were widely advertised and reviewed. The S&L scandals, first reported in 1985, continued to drag on and ensured a steady stream of bank frauds, bankruptcies and, of course, bankers themselves to populate the front and business pages of national newspapers.

Wolfe's success at historicization was immediate: When the stock market crashed on Monday, October 19, one week after the book's publication, the *New York Times* "Metro Matters," column opened its report on the crash with the story of Wolfe's protagonist under the title "Life Imitates Art in a City of Wealth and Welfare."[16] Wolfe's transformation into a spokesman of financial culture transpired in similar form. Some days after the crash, *The Wall Street Journal* ran a piece, "Publishers View Wall Street Plunge as Selling Opportunity—for Books," which described how publishers might be in a position to benefit from the crash.[17] The article mentioned that Tom Wolfe had already been asked to write a novel about the crash, a request to which he demurred. Indeed the crash would hang uncomfortably over the fictional representation of finance so that when Oliver Stone's film *Wall Street* was released six weeks later, he complained that "people accused me of trying to exploit the stock market crash with my film."[18] Wolfe thought it would be in "poor taste" to capitalize on the loss of billions of dollars of stock market wealth. He instead had wanted to historicize the event and to use the reality of the crash as further evidence for the contemporaneity of realism to depict accurately, if not prophetically, the world it represents. "Realistic, even naturalistic fiction, not only [can] but should be written in a period like this," he declaimed in a publicity piece concurrent with his novel's publication. In features-oriented journalism, which was Wolfe's first métier, the "now" of representation, a period "like this," was a financial period.[19] In my retelling, the realism that this financial present demanded is specified as a capitalist one, in that it records and celebrates its own commodification, its own ability to become valued. *Bonfire of the Vanities* has been canonized by both its boosters and detractors for its amendments to literary realism. I argue that the novel's imbrication in financial print culture is the most generative site for the consideration of its canonization. Methodologically, what is demanded is less a close-reading than attention to its circulation.

Black Monday, the one-day stock market crash and subsequent three-year recession, was crucial to both *Bonfire's* and *Wall Street's* circulation and historicization. The crash itself interrupted and called into question the conditions under which a remarkable spate of financial accumulation might continue. This is what the *New York Times* had meant when it linked the novel with the crash. The article questioned whether Wolfe's text about a bond trader whose Wall Street life is destroyed after an illicit car crash somehow augured the post-crash life of the market and the new financial class. What is more interesting here is that Wolfe's novel has nothing to do with stock market crashes or even the stock market itself. Wolfe focuses on the bond market, a technical but important distinction. *The Wall Street Journal* read *The Bonfire of the Vanities* as "a novel of New York real estate," skipping the language of stocks and bonds altogether.[20] In doing so, however, the newspaper did draw a connection between realism and real estate, an important link in Wolfe's text and others in my archive. The rhetorical conflation among stocks, bonds, and real estate demonstrates the seamlessness with which Wolfe's text, designed to be a historical text that could speak typically to and of the economic as such, was, within a week of its publication, read precisely as intended. Different sites of value, risk, and profitability became attached narratively and discursively to this one form: Wolfe's realist novel. That novel then became part of an economic, historical event, the crash, that—while the author certainly could not have predicted would actually happen—the text was nonetheless designed to represent: namely, the limits and possibilities of representation itself in a financial era.

But represent in a certain way. According to Wolfe, *The Bonfire of the Vanities* was written to make an intervention in literary aesthetics and produce a radical change in novelistic form. "I just felt that contemporary novelists who were avoiding realism were missing the boat." He continues:

> The past three decades have been decades of tremendous and at times convulsive social change, especially in large cities, and the tide of the fourth great wave of immigrants has made the picture seem all the more chaotic, random and discontinuous, to use the current literary clichés of

the recent past. The economy with which realistic fiction can bring the many currents of a city together in a single, fairly simple story was something that I eventually found exhilarating.[21]

Wolfe goes on to explain his periodization and to foreground New York City as his object. "It was strange to me that in this really bizarre period there are no novels *of* New York."[22] However, Wolfe's hero is not the city: It is realism itself, a realism that can capture and contain the different social, historical and aesthetic levels sedimented within a physical space or a historical moment. Wolfe's approach to realism and his ability to transform his own musings on the matter into part of his realist text were heightened with each new iteration of his narrative. In 1989 he published a manifesto in *Harper's* entitled "Stalking the Billion-Footed Beast," which presented his motivations for writing a realist novel. (*Harper's* would publish a similar realist *cri de coeur* by Jonathan Franzen in 1996 entitled "Perchance to Dream: In the Age of Images, a Reason to Write Novels"). When Brian De Palma released his film adaptation of Wolfe's text in 1991, the novel was reissued in hardback form from Farrar, Strauss and Giroux and contained Wolfe's bravado-filled manifesto. Still, Wolfe distanced himself from the film; in an interview that probed his involvement with it, he said "I cashed the check [for the rights]."[23] The circulatory afterlives of *Bonfire* are just as important as the financial print culture out of which it came. They are part of its narrative and the story it wants to tell; indeed, they are part of its financial form. For some time books and cultural artifacts have been understood to be commodities. But they are also sites of financial expansion. They continue to produce new content, new meaning, and new material any of which may ultimately become valuable. In the case of *Bonfire*, almost all did.

With the rerelease of his novel for the filmic event, Wolfe clearly opposed realism to postmodernism, a standard enough literary dichotomy (even as it omits modernism). In his description of his authorial approach he offers an understanding of what he perceives as the transmogrification of social forces into aesthetic forms. The presence of nonwhite racial and national others, primarily immigrants from the developing world, is considered by Wolfe to be a form of social disorganization, and the vocabulary in which Wolfe describes it is that of postmodernism. In *Bonfire* the main dichotomy is not between immigrant and native, but between black and white. Still, in his manifesto about realism, it is the former pair that is homologously positioned. Both immigration and postmodernity can be historicized by realism, he argues, whereas postmodernism can only be a sympto-matic expression of the very confusion and social flux it is designed to capture. Wolfe believes, then, that his own type of realism has two re-lated obstacles to surmount: first, a changing demographic and its social and cultural norms; and second, a postmodern aesthetic mode that is formally similar to social disorganization and whose very simi-larity renders it unable to capture the content of a postmodern world.[24]

Wolfe's protagonist for this project, Sherman McCoy, attempts to use finance to control the chaos of urban Otherness in a manner sim-ilar to how Wolfe seeks to position finance in his own realist effort to intervene in literary postmodernism. A "master of the universe" who is overconfident about his upcoming international bond sale to a trader in France, Sherman flaunts the affair he is having and his ro-bust ego even as he walks around the city reminding himself to "insu-late, insulate, insulate" from "those people" of color (*BV*, 65–6).[25] His name can be read as indicating that he is a "sure man" and "the real McCoy"; as such he is an exemplary character of financial mascu-linity. The novel's fundamentally dichotomous plot between white, financial privilege and its accidental, surreptitious interaction with black, deindustrial loss is set in motion when Sherman drives his mis-tress, Maria, home from the airport. The two become lost in the South Bronx and while trying to extricate themselves from the various, par-anoid racial dangers that they perceive in the presence of African-Americans, Sherman briefly gets out of his car. In their desperate attempt to flee what they perceive is an imminent robbery, his mis-tress takes the wheel in order to expedite their escape, and the two unknowingly back over a black high school student, Henry Lamb. Ultimately, their crime is revealed and becomes the print-based scandal of the city, circulating in the text's own depiction of financial print culture. Sherman's Wall Street career is ruined; his wife and mis-tress leave him, and, of course, his anticipated bond deal fails. At his moment of complete collapse within the narrative, he is described as "beyond speculation" (*BV*, 467).

Within Wolfe's economy of realism, however, there lurks a certain pastiche. His understanding of realism is as a nineteenth-century European form, as he makes clear in his admonition to his literary contemporaries: "it struck me that nobody any longer seemed to be writing novels of the city, in the sense that Balzac wrote about Paris and Dickens and Thackeray wrote novels about London."[26] Wolfe tries to retrieve, replicate and revive this historical, realist mode, and there is something wonderfully postmodern about Wolfe's project.[27] For all his interest in the historical novel, he seems to understand it as fundamentally unattached to a specific time and place. The historical novel is an ahistorical form. Wolfe, too, can produce novels like Dickens and Balzac because it does not take a historical moment to produce historical realism, only dedication, primary research, and a command of mimicry. Wolfe's realism might be read as a performative one. When his first serial imprint appeared in the July 1984 issue of *Rolling Stone*, a highly stylized Tom Wolfe donned the table of contents page wearing his trademark white suit, holding a hat and cane. With a wry smile, he appears as a costumed nineteenth-century gentleman, a kind of 1980s flâneur. An editorial comment explains that just as the aspiring young novelist Charles Dickens had been commissioned to write and publish serially novels such as *Oliver Twist* and *Nicholas Nickleby*, the reporter turned novelist Tom Wolfe would be undertaking a similar project with *Rolling Stone*.[28]

If Dickens was Wolfe's model of circulation, then Theodore Dreiser was his model of factual accumulation. Wolfe insinuated himself into the leading bond trading firm of the 1980s, Salomon Brothers, much as Dreiser had done in the Chicago trading pit 80 years earlier.[29] One of the young Salomon traders was Michael Lewis, who would go on to write the definitive journalistic account of 1980s finance, *Liar's Poker*.[30] It was Lewis who provided to Wolfe one of his most enduring phrases, the financier as a "master of the universe." Other monikers that Lewis records, such as financiers as "members of a master race" and "big swinging dicks" have had less staying power in the public imaginary. Lewis's impressionistic account of 1980s high finance is saturated with the sort of racialized and sexualized tropes already evident in the foregoing phrases. In the archive of capitalist realism, these scenes would be fictionalized by Wolfe. Amid the big swinging dicks on the bond-trading floor, Lewis in *Liar's Poker* notes the presence of Tom Wolfe at the firm. Lewis, a master of what Marx called fictitious capital, was recording impressions for his soon-to-be career in narrative financial journalism; Wolfe, a former journalist, was documenting facts for his soon-to-be career as a social novelist. Lewis and Wolfe worked together to suture each other into the decade's hegemonic narrative financial texts. On the cover of Lewis's book is a blurb by Wolfe that declares: "this is the funniest book about Wall Street that I have ever read." In Lewis's nonfiction version, the bond-deal succeeds and the bond-trader becomes a multi-millionaire. In Wolfe's fictionalized account of the same trader, the bond-deal fails, the protagonist kills a poor black teenager, and consequently becomes entangled with New York City's political and criminal apparatus.

At the local level, Wolfe used the power of documentary fact to capture the capital that has been called fictitious, but he transformed those facts into realistic fictions. This transposition from the real of fictitious capital to the fiction of historical realism replicates the kind of interrogations between forms of value and forms of realism to which so many cultural critics continue to return. In an era in which value is future oriented, in which we await a future realization, is our shared present one of fiction? Or is fiction somehow rendered less fictional by the ascension of this value form? The methodological point to be made here is that the disciplinary boundary between literary and social scientific writing, particularly economic writing, is porous, as Mary Poovey has recently argued. Furthermore, the division of the literary and the economic might demand a quite different theorization of value, as Ian Baucom has suggested and as I intercept here. Much as realist fiction is like reality, finance is like value, Baucom has argued. Neither is entirely real in the moment of its announcement or iteration, but both depend on some conception of "realness," some uncompromising and objective corporeal world from which financial transactions can be elaborated and which fiction can represent typically.

For Baucom, the insurance contract is symptomatic of the typical, and I introduce it here to provide an example of how value can take both fictional and economic forms. The insurance contract is both a cause and an effect of a newly novelistic and financial eighteenth century in which one's ability to ascertain a type of person (as risky or credit-worthy, for example) would render one both a better novel reader and also a better insurance broker. Fundamental to his argument, then, is a theory of value that, like fiction, is fictitious, a theory of value that is structured by discourse, agreement, codes of representation, and evaluation. The sense of futurity involved in waiting for a fictional construction to become real is categorically financial. The sense in accepting that it never will become real, but will persist in an asymptotic form of like-real, is fictional of the realist variety. In this scenario, both fiction and value have to be represented and both have to be read. It is the description of value that brings it into existence while the anticipation of its arrival functions almost simultaneously as retroactive confirmation of that existence. As with many post-structuralist accounts of economic activity, labor is deontologized and communication is valorized.[31] Baucom explains:

> Central to that theory was a mutual and system-wide determination to credit the existence of imaginary values…and central to [eighteenth century] value was a reversal of the protocols of value creation proper to commodity capital. For, here, value does not follow but precedes exchange (not, to be sure, as the classical Marxist account has it…). Such value exists not because…an exchange has been made…but because two or more parties have agreed to believe in it. Exchange does not create value, it retrospectively confirms it.[32]

Baucom argues that in the moment of the long eighteenth century, to accept this logic of financial value must have required something like a logic of fiction, a relationship that obtains in both directions. Drawing on Arrighi's claim that eighteenth-century finance capitalism will return and intensify in the twentieth century, Baucom suggests that the late twentieth century—and particularly the 1980s, which Arrighi reads as the moment of signal crisis of the long twentieth century—should see a rearticulation of this financial form, dwelling somewhere between pure futurity, realistic fiction, and historicist methodology. This is the precise point at which I want to interrupt Baucom's argument.

Finance has been called fictitious because it is, among other things, a claim on future wealth. That renders it risky.[33] To count on or to account for something not yet in one's possession introduces uncertainty, but to be waiting for something that one expects to arrive introduces the kind of consistency proper to narrative temporality.[34] This tension is evident in Marx's writing on the subject. Depending on what Marx one reads, finance is either the "germ of automatic progression" (vol. 1, p. 921) or "the height of all insane forms" (vol. 3, p. 519).[35] In the first case, in its historical form as alienated state debt, finance was coincident with the rise of the realist novel. Yet the first recorded use of the word "fictitious" was economic not literary. It was employed to discriminate between "natural and fictitious precious stones."[36] Much like in the 1980s, when finance became a metonym for "the economy," fictitious capital seems destined to become a metonym for finance in literary studies in the sense that finance is representational, discursive and performative.[37]

While each of these qualities is certainly an aspect of finance, it would be too easy to focus on the uncertainty and in doing so neglect the certainty that finance offers, just as it is too easy to consign finance to the realm of pure abstraction without noting its many and necessary concrete correlates. What both *The Bonfire of the Vanities* and *Wall Street* suggest is that finance is a sure thing. This suggestion is made first at the level of plot and it manifests at formal levels as well. By the 1980s, finance has become less risky and more real; capitalist realism follows this form by not taking any aesthetic risks. Indeed, the capitalist realist archive directs our attention toward the non-aleatory nature of finance.[38] One of the problems in need of historical resituating in contemporary work on cultures of finance is that for many critics' quotations of Marx on the problem of fictitiousness, he had in mind a kind of finance ("interest-bearing capital") that is not operative today. The point is not to quibble over Marx, but to note that the relationship between financiers, the state, and the anticipatory nature of finance is multifaceted and needs to be updated.

For example, Marx argues that at the end of a typical financial expansion, after the crash has arrived and the crisis is in present form, "The entire artificial system of forced expansion of the reproduction process cannot, of course, be remedied by having some bank, like the Bank of England, give to all the swindlers the deficient capital by means of having it buy up all the depreciated commodities at their old nominal values."[39] Marx explains that through the crisis-ridden logic of capital, the fictitiousness of certain capitals will be revealed and the speculative boom will end. Michael Hudson, however, notes that "Marx wrote this *reductio ad absurdum* not dreaming that it would come true in autumn 2008 as the U.S. Treasury paid off all of A.I.G.'s gambles...followed by the Federal Reserve buying junk mortgage packages at par."[40] In the moment of Wolfe's novel and Stone's film, the new certainty of finance was attached to the S&L scandals (which I treat in chapter 4), in which lousy and more often criminal investments were insured and recompensed by the federal government. In both examples, then, the crisis enabled certain fictitious values to become scrutinized, evaluated, and, ultimately, realized. Far from exposing finance as en empty shell of performative futurity, the very announcement of it as such seems to have the effect of instantiating it as material. In our contemporary moment, for example, David Graeber has argued that "in the wake of the subprime collapse, the US government was forced to decide who really gets to make money out of nothing: the financiers or the ordinary citizens. The results were predictable. Financiers were 'bailed out with tax-payer money' which basically means that their imaginary money was treated as if it were real."[41] Our present crisis (2008–2012), then, is one that has redistributed not only wealth upward, but the burden of fictitiousness, away from a corporate class and onto the working and middle classes.[42]

Of course there is always a risk that value will not be realized for certain individual investors, and this risk tends to lead some critics to understand finance as fundamentally fictitious.[43] But that risk too must be reconceptualized. The fictional texts under consideration here register the process of finance becoming less risky for the institutions of high finance. In an era of "monopoly finance capital," following the instructive terminology of Fred Magdoff and John Bellamy Foster, finance has a new certainty attached to it.[44] "Monopoly" implies certain basic conditions that are not risky—it does not mean these conditions are well designed or that there will not be interruptions, which was precisely the case in 1987.[45] In the world of 1980s finance, risk seems far off and many financial transactions actually appear as a sure bet, for financial tendencies if not their customers.

In my archive for this chapter, then, finance assumes another dimension where it is not necessarily risky because any existing risk is in the process of being isolated and redistributed. There might be individual risk to the financier, and that is what both cultural objects under consideration in this chapter highlight, but those risks are incurred amidst historical certainty and social and aesthetic entrenchment. And although finance is risky for individual financiers, that risk is not necessarily financial. *Bonfire* and *Wall Street* disaggregate financial risk and personal, often racial and sexual, risk accrued in a financial setting. Under conditions of monopoly finance capital, capitalist realism too seems like a sure bet. The very companies whose cultural objects represent finance also finance representation and there is institutional safety in that, too. The stock market crash no doubt helped the sale of Wolfe's book, as did the multiple features on, interviews with, and reviews of both author and subject. Wolfe's book was all but guaranteed to make money as the publishing industry was consolidated and restructured throughout the decade, and as Farrar, Straus and Giroux made the decision to market *Bonfire* as a bestseller.[46]

Wolfe's realism that records finance may similarly be read as a finance that produces realism, in that a publishing house under the dictates of finance capital molded and released the book. In planning to write a historical realist novel, Wolfe followed all the rules: conduct research, canvass a broad swath of society, locate subjects and objects, situations and institutions that are typical.[47] For practitioners of realism this has always been understood as the goal as well as the unique challenge of their mode. Capitalist realism, however, in its periodization of typicality, confronts the fact that much of what is typical is also proprietary, and those subjects and situations are available for a different commitment of mimesis than content that exists in public domain. Sherman, for example, works at a fictional bond-trading firm, Pierce & Pierce, that is based on Salomon Brothers; his dalliances that become a citywide news scandal are recorded in the tabloid newspaper, *The City Light*, a fictional paper based on the *New York Post*. Wolfe's novel requires the reader to be able to make these matches, as perhaps all realism (and satire) does.[48] But Sherman's car is a Mercedes, his shoes are New and Lingwood, and he attended Yale, and these crucial, proprietary identifiers are not fictionalized. If the brand is a financial form, as I argued in the previous chapter, then Wolfe's use of it points to a tension between the typical and the particular as representative of "the economy" in an era of financialization. Throughout this study, we will note that capitalist realism declines to intervene formally in what is proprietary, to the effect of further consolidating the very structure of the proprietary through its representation. Brands for Wolfe are nondiscursive; they are respected and not subject to aesthetic intervention. They are not subject to transaction. Indeed, the conservative *National Review* selected the novel's lack of branded language for special praise.[49] Rather, Wolfe's text itself is a catalogue of what may be and may not be taken out of proprietary context in a new financial age.

Wolfe explains that the challenges of realism have been updated and expanded in a financial era: "American society today is no more random, chaotic or discontinuous than [previous times]. It is merely more varied and complicated and harder to define."[50] This historical state of affairs "makes the task [of the writer] more difficult." While there are many ways to engage this problem, such as reportage or a "nonfiction novel," neither could "reach into Wall Street or Park Avenue."[51] Two words deserve special attention here: "complicated" and "difficult." Wolfe was among the first to provide a site for the fictional elaboration of these properties that were, through the concurrent

S&L scandals, becoming some of finance's most important adjectives in public discourse. In my close reading of his text, therefore, I focus on how notions of complexity relate to his realist project and distinguish it from the postmodern intrusions around him.

In his polemical text, Wolfe offsets the geography of finance, where financiers work and where they retire when the working day is done, as singularly difficult and important to represent. This "difficulty" in his nonfiction prose is tied not to the properties of an object but to rituals of social exclusion. A financial elite would ostensibly have little reason to admit a reporter/novelist into its world to record and review its private behaviors. Yet *Bonfire* includes a careful cataloguing of the difference between styles of town cars, codes of cordiality and comportment on the bond-trading floor, rules for private school kindergarten admission, and how to hold *The Wall Street Journal* in public space, one of the text's many engagements with financial print culture.

What those who had allowed Wolfe to observe them received as compensation was a conception of finance as complicated, difficult, hard to define, and reserved for wealthy white men. In Wolfe's realist project, however, this exclusive and complicated reality would be transformed from a space into a financial transaction, which would come to signify all that is typical and historical. Simultaneously, the representation of finance would distinguish his realism from other modes. With the locations of Wall Street and Park Avenue well represented, the singular locus of complexity migrated to the financial object itself. "The only problem was the complexity of the whole thing," his protagonist, Sherman, thinks of his impending bond deal. Wolfe grounds his realism in the ability to represent accurately the complexity of society through the representation of finance, the most complex economic form. Conversely, as the novel begins to capture such complexity and attach it to a financial object, Wolfe's realism also begins to produce a discourse of finance as complex. He amplified this relationship between finance and complexity in his public speaking and writing. Brian De Palma's 1991 film adaptation of Wolfe's novel was a debacle whose financial plot line was eviscerated from the story. Commenting on this in a retrospective piece concurrent with the film's release, Wolfe asked, "How could a film be made about something so complex?"[52]

The 1980s are not the first time in American literary and cultural history that realism has turned toward finance. But it may be the first time finance has turned toward realism. Wolfe's recapitulation of the

realist, even naturalist, novel offers a chance to historicize the representation of finance and realism in two different eras of capital. He
hews closely to his predecessors by using the temporal properties of
finance to structure the narrative suspense of his text, a temporality
that becomes his chief financial form. Like those earlier novels, tension is located where plot and profit (or loss) may mirror and substi-
tute for each other. *Bonfire* exhibits striking similarities to the early
twentieth-century American naturalist works of Frank Norris, particularly his "trilogy of wheat," and Theodore Dreiser's *The Financier*
and *The Titan*. (Sherman is described sarcastically as a "titan of finance"
[*BV*, 582].) In *The Financier*, for example, finance structures narrative tension through the same device of repeatedly delayed and suspended information that Wolfe uses.[53] Dreiser deploys print-based
information about finance to connect Philadelphia to Chicago and
its commodities market as well as to New York and its stock market.
Similarly, in *Bonfire*, print-based representation of finance connects
New York's disparate ethnic and racial neighborhoods, and it now
offers global connectivity to London and Paris as well.

The moral suppositions of the two texts, however, are quite different.
Sherman is not particularly greedy, he is only trying to keep up; and
there is no delimited, outside force that overdetermines Sherman's denouement. The Philadelphia fire that destroys Frank Cowperwood's
empire in *The Financier* is here replaced with an impoverished, black
adolescent and a white Southern seductress—the factors that contribute to Sherman's fall. These moral and moralizing suppositions loop
back into the role of financial print culture within the novels themselves. Cowperwood, for example, reads about commodity prices in the
financial press. Sherman reads about bond rates in the financial press,
but he also reads about himself through the scandalous, investigative
reportage of the drunkard Peter Fallow. This elaboration of financial
print culture into a site of reflexiveness suggests a less hierarchical and
more co-constitutive relationship between finance and its representation. Indeed, Peter Fallow's job as a reporter is to generate scandals, and
here he generates a financial scandal—or a scandal about a financier.
I will continue this specific line of argumentation in the next chapter.
For my purposes here, however, I note that for both Dreiser and Norris
finance is not complicated. Rather it is purposefully surreptitious.
Norris had described a financial "trust" in *The Pit* as "silent, its ways
inscrutable, the public saw only the results. It worked on in the dark,
calm, disciplined, irresistible."[54] The trust was secretive and conspiratorial

because Norris understood it as a kind of criminal syndicate, not because of an essential, objective property attributable to an economic
form. Norris wanted to demonstrate finance's relationship to labor.
Wolfe wants to demonstrate its relation to prose and to the possibilities
of realism to succeed in a postmodern era. In literature or film, realistic
representation bestows a kind of gift on its object: It grants it the seemingly impartial confirmation of its existence under definite social conditions. In the case of finance and capitalist realism, the two nourish
each other. Finance proves capitalist realism is adequate as a mode of
representation while capitalist realism establishes finance as a complex
network of power, possibility and intrigue. Together they make the fictions of fictitious capital not real, but realist.

The "difficulty" of finance—both working in it, for the protagonist,
and representing it, for the author—reveals several important structural and rhetorical aspects of Wolfe's realist project. Finance works
as the central challenge to realistic representation for Wolfe in its
contemporaneity and its mechanics. These two features function as
the central underpinning of Sherman's financial masculinity. The text
suggests that one requires an instrumental, specialized knowledge to
understand or represent finance. Then it offsets its descriptive force
against that assumed knowledge. Sherman's bond deal paces the first
half of the novel and serves as a nodal point to manage narrative
transition to and from various plot lines. In deciphering and articu-
lating that complexity, the successful representation of finance serves
to legitimate the very realism that Wolfe espouses. Finance becomes
a site of narrative control and possibility. Conversely, at a time when
Wall Street was socially and culturally portrayed as the zenith of
capitalist success, one who could explain it might also have critical
insights into the capitalist failures of the period: unemployment, poverty, and deindustrialization. Wolfe deploys the credit received from
his representation of finance into a series of racist depictions about
the reasons and effects of capitalism's uneven distribution of wealth.[55]

The novel's early description of Sherman's upcoming bond-deal
orients the reader to Sherman's professional life, to the difficulties
that Wolfe's own realism must overcome and to the novel's structural
division between the subject of finance and the institution of finance
capital.

[In 1973,] the French government had issued a bond known as the
Giscard, after the French President, Giscard d'Estaing, with a face

value of $6.5 billion. The Giscard had an interesting feature: it was
backed by gold. So as the price of gold went up and down, so did the
price of the Giscard. Since then the price of gold and the French franc
had shot up and down so crazily, American investors had long since
lost interest in the Giscard. But lately, with gold holding firm in the
$400 range, Sherman had discovered that an American buying Giscards
stood to make two to three times the interest he could make on any
government bond.... The big danger would be a drop in the value
of the franc. Sherman had neutralized that with a scheme for selling
francs short as a hedge. The only real problem was the complexity
of the whole thing. It took big, sophisticated investors to understand it.... You had to have talent—genius!—mastery of the universe.
(*BV*, 65–6)

The paragraph presents the two perspectives that structure and bifur-
cate the novel. The first is the narrator's as he explains the architecture
of Sherman's bond deal. It is the narrator who offers the perspective of
institutional, high finance, and who speaks from a site of racial, geographical and technical exclusivity that Wolfe understood to be the
essence of his novel. The second perspective is Sherman's own as an
individual financier, albeit one who has an inflated sense of himself.
He presents his excitement at having discovered the bond, his belief
that his knowledge is secret, and his expectation of riches if he is successful in his management of this covert, time-sensitive information. These
two perspectives will never fully cohere in the novel. And Sherman
is the only character to receive the benefit of free indirect discourse,
which is evident here. In providing a dispassionate history of the
Giscard, the narrator notes that it has "an interesting feature." But, of
course, it is only interesting to Sherman, who is seemingly not present
in the narration until the paragraph's emboldened declarations of talent
and mastery appear through free indirect discourse. Simultaneously,
in the paragraph's latter section, ostensibly told from Sherman's perspective, the bond is described as a problem of "complexity." It is not
complex for Sherman, even though he deploys the discourse of complexity throughout the text. Here, rather, it is complex for the reader
who is given no explanation as to the importance of the phrases "selling short" or "hedging" the franc, both of which are key to the novel's
denouement.

Like all financial deals, Sherman's is dependent on information
that carries risk and which is spread unevenly over time, wherein lies
the chance of profit.[56] The twin underpinnings of his financial deal

are, first, the time gaps between the date of bond issue, the date of bond maturity, and the novel's present; and, second, the information that Sherman has acquired about the bond in relation to that uneven temporal progress. As with a detective story, these slips and gaps in time and information—the requisite nonsynchronicity of finance— are rich for narrative representation.[57] Indeed, the narrative structure of a detective story offers an interesting site for comparison. Recall Walter Benjamin's insight into the temporality of the commodity and its generic equivalent in the detective story: Labor, hidden and objec- tified in the commodity, can in fact be located through proper dialec- tical study.[58] The detective searches out clues as a way to unobjectify the past, much like the historical materialist does. But a financial logic is different: it is future oriented, and one does not discover what was hidden, rather one waits to see what will be transacted, what financial future will become of the present. Wolfe uses the representation of these financial properties to configure the temporal development of his narrative. The expectation of future profit gives Sherman the credit to have his affair and not to report his hit-and-run car accident. The expectation of his forthcoming success repeatedly suspends into the future his own, and the reader's, anxiety about the early, fore- boding complications that might interfere in his life, such as his wife's knowledge of his affair.

It is the open, anxious temporality of finance that is given the most substantial formal treatment in *Bonfire*. When Wolfe needs to mark the novel's temporal progress, he returns to the bond deal because it serves as a transitional device between the novel's various story lines—politics, community organizing, criminal investigation. Once the bond deal has collapsed, Wolfe is forced to manifest the elapse of narrative time in a new manner. He describes "time rolling, rolling, rolling" to set the pace because finance no longer opens a future (*BV*, 325); a page later he inserts the phrase "time, rolling by, rolling by" twice into one paragraph (*BV*, 326). Such declarations might be read as a struggle to unify content and form or qualify their relationship to each other as it manifests in the novel. But much as the selected appli- cation of free indirect discourse circumscribes the novel's representa- tion of "totality" to a financial class, only certain properties of finance may be conveyed formally in a complementary manner to which they are conveyed thematically. Temporality, as we have seen here, may be both formal and thematic. Risk, too, may be elaborated both themat- ically and formally.

Finance's so-called complexity, however, is not given narrative form, rather it is repeatedly described as such. The plot, the experience of reading *Bonfire*, from the sentence structure to the chapter structure to the book as a whole, is anything but complex. Rather it is long, it is fast, and it is emphatic. Frequently words are skipped in favor of pure sounds as onomatopoeia is deployed throughout the text: "RRRGGGGhhhhh!" "hmmmmmppphhhh!" "thuuuuummmmmpppp!"; the exclamation point is a regular feature. Yet the object of the emphasis is not the economy, financial or otherwise; it is affect itself, as Wolfe records sensations of speed, sexual excitement, anxiety, and pleasure. In this world of masculine sensation, finance finds it form. Men understand it. As he glares at his wife across the table, alternately planning a bond sale and justifying his affair to himself, Sherman thinks: "Judy understood none of this, did she? No, none of it" (*BV*, 262).

It is from this masculine gendering of finance that *Bonfire* locates the risks that accrue to the financier. The narrator focuses on the loss of heritage and tradition men must endure in order to enter finance and on how institutional finance seduced a whole generation. He laments that "these sons of the great universities, legatees of Jefferson, Emerson, Thoreau…Frederick Jackson Turner…how these inheritors of the *lux* and *veritas* now flocked to Wall Street and to the bond trading room of Pierce & Pierce" (*BV*, 60). Finance is unable to perpetuate this tradition precisely because it is risky, but none of that risk is financial. Risk is racial (one might encounter an African American on the street), or sexual (one might be seduced by a buxom southern belle).

We see this racial risk that adheres to finance first in the prologue, which presents the fantasized anxiety of New York City's mayor as he speaks to a disruptive black audience in Harlem. As audience members grow increasingly insolent, the mayor's anger is transformed into a rambling threat that he imagines making to his wealthy, white constituents.

Do you really think this is *your* city any longer? Open your eyes! The greatest city of the twentieth century! Do you really think *money* will keep it yours? Come down from your swell co-ops, you general partners and merger lawyers! It's the Third World down here! Puerto Ricans, West Indians, Haitians, Dominicans, Cubans, Colombians, Hondurans, Koreans, Chinese, Thais, Vietnamese, Ecuadorians, Panamanians, Filipinos,

Albanians, Senegalese and Afro-Americans!...And you, you Wasp char-
ity-ballers sitting on your mounds of inherited money up in your co-ops
with the twelve-foot ceilings and the two wings, one for you and one for
the help, do you really think you're impregnable? And you German-
Jewish financiers who have finally made it into the same buildings...do
you really think you're insulated from the *Third World*?... They'll come see
you at 60 Wall Street and Number One Chase Manhattan! (*BV*, 7-8, italics in
original)

This introductory passage introduces not only the theme of racial
interpenetration but also of money's contradictory role in enabling
and defending against it. To read only the italicized words produces
the phrase *your money third world,* and indeed the novel is concerned both to link and to disaggregate the objective conditions in
which the two—money and nonwhite bodies—come together and
the subjective conditions under which such objectivity places one.
Those objective conditions such as the end of the gold standard and
1970s inflation, which Wolfe is careful to date and specify, are very
much coincident with a flow of money and people from the Third to
First worlds and with the flourishing of new financial devices and
opportunities. The transformation of money into finance and the
confrontation between the white owners of money and the social
conditions under which money becomes finance are not only historically accurate, they provide the narrative structure of Wolfe's novel.
Just as there is "too much money" there is, in the above quotation, a
surplus of races, ethnicities, and nationalities.

In *The Bonfire of the Vanities,* finance might be defined as money
connected to the future. The representation of money as it is located
in the foregoing quotation, as it is embodied by Sherman McCoy, and
as it is elaborated throughout the novel, presents finance as enriching
but too involved with the source of enrichment and thus unstable.
One cannot be insulated from the Third World if one's money is coming from the Third World. The suggestion is that "they" will find "you"
on Wall Street and that "you" would not be on Wall Street were it not
for "them." Wolfe reiterates the argument in documentary form. In
capturing the many currents of the city, Wolfe does provide evidence for a historicization of the site of finance as newly globalized
and racialized. This tension brings to the fore the dialectical and historical properties of finance that structure the novel: risk, contingency,
profitability, and the traversal of temporal and spatial boundaries.

To enjoy the social inequality one has to endure the social proximity, a problem that an earlier generation of urban, white upper class men did not face. This pattern is repeated throughout the novel: White involvement with finance leads to white confrontation with Otherness (blackness is the main focus); white confrontation with Otherness is risky and leads to individual white loss.

As the novel begins to be melodramatically compromised toward its end, financial institutions are themselves seen to have been racially penetrated by the same otherness that financiers individually want to avoid. Much as institutions are safe from fluctuations in financial markets to which individuals are vulnerable, institutions are safe from the risk that inheres in dark bodies and white individuals are vulnerable to them. In fact, one of the chief moral indictments of Sherman's firm, Pierce & Pierce, is not that it fires him after his hit-and-run accident is revealed and he is arrested, but that it too is involved with a black agitator and proximate cause of Sherman's downfall, the Reverend Bacon, through a fraudulent municipal bond-selling scheme (*BV*, 570).

It is this denouement that provides a site to link risk, race, and masculinity to Wolfe's capitalist realist mode. The real problem with institutional finance is not that it is too masculine, rather that it is not masculine enough. Similarly, finance has a problematic relationship to the racial body not because it is too white, but because it is not white enough.[59] In the most vernacular of phrases, finance has sold out. But Wolfe's realism has a unique relationship to finance. His realism depends on mirroring and capturing its truths and claims. In the introduction to this chapter, I suggested that capitalist realism includes the process of the realist mode commodifying itself, of realism selling out. Wolfe's text may be understood to do so without any seeming awareness or self-referentiality. On the one hand, finance is bad, because it has no heritage and it is not masculine—after all, masculinity is not for sale, nor is realism. On the other hand, in an era of financialization, masculinity is for sale—everything is—and so is realism. The text does not resolve this contradiction. Rather, it concludes with a hysterical, incoherent scene in which Sherman declares that "I've broken with Wall Street. Or Wall Street's broken with me.... [I]n an odd way I feel liberated" (*BV*, 645). Just as Wolfe succeeds in suturing his text to a personal financial event that doubles as a historical financial event, in establishing a new realism through representing what is too complex to represent, his character succeeds in overcoming finance and returns to a real masculinity befitting his name.

"Today Was the Big Crash"

Oliver Stone wanted the title of his film *Wall Street* to become eponymous and, in certain quarters, he seems to have succeeded. Much as Wolfe became the fictional spokesperson for a certain financial class as a result of his perceived prescience, Stone was elevated to a similar status vis-à-vis his moralizing, retrospective gaze. "Greed...is good," his financier protagonist Gordon Gekko memorialized—but not entirely, the tone of his film assured its audience. And when the Great Recession of 2008–2012 was underway, its place in financial history surely established, plans for *Wall Street II: Money Never Sleeps*, a sequel, and another one of Gekko's sayings, were announced.[60] Stone would be available to historicize the Great Recession much as he was there for Black Monday. Except that Stone made his film well before the 1987 event. Released six weeks after Black Monday, the film's timeline placed him in a position rather different from that of Wolfe. If the latter had the good historical fortune of coincidence, then the former was burdened with the bad timing of the transaction itself. Tom Wolfe could politely decline to represent Black Monday, which is what his agent conveyed to *The Wall Street Journal*; Stone was accused of exploiting the crash for personal gain.[61] A film's production time assures that in any local or immediate sense this accusation could not be true. But because finance is so imbricated in representation and inside information, it seems that the accusation could not be entirely untrue, either.

In one of the opening sequences of *Wall Street,* the date "1985" is superimposed across the screen with the New York Stock Exchange (NYSE) trading pit visible in the background. It takes a Hollywood film two years to move through the requisite channels of development, production, distribution, and release, and it is this long dureé of corporate filmmaking that makes it the most capital intensive of representational media. Indeed, that makes film reliant on institutional financial operations. It is fitting that the single most cited cultural narrative of finance in the 1980s is *Wall Street*, a film about finance that necessarily draws attention to the financing of film. Deleuze suggests that "what defines industrial art is not mechanical reproduction but the internalized relation with money... [such that] films about money are already, if implicitly, films within the film or about the film," a relationship that obtains here.[62] In one *mise-en-scène* during which a financial deal transpires, the frame splits into halves, then quarters, then eighths, as various members of the transaction are all present simultaneously. In the upper left of the frame, Stone himself appears and says "Anacot steel, buy it? I take it." When the transaction ends the film returns to a single frame. The idiosyncrasy of Stone's cameo alludes to two relationships that the film allegorizes: that of the difference between a viewer and an investor, and between a financier and a filmmaker.[63] In turning his lens on Wall Street, Stone was necessarily turning his lens on filmmaking and film-viewing in a financial era, much as Wolfe had returned to the scene of reading financial print culture in his novel about finance.

Julie Salamon, a *Wall Street Journal* banking reporter turned film critic, dismissed Stone's film as a lackluster melodrama in the *Journal's* pages. She went on to author *The Devil's Candy: The Anatomy of a Hollywood Fiasco,* a book about the adaptation of Wolfe's novel into Brian de Palma's 1991 film, *The Bonfire of the Vanities.* Mixing fictitious financiers with real ones, she notes that by the late 1980s "variants of Michael Milken and Sherman McCoy" were just as likely to be employed in Hollywood as on Wall Street. And she suggests that one consequence of the end of the 1987 stock-market crash was an increased presence of financiers in the filmmaking process. Banks had laid off

FIGURE 2.1 *Anacot Steel, Stone in upper left*

financiers and they migrated into film. Salamon meant that financiers became involved in the production side, but they were increasingly present thematically, too.[64] Indeed, the film industry itself underwent a series of mergers and acquisitions, of corporate and hostile take-overs during the period in which it represented those otherwise obscure activities with such frequency.[65] Some of the most publicized corporate mergers of the era were of entertainment companies, including the acquisition of Columbia Pictures by Coca-Cola and that of Twentieth-Century Fox by the oil tycoon Marvin Davis. John Nichols's film *Working Girl* and Herbert Ross's *The Secret of My Success* provided meanings and narratives for technical terms such as arbitrage, stock buyback, commodity futures, poison pill, takeover bid, and so on. *Working Girl* is unique in this collection in that the film self-reflexively narrates the acquisition of an independent media company by a conglomerate via an investment bank.[66] Each of these films uses the scale of individual competition to orient viewers to an age of monopoly finance capital. I focus on *Wall Street* because of its canonical presence and because that presence was achieved through its representation in and circulation through financial print culture in a series of features and interviews more so than in actual film reviews.

Wall Street's capitalist realist logic is perhaps best communicated by single directorial feat. Lauded in financial print culture for its uncompromising verisimilitude, *Wall Street* represents the New York Stock Exchange's trading floor—perhaps the most iconic space and consequently image of finance that we have. Stone himself was the first director given permission to record this private space. In a sense, he was given proprietary permission for the iconicity of his realism— a realism that was more real precisely because it accurately captured the proprietary. In this version of capitalist realism, the proprietary becomes more real through its representation and representation becomes more real as it captures and respects the proprietary. Like Wolfe, Stone avoided representing or engaging the brand form, a task already rendered difficult by the medium of film in these years before product placement. Instead *Wall Street* is organized around a process through which all content may function as information, or content that is profitable.

Thus, much as in *White Noise*, in which association and evaluation are co-constitutive, in *Wall Street* description and transaction become co-constitutive. This is a more realist engagement with financial form, and the result is that within the film all representational content may become value producing. If all content did become value producing within the fictional world of the film, we would be in a moment of "realist subsumption." Real subsumption, following Marx, refers to the total incorporation of labor into capitalist production. In more casual theoretical parlance, it is commonly taken to indicate a moment in which "there is no outside." We might say, then, that realist subsumption refers to a fictional scene in which all content within a text/film functions as information rather than content.[67] *Wall Street* does not accomplish that feat, as perhaps no cultural text can. But it does aspire toward such a state of affairs; there is little content in the film on which a transaction cannot be based.

The trajectory of *Wall Street* narrates the rise and fall of young and ambitious New York University MBA Bud Fox (Charlie Sheen), who attempts to break away from his father, a unionized shop steward airline machinist, for a career in high finance. He temporarily succeeds in replacing his father with Gordon Gekko "The Great," a notorious corporate raider (played by Michael Douglas and based on Ivan Boesky). In a case of confused paternal allegiances, Bud fantasizes that Gekko's loyalty toward him will trump Gekko's loyalty toward financial accumulation. Bud offers Gekko "inside information" on Blue Star, the airline for which his real father works, in hopes that the two might take it over, make some money, restructure the company so that all parties benefit, and, ultimately, work together to "build a better airline." Bud's structuring fantasy is of finance working to make production better and of having two fathers: the financier and the machinist, each of whom represents opposing moral positions on women, money, honor, stability, and so on. Instead, Gekko decides to liquidate the airline and appropriate its pension fund, and begins the process of doing so behind Bud's back. Bud learns of his betrayal and retaliates. He does manage to save Blue Star Airlines, after secretly arranging to sell it to one of Gekko's competitors, and his father's job, but his months of illicit brokering for Gekko catch up with him and he is led away in handcuffs and in tears by the Securities and Exchange Commission. The film's opening shot is a hovering aerial of Wall Street; its long closing shot is a similarly hovering aerial of the Federal Courthouse in lower Manhattan. Like so many morality tales, the film celebrates what it claims to criticize and makes normative what it aspires to isolate.

The dichotomous moral compass of the film is organized on an axis that positions production as good and finance as bad. In the film's closing moments, the protagonist and the spectator herself are advised to "stop trading for the quick buck and go *produce* something with your life, create, don't live off the buying and selling of others." This is a notable vernacular twist on the phrase "make something with your life." In the film, "production" functions as the trope of goodness itself. Good people produce: They create a world of things, jobs, and respectability. Bad people finance: They dematerialize the world and remove selected objects from the private commons of the capitalist public sphere: money, jobs, women and contemporary art.[68] Yet the film also conveys the message that production may be good but it is fundamentally obsolete: historically, morally, and psychically, and *Wall Street* is there to memorialize its obsolescence. At the level of plot, the unionized airline workers—the producers—have two choices: (1) lose their jobs at the behest of one financier or; (2) work for lower wages and with less security at the behest of another.

Wall Street, in fact, continues a long, Euro-American history of condemning finance as a gendered and immoral economic form—a tradition most famously represented by Lady Credit.[69] However, financial transactions were once judged as such because they were thought of as flippant, feminized, and excessive. In the 1980s, that same judgment derives from their hyperviolent, sexualized, masculine tendencies. More so than the film's financial terminology, sexual violence is its chief vernacular. Indeed, frequently, the two idioms occur simultaneously, as when Gekko threatens Bud over the latter's conveyance of financial information to a third party by telling him to "take it in the ass you scumbag cocksucker." This transposition of the gendered language and assumptions of finance from female to male, from ballerina-like to warrior-like, is surely one of the most dramatic reversals in the representation of value that the Modern period has witnessed. Its occurrence alongside a similar transfer of moral condemnation from usurer to debtor is similarly striking.[70] In Stone's film, however, finance is ultimately rendered as only metaphorically violent and indeed as only metaphorically bad.

Wolfe's text is a structurally compromised novel that was well reviewed and subsequently transformed into a dismal film. Stone's movie is a structurally compromised film that received poor reviews and its subsequent novelization by a retired financier was not reviewed.[71] And yet, like Wolfe's text, Stone's film spoke from a position of institutional authority to financiers about finance; then it invited audience members to listen in on a private conversation. A film structured around a plot of "inside information," that's exactly what it promises its viewer. That inside information is a realistic narrative that exposes how the infrastructure of the corporate financial services industry operates, and for whom. But that inside information is also an organization of past, present, and future. Each is transacted into either profit or plot in the world of finance and fiction. And, surprisingly, *Wall Street* does make an interesting contribution to historicizing and elaborating a representational financial form though its tripartite use of information. In the film, information exists on three levels: (1) information as difference in realist narrative structure, a difference that makes a difference in the succinct words of pragmatist Gregory Bateson; (2) information as moral allegory: Who has it, why did they get it, and how are they compromised by it, a concern that applies to viewers and characters alike; (3) and, most importantly, information as the requirement for and result of a financial transaction and thus a location of financial form. In my reading of *Wall Street*, I attend to each mode of information.

Wall Street is a film "about" finance, but its latent and nonetheless central focus is "information" and the metabolization of information through a transaction that is both aesthetic and economic. Indeed, the film's deployment of information complicates the very distinction between content and form. In one mise-en-scène we see Bud walk past a rather disjunctive sign that reads simply: "Infoquest." In another scene, Gekko tells him that "the most valuable commodity I know of is information. Wouldn't you agree?" During their final confrontation, Gekko reminds him: "I took you in, showed you how the system works; the power of information and how to get it." When Bud is arrested, the agent tells him he has violated the "Insider Trader's Sanction Act," a law against the use of "inside information." That law, passed in 1984, was indeed used to prosecute many of the financial criminals whose scandalous deeds throughout the 1980s resonated with the denouement of *Wall Street* and whose own narratives will be introduced in the next chapter. There is no finance without information and in *Wall Street* "finance" is a representation of the speed at which information is valorized. The structural import of this claim will become obvious, however, only after information within the film has been theorized. Bud will find out about something about Gekko's liquidation of Blue Star Airlines, and he will have to make the decision to whom and how to convey this information.

For the viewer to follow this story, however, she must herself have some knowledge about the structure of the financial world. If the viewer does not have that knowledge, the film offers a parallel, Oedipal romance plot. Unlike DeLillo's "around the house and yard" aesthetic, *Wall Street* provides two distinct story lines, one for a women's public, one for the subject of financial masculinity. As the financial plot unfolds, the film provides varying degrees of technical language and data about the contemporary financial world, which is both fore-grounded in the script and continually present in the film's office-based banter. For example, one colleague casually mentions to Bud that there is "too much cheap money sloshing around the world. The biggest mistake we ever made was letting Nixon get off the Gold Standard." This is, of course, a rather sophisticated comment, a refer-ence to the end of the Bretton Woods Accords and the perceived dan-gers of inflation. But the viewer would already need to know about the Bretton Woods Accords in order to recognize the comment's so-phistication. Such comments, and much of the technical language that the film selectively employs, might be read as a different, non–plot-based type of inside information, valuable to those who know how to appreciate it in advance and who already possess the channels to render it useful.

This bifurcation of how information may be interpreted within the film replicates the circulation and reception of the film. The *New York Times* reported that "the film is noted for having accurately cap-tured the ambiance of New York's financial center and its manic, electrifying pace." But the passive voice in this yet-another-feature-about the film and its making, is suspicious. The article includes no quotes and most reviewers condemned the film as excessively melo-dramatic. When paired with the following comment, however, its inclusion makes more sense: "If anything, the production [of *Wall Street*] errs in re-creating the ambiance too faithfully, and the film-makers purposely leave much of the business jargon unexplained . . . it may have been a costly victory for authenticity: the film is doing well in cities with large financial centers or white-collar populations but is not the broad box-office hit that its makers had hoped."[72]

Indeed, the film's circulation further paralleled the circulation of the event of the crash itself, and together they mark the elevation of a certain economic niche to the position of metonym for "the economy" as such. It was a crash of Wall Street that would affect Wall Street but that would come to represent more than Wall Street. "All this bolsters the widespread belief that Wall Street itself was by far the biggest loser in the crash," summarizes one article in *The Wall Street Journal*.

"We've searched high and low to find signs that Main Street is as concerned [about the crash] as Wall Street, and we can't."[73] Just as *The
Wall Street Journal* reported that only financiers were affected by the
crash, only financiers were reported to have watched the film and to
have developed an opinion about it that might be worth soliciting—
and they endorsed it.[74] I have claimed several times that finance is
more dependent upon representation than other value forms. Here,
we see a specific result of that relationship: Finance is able to occupy
a space of eventfulness, change, and drama in a manner that other
forms of value are not. "Labor," for example, never has a crash, nor is
its price run up or depreciated daily, hourly, and so on.

Financiers would have had a quite different experience of viewing
the film from those on "Main Street." Wolfe said that all realism required reporting. A multi-million-dollar film budget allows a director
to outsource that reportage and Oliver Stone hired a native informant.
Salomon Brothers financier turned cineaste Kenneth Lipper was brought
onto the set to liaise between the production crew of *Wall Street* and
the men who inhabited the actual physical locations that would be
filmed. His own novel, *Wall Street*, was published concurrently and
his filmic efforts were at first successful in allowing him to bridge two
worlds. He became a financier to Hollywood stars. But like the form
of finance itself, his fortune was quick to change. He was involved in
a series of scandals and when he was given his own *Business Week*
cover in 2002, it declared in a red, block-lettered headline: "Fallen
Financier."[75] It was Lipper who helped secure the NYSE as site for
filming and it was he who ensured that the film was not too critical of
its perceived object. "'It's not Wall Street bashing,'" he explained in
one of several profiles on the mixing of Hollywood aesthetics and
Wall Street technical knowledge in *The Wall Street Journal*. "'It starts
with the premise that Wall Street has a critical and necessary function
and that it has an ability to heal itself.'" Besides, he informed *The
Journal*, the film would be "kinder to Wall Street" with its own partic-
ipation than without it.

The negotiated settlement between Lipper and Stone about how to
represent Wall Street kindly, critically, and realistically produced a film
carefully tethered to institutional finance's icons and symbols. Famous
contemporary art dealers played themselves in the film; in addition
to access to the New York Stock Exchange, members of its trading
floor including traders, runners, and brokers morphed into extras who
played themselves in the film. Ivan Boesky's 1985 commencement

speech at University of California, Berkeley, Business School was transformed into Gordon Gekko's Oscar-winning "greed is good" exalta-
tion in a stockholders' meeting. The Blue Star Airlines deal was modeled
on TWA's corporate history.[76] Yet for a viewer to ascertain any of this,
she would need already to have been familiar with it. Still, the film
does allow for some political economic linkages to be revealed. For
example, a viewer with little information about finance would leave the
film realizing that financial operations do exploit productive operations—although she would not leave it understanding why finance is
necessary to production, and why its importance is so relevant in 1985.
Likewise she might realize some operations on Wall Street assist
companies ("scientists, researchers, bridge-builders") to raise money.
She would also leave understanding the laws against inside information are treated gingerly, that it is possible to make money by putting
together "deals" that simply remove capital from the sphere of commercial circulation, and that all financial deals essentially involve some
amount of inside information. "If you're not inside, you are outside,"
Gekko explains. Those who do not follow the references should harbor
no hopes of making money in the market. Those who do follow should
be flattered with inclusion, but also ready to accept a certain amount
of moral disapprobation as information also functions as a site of
moral discourse.

To acquire inside information one does not necessarily need to be
wealthy or well positioned, but one must be morally compromised.
When Gekko asks Bud to engage in corporate espionage, Bud pro-
cures a motorcycle and trails a British financier's limousine around
New York City. He voyeuristically observes the financier eating lunch
with other financiers, he sees him walk into an investment bank, and,
finally, he witnesses the man departing in a private jet from LaGuardia
airport. Consequently, Bud is able to deduce his position in a certain
deal. Information here is embodied and, conversely, it can be read
on the body. Inside information is found inside buildings and the
corporate interior is a lively, almost animated presence in the film. Bud
dresses as a maintenance man and walks through corporate law offices
at night. Peep into filing cabinets, stand furtively in elevators, hang
around certain bars, and you will learn enough to exploit what no one
knows you know. In contrast to *Bonfire*, the instrumentality of finance
and its constituents are not described as complicated or complex in
Wall Street. Inside information is not hard to ascertain; it is textured
and environmental and flows freely through urban space. The fact

that information is omnipresent in the mise-en-scène and that finance and information are structurally dependent renders a situation in which all representation in *Wall Street* may be transacted into value at some future point.

The film is shot in a strikingly conservative, almost sepia-like, color scheme with little contrast and muted shades of gray, brown, and beige—and so are the financiers, whose suits seem to grow out of the carpeted floor and whose ties become indistinguishable from the lines of the boardroom's walls. The effect of this color scheme is that there is little distinction between inside and outside, between office space and the exterior environment, between the office itself and those who populate it. All spaces are alive with information because information circulates freely and openly. Any of it might become financial. The physical environment of Wall Street—both interior and exterior—exerts an overdetermining presence in the film, and nameless financial workers and support staff populate the mise-en-scène. In the penultimate climactic moment of the Blue Star deal, random, suited, white men are seen and heard speaking the information that will transform the narrative. Who are they and where do they come from? The viewer has not once seen them before nor will she see them again. But certain viewers will know that many of them are real financiers, playing real financiers in the film.

As it is subject to financial form, information doubles as an object of transaction within the film and an object of narration for the film. Information "about" the Blue Star Airlines and Anacot Steel deals, deals which themselves are based on information, becomes for the viewer, information about the plot and a way to follow it. Consequently, the viewer herself is implicated in the location and distribution of information. A financial transaction, for example, requires information "about" a commodity. And any thing, node of content, or commodity that can be represented as nonidentical to its own future profit may become a site of financing. When the transaction is over, information has been either monetized, commodified, or, in the case of fictional narrative, emplotted. Who may say what might become an object of such an operation, or for how long such an operation might endure? No one, of course. Information is whatever one can make money from. All content has the ability to become information at some point in time, past, present, or future, thus all content must be saved, collected, and catalogued—a peculiarly postmodern problem. Yet capitalist realism has as part of its raison d'être a distinction from postmodernism.

Likewise, information has its own critical theoretical tradition that amplifies my local usage of it here. Both Walter Benjamin and Georg Lukács were concerned that it would be incorporated into realism to deleterious effect.[77] Lukács does not use the same term, but in his critique of Naturalism, he suggests that literary content comes to look very much like what Benjamin calls "information." In that essay, the social world of high capitalism, and its newsprint culture in particular, befits and produces something called information in "The Storyteller". Benjamin notes this is "a new form of communication" that for him is associated with the novel and that he carefully differentiates information from narrative. "Narrative has an amplitude that information lacks," he explains.[78] Information does not survive the present and, like "description" for Lukács, it is a force to render the world contemporary, equal, and commensurate. Of "description" Lukács says, "narration establishes proportion, description merely levels," and that "description contemporizes everything" while "narration recounts the past." Both accounts resonate with the way that Geoffrey Nunberg defines information in a literary capacity some eighty years later.[79] Nunberg argues that information is a term of aggregate, that it has a "metaphysical haeceity," a "thereness," and a "transferability." Finally, Nunberg explains that information is a "quantized and extended substance" with an "interpretative transparency or autonomy."

Taken together, these theoretical texts render uncertain whether realism is a consequence of information and a mode that can represent it, or, conversely, whether information is a consequence of realism and a mode that can represent it. Establishing a hierarchy is less important, however, than establishing the relation between realism and information. What these theoretical texts do make clear is that within capitalism, knowledge and commodification overlap and therefore that realism's ontological guarantees and ever-expanding categories of knowledge present a world ready to be bought and sold.[80] Capitalist realism embraces the threat of ceaseless commodification and self-consciously participates in a process in which narrative and information become substitutable for one another.

Indeed, the structuring ideology of financialization is that information circulates freely and democratically. The capitalist realist project is sympathetic to this claim, which is found in everything from E*Trade advertisements to Thomas Friedman's columns. The notion that information must be equally accessible is precisely what the Insider Trading Sanctions Act legislates when it forbids trading on "inside information." And this condition of information equality is what is required for "the democratization of finance," as Joseph Nocera has called the ever-widening involvement with all forms of personal banking.[81] Yet what financial ideology requires of information is inimical to realist narrative structure in which characters and viewers or readers receive unequal and often conflicting information. (Although it does map onto narrative omniscience quite well.) Realist narrative requires the selective assignment of meaning and consistency to certain textual content in the hope that those semantic investments will pay off narratively in an emplotted future.

Wall Street must confront an aporia. The film can present information as uneven but realistic and plot-driven as it reflects how information is monopolized by a certain class during an era of financialization; or it can present information as even and therefore ideologically consistent with financialization but narratively incoherent. This is a contradiction that the film locates but does not resolve, preferring instead a Socratic apology by Gekko in the film's climactic minutes in which the structure of information dissolves. In my close reading of this film, I argue that although it aims to record the uneven production and distribution of wealth, *Wall Street* is fundamentally egalitarian. For its realism to operate in the manner that Stone desires, he is thus forced to break this equality and to introduce a distinction between information, which may be transacted, and fact, which is only declarative, in the film's closing and incoherent moments.

The film's dedication to the evenness and democratic aspirations of monopoly finance capital is particularly evident in two discrete scenes of financial transactions (those of Blue Star Airlines and Anacot Steel; see images 2.1 and 2.2). During both sequences, the speedy circulation of information, in part through financial print culture, raises a stock's price quickly in one day. Each scene is edited so that every new nodal point in capital's circulation is given its own place in the screen. First the screen splits in two, then four, then seven parts, as every person, phone and computer terminal involved in the transaction is allotted its own visual placeholder. As the stock's price increases, the rapidity of the editing and the number of jump cuts increase as well. This is when Oliver Stone himself makes an appearance. Like Kenneth Lipper, he moves seamlessly between the financial and filmic worlds. Finally, the screen is split between eight different shots, and a seeming multiplicity of perceptions is offered. But of course there is no multiplicity of perceptions, only the illusion

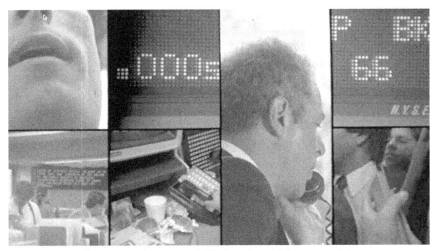

FIGURE 2.2 *Blue Star Airlines, note NYSE trademark in upper right*

of it. The uneven times of a financial transaction are made even and commensurable in their spatial and visual representation. The financial deals are both frenetic and seamless. Information accumulates smoothly and rapidly; it goes where it is supposed to and money is made in neat correlation. Then the transaction ends, as does the split screen.

The film's moral and structural apex arrives when Bud pleads with Gekko not to destroy his father's company, Blue Star Airlines. Bud, of course, had been so impressed by Gekko precisely for his ruthlessness and financial instrumentality. Bud had given Gekko the inside information needed to destroy the company. Predictably, however, when Gekko's ruthlessness is turned toward Bud and his family, he asks to be exempted from it. Yet he does not foreground his plea as personal: He doesn't initially say "don't do this to me." Bud, in a mixture of anger and desperation, authors this exchange:

> BUD: Tell me, [Gekko]—when does it all end? How many yachts can you waterski behind? How much is enough?
> GEKKO: Buddy, it's not a question of enough. It's a zero sum game, sport. Somebody wins and somebody loses. Money itself isn't lost or made, it's simply transferred from one perception to another. Like magic... The illusion has become real. And the more real it becomes, the more desperately they want it. Capitalism at its finest.
> BUD: How much is enough Gordon?

GEKKO: The richest one percent of this country owns half the country's
wealth: 5 trillion dollars. One third of that comes from hard work, two
thirds of it comes from inheritance, interest on interest accumulation
to widows and idiot sons and what I do—stock and real estate speculation. It's bullshit. Ninety percent of the American people have little
or no net worth. I create nothing; I own.

Theirs is an unspectacular dialogue. Indeed, it is rather nonsensible
as dialogue, and it has to be taken out of context, which the film
accomplishes formally. Gekko issues a collection of statements and
documentary facts about the social requirements and effects of an
era of monopoly finance capital. Within the diegesis of the story, the
exchange constitutes a rupture. And yet this is the information that
Stone wants to communicate, as it is the heretofore-repressed condition of possibility for Gekko's success and for what makes finance
so relevant "now" in 1985. In this final representation of information, however, there is no possibility of a financial transaction. In this
scene, information cannot be valorized into money within the diegesis nor can it be integrated into the viewer's experience or comprehension of the plot. Indeed, it is no longer information.

Wall Street is structured around information management so it is
unsurprising that at its narrative climax it is real, factual content that
becomes the star. Fact breaks free from information. Facts are non-
plotted and noncharacterological. The historical facts are "speaking"
for themselves and making a nonrefutable social claim. That they are
speaking through Gekko in the film's climactic moments is distinct
from the film's narrative trajectory. The viewer is given a choice: do
we disavow the content because it is Gekko who is saying it, or do we
disavow Gekko and focus on the content itself? Gekko would certainly be knowledgeable about such things, but he uses such statistics to justify destroying companies, assuming their pensions, and
firing their workers. He may not be a judicious social historian. But
this is rather a nonchoice and here that the film's form and content
diverge. At the level of content we realize that enough is never enough
and it is always too much, a logic which replicates the stasis and impossibility that sustains capitalist ideology as a whole. The individual
and the structural can never appear as a unity: Rather one can always
be disavowed.[82] Bud knows perfectly well that Gekko "does this to
everyone" but that knowledge fails to answer his question, "why [are

you] doing this to me?" Gekko's answer is as simple as it is honest: "Because I can." Much as Stone himself wasn't "exploiting" Black Monday, Gekko is not "doing this" to anyone.

At the level of content, the climax is moralistic and unspectacular; at the level of form, this scene is the film's most distinct. Bud and Gekko's heated exchange, which endures for four minutes, is presented in one seamless shot—the longest and most intimate of the film. The door opens as Bud barges into Gekko's office, having learned of his financial betrayal, while the camera moves between them with no sure sense of commitment. The film's dark and shadowy hues are wondrously transformed by the bright greens and reds of Gekko's conceptual artwork. (He appraises it for us during the scene; its value has increased tenfold since its purchase.) For the first time in the film, sunlight now floods the office, and the space and content that it illuminates may not be transacted. The camera provides the vantage point of a third person, following the two protagonists as they pace in the office, alternating its focus between them as they scream, stare, and turn away, gaining and losing interest with each moment of the exchange. In the mise-en-scène, but just for a moment, a window washer is perched outside the building. Gekko tells us that money is never made or lost, only "transferred from one perception to another." At this moment money and perception are undifferentiated and social. They are both being contested and hopefully "cleansed," as the window cleaner in the background reminds us. The length of the shot and the camera's dedication to recording the entire exchange, its self-conscious presence and verity, are in marked formal contrast to the film's financial deals. The camera dwells impressionistically in documentary fashion.

The spectator may have been seduced by the power, money, excitement, and quick editing of the film thus far, which now seems to have been necessary in part to prepare her for this contextless, formless information about the causes and effects of the financial present in which she dwells. In the crucial narrative climax, the film offers a form of cinema vérité. The content that results from that scene is unconnected to plot or character, indeed it is unconnected to information as the film has theorized and distributed it. It is presented as outside the process of financialization that the film attempts to capture realistically. Like Wolfe's novel, Stone's film is haunted by the capitalist realist imperative to transact all content alongside the awareness that once transacted, the content will be less trusted as real. Wolfe's realism turns to melodrama to free itself from this duality; Stone's film turns to melodrama as well, but also to a kind of dispassionate social historical declamation in which the film presents statistically how divisions of wealth appear in a financial society.

Humiliated by Gekko's financial betrayal and his own criminal indictment, at the film's end, Bud has returned to his machinist father. He has been abandoned by his decorator-lover, who also was Gekko's former lover and an advisor to both men in the contemporary art market. To all this Bud can only say, "Today was the big crash." The two fathers present structurally the choice between two corporations, two modes of accumulation, two styles of financial masculinity. The Old Conservatism and the New Conservatism, the old patriarchy and the new patriarchy, the industrial monopoly capital of airlines and the monopoly financial capital of a corporate raider. Perhaps the film's most radical critique and uncertainty is that both paternal men are respectively ill. Gekko has the high blood pressure that befits financial accumulation: It is able to be continually monitored, the sphygmomanometer is an instrument for the continuous conveying of exact information, diastolic and systolic ratios rise and fall in different social contexts. Bud's father is made sick by an old-fashioned, industrial heart attack—his illness is a consequence of the steady accumulation of arterial plaque.

"The Men Who Make the Killings"

AMERICAN PSYCHO AND THE GENRE OF THE FINANCIAL AUTOBIOGRAPHY

"Murders on our highways I consider charitable acts
compared to some financial deals."*

The Art of the Deal

If Bret Easton Ellis's 1991 novel *American Psycho* is the ur-financial text of our time, it is because the novel introduces the very genre of the financial text as such.[1] Indeed, it reframes the literary, journalistic, and filmic works of the preceding chapter as a generic opportunity that was seized upon but ultimately missed by the capitalist realist intention, a generic opportunity that *American Psycho* will now exploit primarily through the problem of metaphor. In exploring how *American Psycho* became genre creating, we would do well to remember Walter Benjamin's claim that a great text both invents and destroys a genre.[2] Benjamin meant this in a progressive sense; a great text participates in the expiration of one genre as it delimits still another. Ellis's novel engages in a similar generic process, albeit in a rather different order. *American Psycho* destroys the very genre that it creates: that of the financial text. The benefit of the novel's simultaneous elaboration and annihilation of its own economic form is that in *American Psycho* there exists a model of historical criticism about finance. Like the economic form around which it revolves, the genre of the financial text is both retrospective and future-oriented, both analeptic and proleptic. *American Psycho* provides a new understanding of 1980s financial print culture while it also extends forward in time to our

*—Honoré de Balzac (in Robert Fitch, *The Assassination of New York*, 32)

current moment of extended financial crisis, a moment during which the problematic of finance as one constituted by representation, abstraction and periodization is as urgent and historical as it was when Ellis wrote his text in the late 1980s.

To make this argument requires a certain conceptual shift in generic approaches to *American Psycho*, which has been canonized as "brat pack" fiction, a compendium of 1980s postmodern works that includes, among others, Ellis's first novel *Less Than Zero*, Jay McInerney's novel *Bright Lights, Big City*, and Tama Janowitz's short story collection, *Slaves of New York*.[3] Unlike the labyrinthine, encyclopedic postmodern fictions of William Gaddis and Thomas Pynchon or, more recently, David Foster Wallace, brat-pack fiction does not overwhelm; rather it underwhelms, reading more like advertising copy than prose. *American Psycho* pushes the brat-pack aesthetic to its limit with rambling descriptions of branded commodities rendered in deadening prose and broken only by the representation of lethal violence.[4] The novel is structured through short, interchangeable chapters whose titles and contents detail the habits and banalities of upper-middle class, urban consumerism (e.g., "Shopping" [*AP*, 176]; "Lunch" [*AP*, 136]; "At Another New Restaurant" [*AP*, 330]).[5] *American Psycho* is chronologically the last of the brat-pack releases; one of its penultimate chapters is entitled "End of the 1980s" and, indeed, the novel seeks to exhaust the period and destroy "brat-pack" writing, one of that period's most contested literary aesthetics.[6]

In this chapter, I take Ellis's text out of its brat-pack grouping to focus on finance rather than consumption as the novel's structuring representation of the economic. I argue that *American Psycho*'s primary stylistic engagement is less with its postmodern contemporaries than with 1980s financial narratives in fiction, film, and economic journalism. All of the texts and contexts to which I have already referred in this book will now be revisited through Ellis's novel. And *American Psycho* introduces an additional genre of text to my archive: the financier's autobiography. *American Psycho* retroactively produces a genre of 1980s financial writing through its intertextual connections to a series of autobiographies by financiers, including Ivan Boesky's 1985 *Merger Mania*, Donald Trump's 1987 *The Art of the Deal*, and T. Boone Pickens's 1987 *Boone*; as well as to Tom Wolfe's 1987 novel *The Bonfire of the Vanities*; and, finally, to 1980s economic journalism.[7] Ellis's novel looks to the recent financial past to make a claim about the financial present, and in doing so it critiques a form of value that always looks toward the future.

Like *Wall Street* and *The Bonfire of the Vanities* before it, *American Psycho* realizes its meaning through its circulation in the same financial print culture that it represents within its diegesis. Wolfe had employed the theme of finance to mark his fiction as global, historical, and realist. Boesky, Trump, and Boone had used their financial experience to shape the content of their bestselling autobiographical works. They demonstrated their ability to master risk and expose the so-called secrets of profitability as a form of economic knowledge and of masculine self-fashioning. Economic journalism had already established violence as the idiom of finance, with *Time*'s captioning of Ivan Boesky as "Ivan the Terrible" on its cover being only one of many examples.[8] Ellis's text synthesizes the content of *The Bonfire of the Vanities*—the story of a financier who becomes known as a murderer—and the form of the financial autobiography—first-person, masculine grandiosity based on successful financial deals—into its own fictional, autobiographical form whose structuring language is violence. Out of this collection comes a novel, *American Psycho*, whose manifest violence caused its circulation to become as scandalous as the 1980s financial world it represented.[9] That it achieves many of its effects through its representation of the automated teller machine and its engagement with the brand-name, the two structuring financial-cum-narrative devices of *White Noise*, only adds to its defining role as the genre-delimiting financial text of the period.

American Psycho, then, is a patchwork of what might be categorized as capitalist realist, postmodern, and autobiographical styles of financial representation. The effect of this combinatory aesthetic is twofold: First, the text challenges the relationship between content and form in the process of genre creation. Ellis's novel re-poses the twin questions: What is a financial text, and what is represented in a financial narrative? We know character, affect, plot, and setting can be generically determinant—can value form? Second, *American Psycho* represents the financial content of the foregoing works such that it renders comprehensible yet another articulation of financial form. Financial form in *American Psycho* becomes an economic and epistemic category of value whose representation foregrounds a series of tensions between the twin financial processes of description and transaction and of association and narration as both pairs negotiate the space between content and information. As in my reading of

White Noise, I base this second claim on the presence of the two most prominent financial/literary devices in *American Psycho*: the branded commodity and the automated teller machine. And, again, neither of these devices will seem immediately "financial" compared with the high finance of mergers and acquisitions represented in financiers' autobiographies or the international bond-trading subplot that grounds *The Bonfire of The Vanities*. High finance is also prominent in *American Psycho*, but it is precisely the reformulation of financial content, of its object, subject and representation, that is the crucial component of *American Psycho*'s narrative and generic strategy. Throughout this book, I have defined finance as a narrative relationship to the tension between content and information that transpires through different devices and aesthetic modes. *American Psycho* reframes this process as well. Much as it disrupts the financial masculinity found on Sherman McCoy, Gordon Gekko, Jack Gladney, and, as we will soon see, Donald Trump, the novel disrupts the very structure of the financial transaction on which the foregoing subjectivities depend.

Genre, Violence, and Value in 1980s Financial Print Culture

In 1988 *The New York Review of Books* published a contemptuous essay by its resident economic critic, the esteemed American economist John Kenneth Galbraith. Galbraith had been given the task of reviewing several memoirs of newly prominent financiers: Ivan Boesky's *Merger Mania*, Donald Trump's *The Art of the Deal*, and T. Boone Pickens's *Boone*.[10] Galbraith begins his review by noting that while some authors publish books to make money, others use book publishing as an avenue to improve their depressed social standing, in this case the result of the authors' money-making practices. "There are books by people who, having made a great deal of money, believe that through a book they can enhance or perhaps redeem their public reputation . . . a book gives something or is thought to give something that money cannot buy."[11] Yet instead of exploring the tensions between real capital and immaterial or cultural capital that these books might contain, Galbraith's review takes a pedestrian turn. He criticizes the split infinitives in Trump's text and the contradictions between T. Boone Pickens's ostensible economic "advocacy" for shareholders and his actual economic actions; he is amused that Boesky's book, supposedly written to bolster his reputation, was pulled off the shelves by its publisher after his criminal indictment for insider trading.

Diminishing the literary merit of these texts is not a difficult task. *The Wall Street Journal* was perhaps the harshest in its assessment: "Everybody knows by now what a fraud CEO autobiographies have turned out to be," wrote Joseph Nocera.[12] For Galbraith, the fact that the texts' manifest aim is not profit somehow makes them more insidious. While they are not literally making money for their authors, their authors' self-aggrandizement cannot be separated from their accumulative dispositions, as the title *Boone*, both a proper name and an unexpected financial windfall, betrays. For Nocera, the autobiographies trespass on the legitimacy of capitalism itself. If these financiers produce fraudulent texts in their extracurricular engagements, what must they do in their actual economic dealings? Perhaps the reviewers realize the futility of their own project as well and thus their overly harsh and general assessments: By reviewing these texts, the reviewers too enter the financiers' world of discursive accumulation. All publicity is good publicity because capital knows no ethical binaries, only forms of value and its subsequent representation.[13]

Indeed, there lingers throughout the decade's popular financial archive of newspapers, magazines, film, and television the suspicion that representation is somehow equivalent to evaluation; that by representing the financial world one, in effect, becomes financial and may therefore benefit from the act of representation. How does a reader or critic distinguish between content, that which may be narrated and represented, and information, that which is profitable? When is the first transformed into the second and under what conditions? Wolfe's novel about a financier's personal downfall was published the week of the spectacular one-day Dow Jones crash on October 19, 1987, with the event serving as publicity for the novel: By the week's end, the crash was being narrated with references to Wolfe's protagonist in the pages of the *New York Times*.[14] This particular pairing may have been coincidental, but its effect would nonetheless be that a collective loss on the indices of Wall Street would somehow be transformed into a gain for Wolfe.

The suspicion that finance is more sutured to the logic of representation than other forms of value is correct, then. Representation is crucial to finance's efficaciousness in a manner that differentiates it from other forms of value. Heretofore, I have substantiated this claim theoretically. The archive of the financial autobiography provides a chance to do so a bit more concretely. Pickens offers one opinion in *Boone*. He implicates daily financial print culture in publishing obviously planted stories designed to move the price of stocks within a single day. The more certain stocks are represented, Pickens argues, the more money will immediately accrue to them in certain situations. He notes that it is the investment bankers themselves who leak this information, and it is investment bankers who benefit. Pickens goes so far as to claim that he avoids investment bankers whenever possible because, he argues, their income does not derive from their fees or salary but from their access to representation in financial print culture and their ability to monetize that content. He does not cite specific examples, but at one point in 1987 the joint site of profit and print culture became self-reflexive. Several "Heard on the Street" reporters for the *Wall Street Journal*, the very columnists to whom investment bankers leaked their information, were themselves implicated in an insider trading scandal for buying stocks based on the information they were supposed to report; they bought first and reported second, with the tenor of the subsequent reporting raising the price of the stock, if only momentarily and incrementally.[15] All representation is evaluative, Boone seems to surmise, and he prefers to be responsible for his own in his writing and in stories written about him.

This concern over the appearance and perception of finance has its own political economy and discursive history. Marx describes interest-bearing capital as "the height of misrepresentation," because it generates an appearance of money begetting money without accounting for the real productive processes that allow such illusions to occur.[16] David Harvey makes a similar visual and perceptual claim about interest rates, noting that they "appear as a representation of value."[17] But we seem to be dealing with a different kind of representation and misrepresentation here, and certainly a different scale. Indeed, we may wonder what actually constitutes the difference between representation and misrepresentation in a financial context. If contemporary financial activity produces a social anxiety different from its predecessors, part of the reason may be specific to its own imbrication in representation itself.[18] While the texts under consideration here all date from the mid- to late 1980s, they prefigure contemporary non-Marxist scholarship on finance. For example, Donald MacKenzie, a leading practitioner of what is called the "social studies of finance," whose work I take up in the next chapter, influentially argues for what he calls "the performativity of finance." MacKenzie is interested in how academic theorizations of finance come to affect and transform financial markets and how financial discursivity becomes effective.[19] This concern with representation itself is similar to the one that motivated Galbraith and those who criticized Stone. They each share the correct assumption that rarely is the consumer of a financial narrative aware of the point in its historical unfolding during which she receives said narrative. This worry is acutely relevant to the precise financial texts under consideration here, but it is also relevant to the form of finance itself. Financial transactions presume an end whose time has not yet come and that temporal gap is a space for risk, profit and the instantiation and avoidance of narration. As we saw in the previous chapter, finance might be conceived of as information spread unevenly over time, but without a full understanding of the duration itself. And because representation can affect whatever end a financial transaction awaits, finance too—whether its particular constituent is an institution, a country or individual—has a stake in narrative compositions *about* finance.

Indeed, there is a contest over financial representation throughout the 1980s, a tension that these autobiographies and their reviews locate but do not resolve: If writing is part of the value, how does one represent a financial operation? Or the culture of finance? Or the emergence of finance as an overdetermining force in the United States' economy as it proceeded throughout the decade? And, most crucially, how does one represent any financial content without succumbing to (someone else's) financial aims of reduced risk and increased profit? If financial autobiographies are fraudulent, if financial journalism colludes with financial institutions, if financial realism is capitalist realism, then what? It is Ellis who first appreciates that this is a contest, and who consequently understands that finance is a problematic which undergirds the aesthetic transformations of the decade. Fredric Jameson has claimed that finance capital "underpins and sustains postmodernity as such." Ellis's text anticipates and refines this claim. It is cognizant of the continual pull between both different types of finance, such as high finance or personal banking, and different types of postmodernity, such as the "technomodernism" of metafiction or the minimalism of the brat-pack novel. *American Psycho* provides a discursive space to catalogue each of these typologies as well as to observe how they intersect with and critique each other in a textual medium.

Ellis chooses a postmodern mode to represent the financial world for which Wolfe had earlier chosen a realist one. But Ellis's novel is about Wolfe's novel, and it is this connection to *The Bonfire of the Vanities*, and particularly to the role that the representation of finance plays in producing Wolfe's realist aesthetic, that Ellis takes as his manifest content. In one of *American Psycho*'s later chapters, "The Best City for Business" (*AP*, 366), Patrick Bateman walks into the apartment of a fellow financier whom he had murdered several months earlier. The apartment is now being shown by Mrs. Wolfe, a real estate agent. Mrs. Wolfe asks Patrick if he has seen the advertisement for the apartment in the *New York Times*. He replies affirmatively, and she then informs him that, "there was no ad in *The Times*." Patrick records their interaction by explaining that, "we stare at each other endlessly" (*AP*, 369). Patrick describes Mrs. Wolfe as "distressingly real-looking." Mrs. Wolfe orders Patrick not to "make any trouble" and "not to come back." This conversation may be seen as a recapitulation of the textual relationship that obtains between *The Bonfire of the Vanities* and *American Psycho* as financial texts: the first is distressingly real and is in the business of selling its realism, and the second endlessly troubles that prospect.

For Wolfe finance and realism had, of course, been deeply entwined, both structurally within his text and rhetorically in the publicity surrounding his novel's publication—ultimately one of the best-selling novels of the decade. For the financiers themselves, the preferred literary approach was nonfiction and the tone was advisory: This is how it is, this is how one should conduct oneself financially. Both T. Boone Pickens and Donald Trump understand their tomes, in Trump's words, as "common sense guide[s] to personal finance." Of course their advice books are not sufficient to emulate the actions described, a fact that constitutes one of the central ironies of the genre. That reality is a result of the impossibility for the reader to access modes of corporate information to say nothing of modes of corporate expenditure, yet another irony which is alluded to in the subtitle of Boesky's *Merger Mania: Arbitrage: Wall Street's Best Kept Money-Making Secret*. Indeed, the best-kept secret was that it was not the technicalities of arbitrage but the endemic culture of securities fraud through which Boesky made his money. These texts are somewhat fraudulent, then; their value comes not from what they claim it does but from something more tangential and symptomatic. As for Boesky's claim that "[he] doubts there are any more exaggerated stories than are told about risk arbitrage" (p. ix), it's almost impossible to say if this should count for representation or misrepresentation but, either way, *American Psycho* accepts the challenge.

American Psycho recapitulates and criticizes texts of journalism, realism, and autobiography, all of which seek to stylize and criticize the relationship between narration and finance. From each Ellis borrows and to each he appends both his own and the other texts, thus pulling a series of seemingly incommensurable texts into a common representational and discursive space whose object is finance. Ellis's is a finance that encompasses both the high finance of the exclusive investment banking firms, the secrets, the world which only capitalist realism can penetrate, the personal banking of the automated teller machine, and the linguistic economy of the brand name. Postmodernism, of course, famously erases the distinction between high culture and low culture; *American Psycho* crafts its postmodernism by rejecting a distinction between high finance and personal banking.

In order to accomplish this task, Ellis mimics some structuring element of the dominant modes of financial print culture that he generically delimits. From the novelistic world, Ellis borrows the financial and violent plot and setting of *The Bonfire of the Vanities*; he takes the financial as literary devices of *White Noise*. From real-life authors and financiers Donald Trump, Ivan Boesky and T. Boone Pickens, Ellis takes the autobiographical narrative form, the cadence, and much of the paragraph structure and the point of view. He also takes the central narrative construct of "the art of the deal," the sectioning of a text with no overall narrative coherence into moments of discrete meaning called "deal-making." A "deal" is an instance in which something happens. Perhaps a company is bought, perhaps it isn't. Perhaps an agreement is made or perhaps it falls through. In a deal, the horizon of possibility is suddenly reconfigured. Boesky's *Merger Mania*, for example, begins with the purchase of stock of Gulf-Western, what would eventually become Paramount Communications. In the opening pages of his text, it remains in doubt whether he can acquire the necessary stock; then he does, and the text begins its narrative. Trump's *The Art of Deal* uses the success or failure of various deals to organize its chapter segmentation. Ellis replaces the content of financial deal, for example that of a surreptitious stock-buying spree, with an act of violence, usually murder. These violent actions are the few moments in *American Psycho* in which something concrete transpires, perhaps the reason why they have left such an indelible effect on readers and critics. And this last fact leads into the text's third financial print-culture borrowing, that of the metaphor of violence. When the *New York Times* reviewed *Taking America*, a history of corporate raiders by Boesky's editor and coauthor Jeffrey Madrick, it titled its review "Cannibals at Work."[20] Subsequently, when Ellis's murderous financier-protagonist eats the brain of a colleague whom he has murdered, we can now see a connection.

Yet the financial print culture into which Ellis's text intercedes already contains a great deal of cross-referencing and seemingly generic consistencies. Many of the authors under consideration here treat the other authors as characters in their own texts: Trump describes the phone calls he makes and receives from Boesky and Michael Milken; Boone mentions the financing he gets from Boesky; Boesky describes Boone's corporate maneuvers and Milken's genius. Wolfe's text, too, is present in this compendium. One of Wolfe's central characters, Peter Fallow, is a reporter, after all, who writes for a tabloid newspaper that generates print culture scandals about financiers. Wolfe, moreover, includes references to the external, historical financial print culture that I have delimited here. Indeed, immediately before Sherman's arraignment—when it is clear that this financier will be publicly tied to his violent act and that his life will be dictated by a media scandal— one of the arresting officers turns to Sherman and, noting his profession, says, "Have you read that book, *Murder Mania*?" The other officer quickly corrects him, "no it's *Merger Mania*!" thus introducing Ivan Boesky and his autobiography *Merger Mania* into *Bonfire'* s fictional world. T. Boone Pickens, Ivan Boesky, Michael Milken, Donald Trump and Tom Wolfe—each an author in his own right—all make an appearance in *American Psycho*.[21]

Read together, and certainly that is how Ellis reads them, these texts begin to gesture toward a kind of generic consistency. This process might be seen to begin with the most basic articulation of the subject of financial masculinity: his name. The characters' names in Wolfe's and Ellis's texts are notable, as is the relationship between the second and the first. Sherman McCoy is a "sure man" while Patrick Bateman, a "Bate Man," is a "Bates," perhaps a kind of Anthony Bates, a previous articulation of another fictional *Psycho*. And to be sure, this is a world of men: I'm not including female financier Nancy Bazleton Goldstone's 1988 autobiography *Trading Up* in this chapter for that precise reason.[22] Then there are the serendipitously referential nonfictional names: Milken might be read is "milkin'"; Trump might be read as a verb, "to trump"; Boone is a boon, and so on. The

titles to which these names are attached also hint toward some generic rule, and suggest a link between the description of financial
qualities and the effects such descriptions might produce. The financial titles under consideration here foreground the problem of subjectivity and particularly the instability of the financial subject: Merger
and mania are both clinical terms, the first of borderline states, the
second of the pleasures of psychosis; *The Bonfire of the Vanities,* an
intimation of narcissistic fortification and its loss; *Boone*, the enjoin-
ing of an author-subject to financial grandiosity; and, of course, *American
Psycho*, a nationalistic detachment from reality.

Now it is possible to specify that it is between these different modes,
texts, names and other denotations that financial masculinity is developed within these texts. Here financial masculinity functions as
a suturing of the effects and affects of finance to a subject position
which traverses and unifies aesthetic modes. A site where ego form
and value form mix, financial masculinity is also the location from
which *American Psycho* intercedes most manifestly into the discursive world of 1980s financial print culture. Thus financial masculinity
has generic implications, and *American Psycho* is as much about writing about finance as it is about finance.[23] Much like the destabilization
of gender on the drag queen renders visible what a stable gender is,
the destablization of financial masculinity in *American Psycho*, its exfoliation, renders visible, too, the normative content and disavowals
of a previously assumed financial masculinity. As *American Psycho*
destroys the genre it creates, it evacuates the subjectivity it frames.

The Men Who Make the Killings

The story of serial killer and investment banker Patrick Bateman,
American Psycho is better known for its harrowing descriptions of interpersonal violence than for its formal financial representation or,
conversely, its engagement with some critique of a financial form. The
novel has an essentially plotless structure as the protagonist describes
his wanderings through New York City: He shops, dines at exclusive
restaurants, and perpetrates brutal and seemingly random acts of violence and torture, which range from intimate acts of sexual violation
to anonymous murder to cannibalism. But we are already within the
discursive world of finance. Soon after the mid-1980s financial run dramatically ended with the stock-market crash in 1987, famous financiers

quickly became infamous for a series of financial scandals, and the language in which their crimes were narrated was that of interpersonal violence. Author and arbitrageur Ivan Boesky had been indicted and sentenced in 1987 for violating the inside information traders sanction act. The prosecutor on that case was Manhattan District Attorney Rudolph Giuliani, who was, as a result of the case, featured in the first inaugural issue of a journal that gestures toward another facet of 1980s financial print culture, *The Corporate Crime Reporter*. Boesky cut a deal with Giuliani and turned in Michael Milken, who was subsequently indicted in 1988 and imprisoned soon thereafter (and who published a cookbook in 1998); one of Milken's colleagues, Dennis Levine, was also implicated when Boesky turned state's evidence and he published a memoir, *Inside Out: An Insider's Account of Wall Street*, in 1991.

The *New York Times* duly covered Boesky's trial, but it also speculated on his sexual and narcissistic tendencies.[24] Reporter turned author Connie Bruck published a book on Milken's scandalous downfall entitled *The Predators' Ball*, the term that Milken and his colleagues had used to describe their yearly, prostitute-laden gathering where they assessed which companies they would attempt to takeover, in other words, the "hostile takeover."[25] After Milken was indicted, *Time* magazine adopted Milken's own lexicon to narrate a cover story about him: "Predator's Fall." Two years later, *The New York Times* described the financial practices that Milken engaged in as those which "introduced terror and mayhem into countless corporate boardrooms [by causing] managements to focus on short-term gains and elaborate takeover defenses rather than the research and development that make for sustained growth."[26] On one *Time* magazine cover, venture capitalist Arthur Rock, the man who arranged the initial financing for Apple, was described as one of an untold number of "the men who make the killings."

From "the killings" to the "hostile" acts to the "takeover defenses," it is this descriptive, metaphorical language of finance that is collected and emplotted in *American Psycho*. Indeed, the book was deemed so violent that it was famously dropped by its publisher, Simon and Schuster, weeks before its publication and after vociferous protest from the National Organization for Women (among other groups).[27] Ellis's text was subsequently published by Vintage Contemporaries, sparking yet another round of controversy. In an op-ed in the *New York Times*, Roger Rosenblatt wondered in his title: "Will Bret Easton

Ellis Get Away with Murder?"[28] If Ellis could use language of violence to describe investment banking then critics, including Rosenblatt, seemed to agree, that he too could be subject to a similar metaphorical substitution. Those who engage in finance are killers, but those who write about the metaphor are killers, too. The clamor against Ellis and his novel, the threatened boycotts of Simon and Schuster and then Vintage, the repeated substitution of Ellis himself for his murderous character in financial print culture, and the substantial publicity turned Ellis's text into the literary scandal of the decade. In its circulation, Ellis's text mimicked the form of a financial narrative, that which is dramatically revealed through a scandal, with all the requisite and performative shock, disbelief, and intrigue. Like the financial scandal, *American Psycho* emerged abruptly, it was an interruption into two otherwise smoothly accumulating literary trends: first, what *The Wall Street Journal* had described as the "fi-fi" genre of the 1980s, that of "financial fiction"; second, of the new, award-winning Vintage Contemporaries series that was publishing much bratpack work and in which *American Psycho* was included.[29] Yet unlike a financial scandal, its publication could have been prevented. After all, when Ivan Boesky, the world's leading arbitrageur, was indicted for securities fraud, the business community was stunned. The business press duly reported the event as a scandal. But *American Psycho* was a scandal only because it was published.

If genre requires a certain character-type, then the financial text requires a violent financier. That violence might either cause *or* narrate a scandal; financial scandals were narrated *through* masculinized references to violence and sex while Ellis's financial text became a scandal *because* of its depictions of sex and violence. That language of violence is present in the financiers' autobiographies, but also in the larger historical record. By 1982, the *New York Times* was reporting on a new type of businessman, the corporate raider. "They have even developed their own language, laced with the images of aggression and sexual conquest: raids, battles, white knights, wooing, shark repellent, bear hugs."[30] The financial autobiography adopts this language, in part codifying it, in part representing accurately the financial world about which it is written. Boesky speaks of takeover "battles" as "war" and designates various financial instruments as types of "weapons"; one subheading in his book is simply called: "What can kill a deal." Trump includes a picture of himself as a military school teenager marching down New York City's 5th Ave. in full military regalia with the caption: "This was my first real glimpse of prime fifth avenue property."[31] Far from being innovative, the language of interpersonal violence to describe financial transactions harkens back to their earliest articulations, when the term finance itself was still able to bridge the intimacy of the feudal scene with the finality of the early capitalist transaction: to finance is to go to the end (*finir*), but of life itself. "There is no more, but death is my finance," relates the *Oxford English Dictionary* in one of the word's first recoded usages.[32] It is fitting that this language is resurrected in the 1980s in a manner distinct from the financial language of the 1910s and '20s, as it amplifies the subjective instability inherent in so much postmodern cultural production. In that earlier financial period, financial trusts were criminal, but it was the capitalist economy as a whole that was violent. Now, when it is finance that stands in for the economy, the discourse of violence has been transferred to finance itself.

Nonetheless the serial killer of Ellis's text is as much about financial form as it is about financial content. Ellis's text is a satire of *The Bonfire of the Vanities*, which was serialized in its entirety in *Rolling Stone* magazine before its publication as a book.[33] At the level of content, *The Bonfire of the Vanities* realistically narrates the scandal of a financier as a result of his involvement with an indirect scene of violence; at the level of circulation, *American Psycho* became a scandal because of its nonrealistic representation of a financier whose direct violence sustains the novel. *American Psycho* presumes Wolfe's text. Then it neatly reverses *Bonfire*'s structural underpinnings, and I am particularly interested in showing how the representation of finance—as a masculine subject position, a scandal-based narrative, and a value form—participates in this process. To Wolfe's third-person, omniscient narrator—one who knows all, literally a "sure man"—Ellis gives us a first-person, paranoid narrator, one who is seduced by false knowledge and one who cannot be trusted, a Bateman. To Wolfe's transformation of global finance into an optic for the mapping of the physical space of New York City, Ellis's gives us the professional space of finance, his firm Pierce & Pierce (the same title as the fictional firm in Wolfe's text), as an optic for viewing the manic, claustrophobic psychic space of his protagonist's violent interior. To Wolfe's international, gold-backed bond trading, Ellis gives us the remarkably quotidian, although deeply tropological, personal banking technology of the automated teller machine. Wolfe's plot of an accidental murder through a hit-and-run is transformed into the intentional violence of a serial killer, a version of *Time*'s "the men who make the killings." Most simply, the satirical presupposition of Wolfe's novel is: how could we ever consider an ineffectual financier a killer? The satirical presupposition of Ellis's novel is: how could we ever *not* consider an ineffectual financier a killer?[34]

The plot and the satirical problem may be taken from Wolfe's fictional world, but the lack of plot in *American Psycho*, its semantic patterns, chapter segmentation, even sentence structure replicate those of Trump, Boone, and Boesky's texts. In other words, some of what is recognizably "postmodern" about *American Psycho* is taken from these autobiographical bestselling guides to "personal finance." One of the most distinct patterns in their autobiographical narration is the combination of first-person statement, third-person declaration, and second-person advice.

From *Boone*:

> A commodity futures play is one of the purest forms of entrepreneurship. The keys to success are an accurate analysis, the willingness to take risk, and the ability to act. Once you've made the decision, just stand by it because you're likely to get your answer quickly. Although I enjoy many types of investing, there's nothing like a commodities play for fast action. (*Boone*, 264)

From *The Art of the Deal*:

> Location also has a lot to do with fashion. You can take a mediocre location and turn it into something considerably better just by attracting the right people. After I built Trump Tower I built Trump Plaza, on a site at Third Avenue and 61st Street that I was able to purchase very inexpensively. The truth is that Third Avenue simply didn't compare to Fifth Avenue as a location. (*Trump*, 55)

From Boesky's *Merger Mania: Arbitrage: Wall Street's Best Kept Money-Making Secret*:

> You are on the line and visible, especially to your Wall Street colleagues. Good Arbitrageurs seem to like it that way. They represent, I think, the best of America's entrepreneurial spirit. (*Boesky*, 202).

In each of these passages, the movement between first, second, and third person creates a mixture of factual assemblage, of radical eco-

nomic objectivity, and from that objectivity a pronounced subjectivity. The effect of such diversity is that it quickly becomes impossible
to discern which point of view is associated with which effect. The
financiers address the readers as though they were colleagues and as
though they, too, might be about to engage in one of these deals.
Thus in each example, the ultimate point is not the accuracy of the
description, but the transformation of description into a directive,
into advice. This movement is most visible in Pickens's *Boone*, but all
three texts offer to interpolate the reader into, in Boesky's words, a
"Wall Street colleague."

Ellis's novel, too, offers such a structure. From *American Psycho*:

> Then I always slather on a moisturizer (to my taste, Clinique) and let it
> soak in for a minute. You can rinse it off or keep it on and apply a shaving
> cream over it. It also helps prevent water from evaporating. Always wet
> the razor. One should use an alcohol-free antibacterial toner with a
> water-moisturized cotton ball to normalize the skin. (*AP*, 27)

The reader who would buy Trump's book would find his advice rather
useless, as would the reader of Boone's or Boesky's. After all, few of us
have access to millions of dollars of credit for our daily business
doings, to the mayor of New York City, or to the national media. For
Patrick Bateman, however, one can't mimic financial actions, only
financial appearances. Except that his text begins to suggest that
maybe finance is an appearance. One could actually take Patrick
Bateman's advice about skin-cleaning and shaving rituals, but in the
context of his serial killing, who would want to? Each of these four
samples is representative of what the reader of the financial autobiography encounters between the deals—those moments of financial
narrative—when the real-life financiers are not acquiring and when
Bateman is not killing. A discussion of the merits of Canadian versus
American business regulation might be interrupted with a thought
about what makes a good hunting dog (*Boone*); a discussion of a tax
abatement is interrupted by a meditation on the nature of cowardice
(Trump); Boesky's book, the most technical by far, includes digres-
sions on the etymology of the word arbitrage, from the German
Arbeit.

Together, these passages form a kind of who's who of the financial
world, and a "how to" of financial comportment and style. The second person address might indicate this presence of other financiers,

who are frequently mentioned in deals. The genre is one of see and be seen, record and be recorded, as the movement between forms of address conveys. Perhaps the premier event at which to be located was the "Predators' Ball," a Michael Milken–hosted event at the Ivan Boesky–owned Beverly Hills hotel, which hotel Trump recounts unsuccessfully trying to purchase in *The Art of the Deal.* The content of the actual event is, importantly, not found in any of these texts. It was dubbed the "predators'" ball because it was an event devoted to Milken's disbursement of credit to precisely corporate raiders like Boone and Boesky who would use the cash to engage in "hostile" takeovers of companies via the purchase of stock. Indeed, it is rather pointed that the event itself is not described in any of these texts; it remains inside information. Nonetheless, we do know that one popular feature of balls were the skits and performances of Hollywood stars and financiers themselves, including the dubbing of Madonna's hit single "Material Girl" into a song about "hostile takeovers" and the presentation of a fake credit card with a "ten billion dollar line of credit" and the slogan, "don't go hunting without it."[35]

Ellis offers his own account of the predator's ball in *American Psycho.* Patrick Bateman goes to Pierce & Pierce's Halloween party dressed:

> as a mass murderer, complete with a sign painted on my back that read MASS MURDERER…written in blood, some of it fake, most of it real…my boutonniere was a finger bone I'd boiled the flesh off. As elaborate as my costume was, Craig McDermott still managed to win…[he] came as Ivan Boesky, which I thought was unfair since a lot of people thought I'd gone as Michael Milken last year. (*AP*, 330)

Ellis's serial-killer protagonist reverses a series of references to financiers who were metaphorically linked to violence by literalizing the metaphor. He goes as a predator, but is unrecognized as such; the winner came as a person who had in fact gone to the predator's ball, Ivan Boesky, which must mean that the winner wore a suit. "What [do] people think?" T. Boone Pickens rhetorically asks in *Boone*, "that [we] show up [to meetings] with a shot-gun?"; at the same time, Pickens, too, makes use of the metaphor. Recalling advice from his father, he concedes that financial success is "like murder, son. Don't try to explain it" (Boone, 97).

But *American Psycho*'s literalization of the metaphor of violence, while it may highlight the labor such a metaphor performs, does not adequately answer the question of why the metaphor is there in the first place. David Graeber might say that finance retains the connections because it *is* violent.[36] Indeed, the etymology of many financial terms—think of mortgage or of finance itself—does contain a link to the violence that undergirds all social relations, including economic ones. Paul Ricoeur might respond that it maintains the connection because it is *not* violent.[37] For Boesky, the metaphor becomes a simile: "it's like war." For Boone, "it's like murder." For former bank reporter turned film critic Julie Salamon, writing in *The Wall Street Journal*, finance is, in fact, not like war. Their "battles" are "pretty tame" she notes, and mostly involve "screaming into telephones."[38]

A new metaphor creates a relational ground of contest; both terms come to have new associations. As *American Psycho* compiles various relationships between finance and violence it creates a discursive space in which the motivations for and relationships between the tenor and vehicle of the metaphor can be examined. In addressing one of the central conceits of Ellis's novel, that the investment banker is also a serial killer, the conservative *National Review* attempted to argue that Ellis's exfoliation of the metaphor itself was groundless.

> Anyone who knows anything about serial killers knows that all of this is perfect nonsense. They are weak, nondescript, maladjusted loners who kill women in order to satisfy their twisted sexual longings, not Masters of the Universe with a taste for human flesh. Bret Easton Ellis would presumably argue that *American Psycho*, being a satire on the Reagan era, need not be overly literal. Manhattan may be crawling with serial killers, but I find it highly unlikely that any of them are doubling as investment bankers.[39]

The *National Review* demonstrates that remaining within the ambit of the metaphor is itself problematic. To repeat the phrases in hopes of disarticulating them establishes some sense of familiarity. For example, the use of Wolfe's borrowed (from Michael Lewis) language here, "Master of the Universe," itself now seems newly violent in this context, maybe because of the assurance that they do not have a taste for human flesh. Perhaps aware that it cannot dislodge the metaphor of finance and violence altogether, the *National Review* offers instead a new metaphorical relationship:

No doubt Ellis spent his undergraduate years steeped in the modish brand of academic nihilism that goes by the name of "deconstruction," a school of criticism in which works of art are verbally hacked to pieces in order to prove that nothing means anything. He seems to have learned his lessons well, if a bit too literally.

For the liberal press, exemplified by Rosenblatt, Ellis should not be allowed to pursue the analogy. He should not be able to "get away with murder." For the conservative press, he should be subject to his own metaphor through a historicization of this particular type of violence. If to make a killing is to kill, then to have come from a literary tradition of deconstruction is to have dismembered cultural capital and perhaps a human body. In either scenario, however, the representation of finance is firmly linked to its language and to violence. Ellis does seem to have exhausted the binary of metaphor, perhaps in favor of a more metonymic understanding of the relationship between finance and language.

Literary critics of *American Psycho* have followed the problem of metaphorical language, and treated violence as the major metaphor if not trope of this satirical text. In a society narrated as being as capitalistic, self-obsessed, and individualistic as the United States in the 1980s—or so the understanding goes—violent acts in plain sight attract no attention or concern. Asked at a club what he does, Patrick answers, "I'm into, oh, murders and executions mostly." The female interlocutor responds, "Most guys I know who work in mergers and acquisitions don't really like it." "That's *not* what I said," Patrick responds, but to no avail (*AP*, 206, italics in original). This quick exchange may be extrapolated into a larger relationship between the text and its reader. The violence is so gruesome, carnivalesque, public, and nonconsequential—dragging a suppurating corpse through a building's lobby in full sight of the doorman, for example—that the reader is led to wonder if it is not fantasized or otherwise unreal. In trying to tease apart the ontological status of Patrick's violence, Jules Murphet suggests that "textually [the violent acts] happen, they affect the reader and the course of narration...at the level of some putative diegetic reality...they probably do not happen...[but] at a higher, allegorical level, they do happen."[40] Murphet follows many of Ellis's critics here and focuses on Ellis's representation of violence as a site to question the text's narrative coherence and the limits of its representation, arguing that the basis of Ellis's satire is the inability of Patrick

Bateman to convey his violent acts to his social and professional world.

I would argue instead that the violence is largely an effect of Ellis's dedication to generic compliance and to the language of finance. But I would also argue that *American Psycho* does not use a metaphor of violence. Rather it reveals how prevalent that metaphor is, and it then kills the metaphor. It is not that finance is narrated through violence in this novel, but that violence is narrated through finance. In other words, the text reconceives of finance as a metaphor for violence or perhaps even of a metaphorical relationship's ability to cede into metonymy as finance and violence become more contiguous than vertical. Consequently, instead of attempting to understand the ontological status of violence within the text's diegetic frame—is it real or not?— I want to pursue a different line of questioning and explore whether the finance exists within this text.[41] This line of questioning is not meant to open a discussion about real versus fictitious economies, as, for example, Richard Godden has suggested the text invites.[42] Rather, I locate the operative financial forms that organize the text and I suggest how their relationship to other texts in my study has the effect of placing the representation of finance at the center of the canonization of 1980s American literature as surely as that literature offers a site to critique what finance is and how it functions.

Financial Literary Devices

Like Wolfe's Sherman McCoy, Patrick Bateman works at the fictional bond-trading firm Pierce & Pierce, but those names now seem to indicate not proper nouns so much as violent verbs; he has a predilection for stabbing his victims. Unlike Sherman McCoy, Patrick never gives us any indication of the work that he does, of his technical knowledge of finance, or of his level of engagement in New York's financial community. In his office, he does crossword puzzles, listens to popular music on his Walkman, and manages his extensive social life with the help of his secretary, Jean. About the only financial object to be found on his desk is a copy of Donald Trump's memoir, *The Art of the Deal*. And like Trump's autobiography, *American Psycho*, too, is a compendium of nonnarrative information: I went here, I saw this person, I wore this, I did this, I made one phone call, I returned another. This repeated sentence structure has a deadening, hypnotizing quality. But unlike those first-person financial narrators, Patrick Bateman can never use accumulated content to foment any *financial* deal. While at work he sometimes looks for "information" on the "Fisher Account" and he claims to be involved with the "Ransom Account," but one suspects the names of those accounts are the point here: to fish for something and not find it might be the extent of the "fisher" account; to demand something by threat of force might constitute his work on the "ransom" account.

Outside of his office Patrick is engaged in the work of personal banking and interpersonal violence; as in *White Noise*, the two are structurally entwined. Indeed, all banking is personal for Patrick Bateman. The world of high finance is rendered in deeply interpersonal terms, as when he randomly calls phone numbers from the Dalton girls' school and, while masturbating, says into the phone, "I'm a corporate raider, I like hostile takeovers." These two constructions—personal banking and interpersonal violence—are the two major tropes of the text, and they cannot be read separately from each other. I use personal banking and interpersonal violence to mark the text's financial masculinity as well as its narrative form. Yet while the manifest content of that destabilizing material is violence—did he do it or didn't he?—the violence is rendered through a financial frame and it is the finance, not the violence, with which Ellis's satirical and postmodern form are concerned.

The automated teller machine (ATM) becomes a crucial site for the elaboration of this problematic. Ellis begins his project of disaggregating finance by turning the ATM—that widely profiled and anxiety-provoking personal financial object—into a narrative device. Although Patrick is ostensibly a financier at Pierce & Pierce, his major engagement with finance transpires at the ATM. The protagonist repeatedly informs us of his visits to the ATM and obsessively checks in with his answering machine. From the machine that tells to the machine that listens, *American Psycho*'s first-person narration is continually questioned if not outsourced to the same mechanized processes that depend on unpaid personal labor for their function. Indeed, *American Psycho* has two narrators: Patrick Bateman, the millionaire financier, and the text's own automated teller, which assumes the narrative function when the narrator is, in his own words, "simply not there" (*AP*, 367). As in Don DeLillo's *White Noise*, the automated teller machine is a phenomenological conduit to financial paranoia, conspiracy, violence, and depersonalization. "I had all the characterizations of a human being, but my depersonalization was so intense…" (*AP*, 282), Patrick explains quite clinically. Jack Gladney panicked that he was not masculine enough in the face of his wife's infidelity; Patrick's worry is that he is perceived as gay. And again, it is important that the machine is unbranded, as the discourse of the brand will have its own structuring presence here, too. If "telling" presented the limits of narration in *White Noise*, here it is the condition of possibility. It is the ATM that allows Patrick to circulate through the city and to be articulated in a financial network. As he moves through urban space, the teller is a continual point of orientation and demarcation. The ATM orients Patrick in his movements and it orients the reader to his impending violence. Fittingly, the first realization of his violence comes after his first visit to what he calls "my automated teller" (*AP*, 81). The standard abbreviation for automated teller machine, ATM, is never used in the text. Patrick is not simply visiting an ATM; rather he is making reference to an alternative narrative structure.

Indeed, the representation of the ATM is crucial to the novel's development of violence. The construction of the interrelationship between violence and automated telling begins with the novel's first sentence and continues throughout the novel's denouement. "ABANDON ALL HOPE YE WHO ENTER HERE is scrawled in blood red lettering on the side of the Chemical Bank…" (*AP*, 1, capitalization in original). The scene is reported by Patrick on a taxi ride from Wall Street to the Upper West Side, by way of introduction. As the city is narrated by neighborhood in this long first sentence, the link between finance, here represented as the edifice of a bank, and violence, here represented in the blood red lettering, is the first connection established. The more obvious reference here is to Dante's *Inferno*; the less obvious reference is the fact that Chemical Bank was the first bank to have a functioning ATM in 1971, and furthermore was instrumental in developing the New York Cash Exchange (NYCE) in 1985, a program which allowed individuals to access ATMs from different banks around the city. Patrick is similarly linked throughout the city to the automated teller machine. He is frequently "lost in my own private maze, thinking about other things" (*AP*, 342). One of his distracting images is "blood pouring from automated tellers" (*AP*, 343). When he thinks in the future tense, obsessively planning his days to come, he foretells that: "I have video tapes to return, money to be taken out of an automated teller, a dinner reservation that was difficult to get" (*AP*, 346).

The first appearance of the machine itself is contiguous with the first appearance of violence, and the protagonist's visits to various ATMs precede many more of his violent acts. When he recounts these acts, the ATMs become demarcating references. "I have misgivings about spending the evening with [my friends]…I wave them off, then cross Houston…and start moving uptown. Walking along Broadway I stop at an automated teller where just for the hell of it I take out another hundred dollars, feeling like having an even five hundred in my wallet" (*AP*, 128). What follows is the first scene of actual murder in the novel. Patrick encounters a black homeless man begging for food and money. Patrick initiates a conversation with the man asking, "Do you think it's fair to take money from people who do have jobs, who do *work*?" (*AP*, 130, italics in original). He then stabs him to death. Soon after, this interaction is repeated when Patrick encounters another black beggar, a woman asking for money, and he decides not to kill her. But as he moves on, "stopping at an automated teller to take three hundred dollars out for no particular reason," he kills a gay man and his dog (*AP*, 163). This killing is for no particular reason, either. Within Patrick's perception, his interaction with the ATM has replaced his violent interaction as an object of evaluation. It has the opposite effect on the reader, however. It is acceptable to have senseless violence. That's the culture of late modernity, after all, one that Mark Seltzer has argued constitutes an important public space, namely the pathological public sphere.[43] But senseless banking? Who would do such a thing? Patrick must really be psychotic. We know that the violence is for no reason but we expect money or its instantiation as finance to have a governing logic to it.

In one of the novel's later scenes of violence, Ellis draws attention to the relationship by explicitly linking the financial credit one receives from an ATM to the basic sense of credible affect required for interpersonal relations. "I make a phone call to check my messages. I return some videotapes. I stop at an automated teller…[but I am] unable to maintain a credible public persona. I find myself roaming in the zoo in Central Park, restlessly" (*AP*, 297). While "roaming" the zoo, Patrick pierces a small child to death. Yet when Patrick becomes nervous or anxious, indeed when he begins to experience a sense of depersonalization and derealization that might compromise his narration, the ATM returns to support him. For example, when being questioned by a private investigator about his murder of fellow financier Paul Owen—incidentally the only time in the novel he kills a social equal and the only time he is asked in even a perfunctory fashion to provide an alibi—he becomes nervous and agitated. As the detective's questions become more specific in their requests for times, places, and dates, Patrick describes himself: "My thigh muscles tense... I'm suddenly confused and scared, oh my god, Bateman, think up something." The "something" that Bateman thinks of is the automated teller. "The...last time I *physically* saw him...was at an automated teller. I can't remember which...just one that was near, um, Nell's" (*AP*, 273, italics and ellipses in original). Since the ATM is used in place of an evaluation of violence, this statement is actually true. The last time Patrick saw Paul was during his murder, but what made the murder possible, narratable, was the ATM. In the context of the ATM, the narration changes. When Patrick can't narrate ("oh god, Bateman, think of something"), the narration is transformed from first to third-person: something has thought of him and that something is the ATM. In the book's last paragraph, Patrick "automatically answers" that "this [the foregoing content of the book] is what it means to be Patrick (*AP*, 399). *American Psycho* is, in part, an automated narrative, a narrative told by an automated teller wherein the metaphor of finance distributes the intensities of violence. Finance is a way to conduct violence.

While dining in one of the many restaurants he visits with his financial colleagues, Patrick reports on the surrounding conversation. The content functions as commentary on the structure of the text.

> The conversation follows its own rolling accord—no real structure or topic or internal logic or feeling; except of course for its own hidden, conspiratorial one. Just works, and like in a movie, but one that has been transcribed improperly, most if it overlaps. I'm having a sort of hard time paying attention because my automated teller has started *speaking* to me, sometimes actually leaving weird messages on the screen, in green lettering, like "Cause a Terrible Scene at Sotheby's" or "Kill the President" or "Feed Me a Stray Cat...." (*AP*, 395, italics in original)

In this paragraph's first few lines, Patrick provides a description of the lack of narrative coherency of the novel itself. The ATM is introduced in the context of a discussion of the text's narrative form. The italicization of the word "speaking" emphasizes the link between the function of a teller and the function of a narrator. It also provides an impartial confirmation of Patrick's psychotic state. The reader knows, for example, that the automated teller has not been leaving such messages. This is the first time such conversations have been relayed to the reader, but the novel has an atemporal narrative structure so we cannot deduce what timeframe "has started" demarcates. Nonetheless, because so many of his murders and executions have been preceded by visits to the automated teller, we are now in a position to wonder whether the automated teller hasn't been ordering murder, torture, and the orchestration of "terrible scenes" all along, and if the novel is not a delusional conversation between a financier and his automated teller. The reader cannot confirm the status of the represented violent interactions, but she can confirm that of the financial transactions.

This final passage contains reference to the most commonly repeated simile within the text, that of the movie. Patrick repeats that things happen, "like in a movie" "as in a movie" that something is "just like a movie." At other times, the simile becomes a metaphor. "Most [of my relationship with Evelyn] is blacked out, bombed, footage from the film in my head in endless shots of stone and any language heard is utterly foreign, the sound flickering away over new images" (*AP,* 343). One of the images Patrick then offers is "blood pouring from automated tellers." There is a movie in his head that he is recording, except when he cannot record it, and then he leaves the job to an ATM. In both instances the labor of conveying mental self-representation and the content that constitutes it is outsourced, automated, and refused. If personal banking is the decision of the banking industry to move into the most intimate domains of private life and to ask consumers to undertake the labor required for it to remain there, then we might ask whether Patrick is willing to engage in this labor or is on strike from it. As we saw in chapter one, personal banking requires the transfer of the work from the banker on to the consumer; but Patrick is a banker.

In this context, the question he poses to the African-American beggar he murders immediately after his visit to the ATM—"do you think it's fair to take money from people who do *work*?"—is, if nothing else, telling (italics in original). The ironic language of the labor transfer is crucial to the text's exteriorization of value and subjectivity. Patrick hates the work of banking but he loves the ATM, only he visits it for no reason. But he works for no reason, too. After all, his girlfriend Evelyn hints that his father "practically owns" the company. When a date asks him about his occupation he responds, "I just

don't want to talk about…I stop…about work." "Why not?" his date
responds. "Because I hate it," he snaps (*AP*, 237, ellipses in original).
He may hate work, and indeed he complains of this somewhat repeatedly, but he obsessively works out. Just like he may refuse narration but he obsessively visits the automated teller even when, or
precisely when, he doesn't need the money.

The repeated use of the teller as a narrative device, as a teller (literally one who speaks about money), reveals a more structural question with which the text is concerned. Namely, how to execute and
refuse a financial transaction at the level of content and form. In this
passage Ellis provides a list of objects through which one could conduct a transaction:

> [I am] lost in my own private maze, thinking about other things: warrants,
> stock offerings, ESOPs, LBOs, IPOs, finances, refinances, debentures,
> converts, proxy statements, 8-Ks, 10-Qs, zero coupons, PiKs, GNPs, the
> IMF, hot executive gadgets, billionaires, Kenkiski Najakima, infinity,
> Infinity, how fast a luxury car should go, bailouts, junk bonds, whether
> to cancel my subscription to *The Economist*.…(*AP*, 342)

This list seems almost free associative. In moving from one financial
object to the next, their connection to each other as an act of cataloguing is stressed, much like the text itself catalogues financial narratives. The final reference to *The Economist* magazine suggests that
Patrick may simply be flipping through it and associating to whatever
meets his gaze, placing the text again within the ambit of 1980s financial print culture. This particular representation of financial devices
and gadgets follows Ellis's satirical strategy of evacuating the content
of his chosen object, and then locating and elaborating new content
from an associated or, in Bateman's mind at least, associative, form.
The Bonfire of the Vanities was serialized in print, and Ellis anchors
his text with a serial-killer protagonist. Financiers were referred to as
violent, and Ellis saturates his text with stabbings, torture, and dis-
memberments. Hostile takeovers between corporations were labeled
a form of "cannibalization," and Ellis's character freezes the head and
then eats the brain out of a fellow financier's skull. In each of these
examples, then, there also exists a destabilization of the identity between financial content and form that obtains through the literalization of metaphorical language. The structure of association becomes
both a site for the designation and reconfiguration of financial form in

the text, a possibility that will become particularly apparent in its engagement with branding.

The problem, indeed, problematic of the text is to apply a similar operation to a financial transaction, to literalize it. To complete this operation the text must possess some notion of a financial form. *American Psycho* reveals how the application of narrative literary technique and its suspension offers insight into precisely what that financial form is, and how the form itself negotiates the twin questions of mode and genre. Ellis's novel is about Wolfe's novel. And Wolfe's novel is about how finance and realism might equally support each other in the production of a capitalist realism. But finance offers more to Wolfe's realist project than its history or its ostensible difficulty of being understood or represented. The very form of any financial transaction—whether in the specific case of a mortgage, bond deal, and so on—already has certain structural affinities with literary realism. Realistic representation distinguishes itself from other modes by its use of accurate information, and so does institutional finance. The manner in which that information accumulates, and to what extent it is transformed into either profit or plot, depends on how that information is deployed in a temporal frame. In the previous chapter, I argued that Sherman McCoy's impending bond deal paces the first half of the novel and serves as a nodal point of narrative transition to and from Wolfe's various plot lines. The anticipation of that successful bond deal is suspended throughout the first half of the novel, only to be called due, and ultimately collapse, at the point in the narrative when Sherman needs it most: the revelation of his infidelity and the ensuing police investigation of his involvement in the vehicular manslaughter of a black teenager in the South Bronx. Much as finance is information spread unevenly over time, so realistic narrative must adopt this same structure. Were it spread evenly or more reliably over time, it might gesture toward other modes such as genre fiction.

I have insisted throughout this book that the content of finance, whatever else it is, is necessarily temporal.[44] An interest payment, a government bond, a debt, the purchase or sale of a stock, a derivative contract—each of these financial instruments reflects a form in which some representation of information is codified and a time period is delimited after which that information may be monetized into profit or loss. In the above passage, which lists financial devices delimited by serial commas, the temporal content of finance is evacuated, and in rearranging the structure of temporality, here realized as narration, the text provides both an understanding and a critique of finance as a temporal form. But, then, this is necessarily a discussion of realist narrative development, too. If realism transforms accurate, or real-like content over time into narrative, much as a successful financial transaction transforms good information over time into profit, Ellis satirizes finance formally by using quotidian financial devices to disrupt temporal structure and ultimately to render suspect whether the information/content within it is reliable, indeed whether it should be understood as content/information at all. For its critique of a financial form, then, *American Psycho* must offer two complementary deconstructions: one of temporal form; the second of content/information within that form since it is the consistency of information within a temporal structure that ultimately makes possible a financial transaction. For Bateman, association itself is this form.

The brand as financial device is *American Psycho*'s second system in place to accomplish its goal of literalizing a financial transaction.[45] Like so many things in this text, the brand is introduced through the language of criminality. The most serious financial crime—really the only financial crime—and one for which Boesky, Milken, Levine, and, fictionally, Bud Fox, were convicted is that of transmitting "inside information."[46] We might define the substance of inside information as a kind of non-synchronous knowledge of how some content will become information and will be realized as profit within a certain temporal frame. The crime of inside information is and was notoriously difficult to prove. If convicted financier turned author Dennis Levine were to say to Ivan Boesky at the Harvard Club, "I might keep an eye on Nabisco," and Boesky were to buy the stock based on the conversation, this might be a crime. But who can prove that it happened?[47] Boesky could just as easily conjecture that it was his research into the structure of Nabisco that led him to buy its stock.

There appears precisely one discussion of legality in *American Psycho* and that concerns the labeling of clothes. At a Christmas party, one of Patrick's financial colleagues solicits his opinion about whether it is legal for a clothing retailer to put his own label (brand) on the wholesale clothing he has purchased from another label. In response to the query, Bateman provides an exegesis on the crime of "label tampering": "It's confusing, I know....Once a line of clothing has been purchased from its manufacturer, it's perfectly legal for the retailer to replace the original label with his own. However, it's not legal to replace it with another retailer's label....Label tampering is very hard to detect and is rarely reported" (*AP*, 185, ellipses mine). In fact, this is a conversation about crimes of inside information (here, literally, what happens on the "inside" of a suit jacket, where the label is affixed), a crime understood by criminologists and financial reporters alike to be "hard to detect" and "rarely reported."[48] In a neoliberal society of radical and financially produced monetary inequality and social violence, that inside information is the ultimate financial crime seems like it would be satire enough.

As with the list form of financial devices, the text provides a similar rubric for understanding its own connection between the brand and information. One way to satirize information is to provide too much, a path taken by postmodern "maximalism" from Pynchon to Wallace; another is to provide too little, as David Markson does in *Reader's Block*. Ellis renders information useless. Through the form of the brand, he takes information out of circulation. If the teller expands and other devices contract how the how narrative unfolds, the brand disrupts whether what is within the narrative is content or information, whether it is reliable or not, whether it could ever transform from the first to the second. If the automated teller transforms the text's first-person narration, then the use of branded language renders suspect its use of point of view as well as its representation of "information," "fact," and "content."

In an early chapter entitled "Morning" Patrick describes his routine as he awakens, showers, shaves, brushes his hair, chooses his clothes, and finally hails a cab down to Wall Street. The chapter's first paragraph is five pages long and reads like a magazine article on personal grooming. It is slightly more narrative than an advertisement, but so saturated with brand names that Patrick's presentation of his own individuality is lost. In presenting himself as unique, the language of self-fashioning that is available to him compromises his very sense of self, a process that is formally conveyed by the shifting point of view in an already cited passage. "Then I always slather on a moisturizer (to my taste, Clinique) and let it soak in for a minute. You can rinse it off or keep it on and apply a shaving cream over it. It also helps prevent water from evaporating. Always wet the razor. One should use an alcohol-free antibacterial toner with a water-moisturized cotton ball to normalize the skin" (*AP*, 27). I return to this passage because in addition to mimicking the prose of financiers' autobiographies, it demonstrates how, through deployment of the brand form, a changing point of view does not destabilize or complicate the narration. The meaning is not lost or reconfigured. The brand itself overshadows any perspectival relationship between object and subject; a brand does not require a point of view. One management theorist describes the phenomenology of the brand as abstract and concrete, both "a means of relationality and relativity" simultaneously.[49] The brand performs similar work in Patrick's narration as it provides a site for the creation of shared meaning between Patrick and the reader, but what that meaning is remains relative.

Initially, the brand seems to be the only thing we can trust in Patrick's narration as it requires evaluation but is not of value to the story, which is accentuated by the move from third to first-person.

> There's a black-tie party at the Puck Building tonight for a new brand of computerized professional rowing machine. I'm wearing a wing-collar jacquard waistcoat by Kilgour, French & Stanbury from Barney's, a silk bow tie from Saks, patent-leather slip-ons by Baker-Benjes, antique diamond studs from Kentshire Galleries and a gray wool silk-lined coat with drop sleeves and a button-down collar by Luciano Soprani. (*AP*, 126)

Here Patrick places himself at a branded event, literally, and proceeds to describe himself accordingly. In its obsessive detail, the paragraph manages to present no detail at all. Indeed, it is difficult to see how branded meaning could be challenged at the level of content. Does the reader believe Patrick? Is he lying or misrecognizing certain brands? The reader is in no position to judge the veracity of Patrick's claims. But she probably is not concerned to judge them, either. They seem extraneous and noninformative to narrative development. After all, were Patrick wearing a waistcoat by X and a collar by Y as opposed to a waistcoat by Y and a collar by X, there would be no narrative disruption to the text. The branded language that Patrick presents mimics but ultimately rejects the form of a financial transaction in which information becomes monetized. It interrupts the accumulative tendency of information to take a temporal form, to be turned into either plot or profit. If finance requires information to circulate over time, then part of *American Psycho*'s disaggregation of that financial form, its literalization of a financial transaction, is to demonstrate how this process may be stalled, reconfigured or even rejected.

The brand in *American Psycho* serves, as it always does, as a marker of social status and class allegiance with all of their attendant anxieties. It provides access to a larger ideology of class fantasy. But that does not explain its rhetorical and structural function in *American Psycho*, in which the level of detail, repetition and insolence with which brands are employed supersedes either individual or collective utopian fantasies of desire. For all of its engagement with the discourse of consumption, *American Psycho* has nothing to do with consumer desire.[50] Indeed, the simultaneous presentation of sheer quantity and quick exhaustion of branded language creates a world apart, a world that can be represented but is not available for temporal development.

The chapter "Chase, Manhattan," provides a site of confluence for branded meaning, literal movement, and narrative stasis. Chase is, of course, a major financial institution. One Chase Plaza is an office park in lower Manhattan, where the bank's headquarters reside and, fittingly, the "Chase, Manhattan" chapter has Patrick being chased through lower Manhattan (*AP*, 347). It is unclear precisely who or what is chasing Patrick—he could in fact be being chased by Chase and, indeed, the movement of the chapter is less that of a physical movement through space than of anxious proprioceptive awareness wherein the place of the banking plaza becomes a state of being chased. The text repeatedly externalizes value, but here we see it ironize its own construction: An external brand turns into a moment of psychic incoherence and narrative disorganization. Formally, this experience is conveyed through a shift in point of view from first to third-person while the use of a financial brand here highlights the financial nature of all brands.[51] Like the financial transaction, the brand is a representation of the movement from information to value but with the caveat that the brand expresses this problem more spatially than temporally.

While Patrick can always recognize a brand (one must, at least, assume), his attempts to identify people are less successful. *American Psycho* contains a sustained dialectic between the recognition of brands and the misrecognition of people, financiers in particular. While moving through the many nightclubs and restaurants he frequents, Patrick has a palate of fictitious and real-life financiers whom he repeatedly identifies, fantasizes, and/or misrecognizes. For example, he and his girlfriend debate whether someone at a bar is a colleague of his at Pierce & Pierce or the actor Michael J. Fox, in the context of Fox's leading role in the 1987 hostile-takeover romance, *The Secret of My Success* (*AP*, 332). In return, Patrick's colleagues constantly misrecognize him, commonly addressing him as "Allen" or "Halberstram."

Much of the text is devoted to recognizing, but doing little else with it—both people (mostly financiers) and brands. The most important cycle of recognition/misidentification comes from Patrick's engagement with Donald Trump, the financier, who is also an author and a brand. (His book, *The Art of the Deal* was, of course, a crucial part of the branding, as Galbraith suggested in his review.) Indeed, Donald Trump seems to be the one "person" Patrick Bateman has any respect for, or about whom he expresses no immediate fantasies of destroying. He describes Trump's autobiographical account of his 1980s New York–based real estate exploits, *The Art of the Deal*, as "very good" (*AP*, 276). He repeatedly thinks he sees Trump and Trump's wife, Ivanna, about town. The status of Patrick's repeated sightings of Trump around the city remains ambiguous, but he is able to recognize Trump in financial print culture (and in media culture, one morning he reports watching Trump on the fictional Patty Winters show; next up was violence). And his recognition of Trump, not the person but the image, empowers him and provides a kind of intersubjective experience. "Faded posters of Donald Trump on the cover of *Time* magazine cover the windows of another abandoned restaurant, what used to be Palaze, and this fills me with a newfound confidence" (*AP*, 226). That he uses that confidence to violent ends is unsurprising. But now, in a reversal of his involvement with Chase, Manhattan, Trump is transformed from branded image into physical space.

In *The Art of Deal*, Trump relates a meeting he had with Judith Krantz, a "best-selling author." He explains that "Trump Tower is the setting for her latest novel, *I'll Take Manhattan*, and I'm a character in the book."[52] Trump describes his pleasure at the publicity that Krantz's book and upcoming miniseries will bring to Trump Tower. He is, of course, branding himself and his building and, indeed, the building and branding of Trump Tower is the narrative climax of his autobiography. Trump is a character in *American Psycho*, too, and the Tower is a constant landmark for Patrick as he navigates his way around the city. At the aforementioned Central Park Zoo murder, he composes himself by scanning the horizon and locating "skyscrapers, apartment buildings, the Trump Tower." (Elsewhere he cites Trump Plaza, too.)

Much as there is a brand "Trump" that is independent from the man Donald Trump himself, Patrick reports that "there is an idea of a Patrick Bateman." He attempts to brand himself through his own work at Pierce & Pierce, but that operation fails to get him the desired recognition. When he brings two prostitutes to his apartment and is playing at a seduction of them he asks "don't you want to know what I do?" One of them simply answers, "no" while the other says, "no, not really." To this Patrick responds, "'Well, I work on Wall Street. At Pierce & Pierce.' A long pause. 'Have you heard of it?' I ask'" (*AP*, 172). This interaction conveys the opposite of a branding operation, which depends on constant and immediate recognition; a misrecognized brand is a failed brand.

Through his own branded logic, Patrick Bateman may be read as a failed character, one who can recognize other financiers but cannot not be recognized as a financier. As he himself explains:

> There is an idea of a Patrick Bateman, some kind of abstraction, but there is no real me, only an entity, something illusory, and though I can hide my cold gaze and you can shake my hand and feel flesh gripping yours and maybe you can even sense our lifestyles are probably comparable: *I am simply not there.* (*AP*, 376–7, italics in original)

One possible interpretation of this claim would be to conclude that Ellis has now chosen to reveal the solely discursive composition of Bateman's character—that he really is a nodal point in a series of post-modern language games. Yet it remains unclear whether we can, quite literally, take Patrick Bateman at his word. The foregoing passage is less interesting for what it reveals about Patrick than for what it suggests about the financial form that circulates throughout the text.

The text now may be understood to confuse the difference between abstraction as a descriptive practice and abstraction as an ontological form, a confusion that has important consequences for the relationship between finance and literature, both in Patrick's textual moment and in our own present. *American Psycho* was written before abstraction emerged as the dominant trope of critical studies of finance, whether in aesthetics or political economy. Most centrally, Fredric Jameson has claimed that we need "new account of abstraction" in order to be able to discern the aesthetic forms generated in a period of dominance of finance capital.[53] Now, in what seems to be an answer to a question not posed to him, Patrick Bateman informs the reader that he himself is an abstraction. For Ellis, the financializing environment of 1980s New York City has interpolated a masculine subject, Patrick Bateman, a financer who can recognize but cannot be recognized, who is more of a teller than a narrator and, finally, who renders finance as a series of material and textual effects but who claims that he himself is an abstraction.

Conclusion

Thus, while *American Psycho* quite rightly has been read as a satire, we now are able to specify what, precisely, it satirizes. Its satirical object is not simply the grandiose though ultimately uncertain and phantasmatic masculinity of the financier (as Mary Harron's 2000 film adaptation so persuasively argues); or the extravagant consumption that both reflects and makes possible a culture of finance; or the all too real and simultaneously obfuscated social violence of a financial order. Rather, *American Psycho* is a satire of a range of financial texts that Ellis himself is the first to collect as financial texts. But at the same time that *American Psycho* introduces the genre of the financial text, it threatens to collapse the unifying feature of that genre by destabilizing the supposedly determinant content, that is, the very representation of finance itself. Part of this destabilization is no doubt expected in a satire, the genre in which *American Psycho* has been placed by most critics; after all, any satire both destabilizes and codifies its object simultaneously. The text's self-reflexive use of it, however, is a historical intervention, and one that goes on to structure and define the novel. One of the many ways that *American Psycho* is as much about writing about finance as it is about finance is that, ultimately, *American Psycho* is a satire of itself. It is only with this understanding that this novel's singularly celebrated and excoriated problematic is rendered newly sensible: *American Psycho* takes the most widely distributed metaphor of 1980s financial print culture—the violent financier—and then it tries to "kill" that very metaphor. The novel attempts this final "killing" by substituting the quality to which the metaphor referred for an action and then, finally, having its own action refer metaphorically to the quality assumed by financial print culture. When Patrick tells his friend, Price, that "you're priceless," he hints at this same process of metaphorical aporia that structures the text (*AP*, 57).

In disarticulating the financial transaction, the novel goes beyond earlier postmodern engagements with finance such as *White Noise*; the novel makes an argument that the possibility of economic transformation is always at hand, and that we can imagine and represent an economic otherness. And in rearticulating finance in a generic realm, *American Psycho* serves as a reminder that an understanding of finance may be derived as much from the discursive realm of print culture as from the economic realm of political economy. Whether *American Psycho* ultimately succeeds in this operation is a question to be answered within our own contemporary financial moment. If the increasing scholarship on the text is any indication, it is succeeding. Yet the novel will likely never "replace *White Noise* on the course syllabus" as DeLillo's text had done with *The Crying of Lot 49*. Indeed, the violent content that is so central to rendering *American Psycho* financial, and thus the reason it is being canonized, is the same content that renders it valuable but not teachable. By this I do not suggest the text cannot be taught, but it seems unlikely to find the broad undergraduate audience of *White Noise*. Perhaps, then, it will replace *Gravity's Rainbow*.

Realism and Unreal Estate

THE SAVINGS AND LOAN SCANDALS
AND THE EPISTEMOLOGIES OF AMERICAN FINANCE

"Cleverness is a savings and loan."*

A Rolling Loan Gathers No Loss

By the time the nascent Savings and Loan Panic (as it was then called) materialized in Maryland in 1985, it had the feel of a scripted event.[1] Baltimore's *The Sun* reported that the Old Court Savings and Loan Association was under investigation for real estate fraud and soon after its customers amassed in the parking lot of the unremarkable building. Their convocation was described by *Newsweek* as a bank run in an article entitled "The Maryland S&L Panic," a text whose accompanying picture's caption notes "nervous depositors" and a hoped for "end to anxiety."[2] The account holders in the image, however, look rather sanguine: Several are reclined in beach chairs while others stand languidly under their parasols. What is a bank failure in 1985? In part, it occurs when depositors make a run on the bank. But the patrons at Old Court hardly seem to think their life- savings have absconded. And the *Newsweek* article ironizes the fact that these customers constituted the event that their presence in front of the bank was intended to safeguard against by referring both to an impending financial catastrophe and the fact that such a catastrophe would likely never occur.

As events similar to the Old Court failure proliferated in and were repeated throughout the decade, they were gradually renamed "The S&L Scandals" in the pages of financial print culture. The surety of

*—Kelly Cherry, "Cleverness Is a Savings and Loan." ANQ 5 issue 4 (October 1992): 184–5).

name might be read as compensation for the lack of a clearly demarcated beginning or end, for the absence of any consistent cast of characters or narrative of the event(s). Between 1983 and 1992 over 1500 savings and loan institutions (hereafter "S&L" institutions) failed. Many of these failures were the result of the involvement of S&L institutions with speculative real estate deals that were, in retrospect, fraudulent.[3] Of course, if we return to that moment, if we did not have to operate in retrospect, then these deals were still fraudulent. And that space between tautology and narrative in the production and representation of value is the one I find so interesting in this archive. This is what I want to take seriously as I explore how discourses of fraud and fictitiousness get distributed through retrospection in the specific temporal and epistemological frame of finance that the S&L crisis (as I will refer to it) delimits.[4] Indeed, some twenty years after the disappearance of these failures from the pages of financial print culture, it remains difficult to articulate what constituted these events other than a series of bank failures unrelated in time and space; it remains similarly difficult to discern what was resolved, uncovered, and memorialized in these scandals that John Kenneth Galbraith predicted "will stand as one of the most appalling events in our civil history."[5] In part, the S&L crisis was a re-creation of a past crisis—the bank runs of the Great Depression—and, in part, it was a rehearsal for the Great Recession (from 2008 to 2012)—in which the some of the country's largest banks either folded or required government intervention to remain solvent. These institutional failures were profitable because banks' deposits were insured by the federal government.[6] If an event is a drama that produces a radically open situation, as Badiou claims, then the Savings and Loan Crisis never became one, and indeed, financial events could be understood as precisely the opposite of Badiou's description. They foreclose temporal horizons and rewrite their own past.

There appeared requisite reporting on the S&L crisis within financial print culture: stories of individual bank failures, detailed descriptions of speculative real estate schemes, analyses of forms of insurance and recompense through the federal government, and so on. But with no certain eventful dates, no graph to coordinate change over a time/space continuum, no central protagonist (Charles Keating is the most notable but—perhaps since he did not author an autobiography—he has not had the staying power of the other financiers in my archive), and no real resolution, the crisis itself remains historically suspended in a kind of nonnarrative form. "The history of the savings and loans is still waiting to be written," claimed political economist and black market expert R.T. Naylor in 2006.[7] In the midst of the scandals themselves, journalist Mark Danner described them in the pages of *The New Yorker* as "remarkable for their inconclusiveness" (appropriately, the scandals dragged on for several years after Danner's comment).[8] One of the few outlets of journalistic self-criticism, *The Columbia Journalism Review*, claimed in 1990 that the story of the demise of S&L institutions had been missed, but it too was unable to say what the story in fact was.[9] In contrast to the 2007–8 credit crisis, when economists claimed their trusted models could not have predicted the systemic collapse and contraction of the global financial system, the S&L crisis never reached the level of having a codified system for prediction and retrodiction. As we will see, the reason for that lack is because the methods of money making that led to the crisis hovered between the legitimate category of economic practice and the criminal category of fraud.

The S&L crisis' lack of distinguishing features, of financial identity, and of narrative coherence is important both to the argument that I make in this chapter and the methodology I employ. The argument is that the S&L crisis reveals a mode and model of writing about finance that may be understood as the apotheosis of financialization: the moment when all writing about finance, no matter how fictitious or, in a different idiom, fraudulent, has the potential to become value producing. The "fictitious" and the "fraudulent" stake out different epistemological territory, but precisely what interests me about this archive is the manner in which these concepts are destabilized and interspersed in the representation of value. The methodology is to read the discrete events that constitute the S&L crisis, such as the individual bank failures that collectively disappeared some 150 billion dollars from the United States Treasury, as an example of a process that is no longer centered around the representation of finance by fiction, but rather the reverse: namely, the use of "fiction" in financial transactions. In that transition, I identify the location of this chapter's financial form and I suggest genre-fiction and allegory function as sites of its representation.

The texts that orient this chapter are the modes and genres of the S&L crisis—and the crisis itself is one of those texts. Thus the categorically representational work that I read herein, Jane Smiley's realist novel, *Good Faith*, does not have the same methodological status as such work in previous chapters. The novel does not delimit a financial object or process through fictional analogy, and I place it in the chapter's second half, where it functions as critique. Rather, the literary work shows the possibilities and limitations of representation when the financial process being represented is representation itself—a larger tension that I label "the descriptive imperative." Under that logic I organize the central tension and the financial form of this chapter: the need for finance to be written about for its own efficacy and realization, and the ability of those transactions to become legible only in retrospect and as they move between different discourses, from the economic, to the journalistic, to the academic. When the money is "lost," or unable to be represented, the money is made.

This chapter follows the myriad sites of the S&L crisis: fictional, journalistic, criminological, and microeconomic. Like its object, the chapter begins with a series of local scandals and ends with an abstraction, the moment in which those scandals can no longer be located temporally or spatially but come to be referred to, in this archive, as "complex."[10] In charting this history, I show how the scandal and abstraction have become our limit and possibility for thinking finance as such, and I highlight certain specifications of value—including types of money and types of loaning and accounting—that complicate this state of affairs. In doing so, I suggest that in addition to revealing the relationship between our rhetorical forms and our epistemologies of finance, the representation of the S&L Crisis might serve as an allegory for the development of academic understandings of financialization in literary studies.

Writing about the Savings and Loan Crisis: The Descriptive Imperative

While the ATM was being introduced into banks, into financial print culture and, indeed, into literary postmodernism, the S&L institution began to circulate as a new kind of economic object in corporate banking and corporate law publications. Ronald Reagan himself had designated the national deregulation of S&L institutions as tantamount to nothing less than "the emancipation proclamation of America's savings institution," when, in 1982, he signed the bill removing the cap on the amount of interest these institutions could pay to their depositors.[11] Soon after Reagan's announcement, one corporate law firm advertised a seminar whose title was the rather odd, although presumably rhetorical, question: "Why Does Everyone Seem to be Buying or Starting a California Savings and Loan?"[12] S&Ls became, in the words of one financial journalist, "money-making machines."[13] And just as what a bank *was* changed with the advent and proliferation of ATMs and the associated technology of personal banking, what money was, what savings were, changed when the governance of S&Ls changed.[14]

Indeed, it would be possible to tell the story of the emergence of financialization and its political order, neoliberalism, in the United States through the comings and goings of money in S&Ls during their celebrated tumescence and scandalous demise throughout the 1980s. Many of the crucial concepts and structures that critics including David Harvey, Jacques Derrida, and Jean Baudrillard have provided to orient us to what we now periodize as neoliberalism—but what was, in the moment, called postmodernism, late capitalism, and/or a regime of flexible accumulation—are immediately present within this story.[15] Such key moments and concepts include the end of the gold standard, which led to interest-rate fluctuation and which produced, among other things, increased transnational capital flows; the expansion of apparatuses of credit and debt at the individual and corporate level, now understood as the beginnings of the financialization of capital; the transfer of risk from the "private sector"—whatever that is—to the state and individuals; and the concurrent privatization of social space.[16] More importantly for my purposes, the critical theoretical tropes used to understand neoliberalism and to translate its content from the economic to the cultural, from the late capitalist base to the postmodern superstructure, to use the language of the original analysis, are locatable here as well: the dematerialization of money, the spatialization of narrative, and an aesthetics of ephemera, pastiche, and fragmentation. Indeed, my reading of the savings and loan crisis may also serve as a critique of more recent theories of "linguistic capital" as advanced by Christian Marazzi, for example.[17]

Simultaneously, the adjustments to this critical theoretical history that I have attempted to make throughout my study are available and necessary, too. To take the example most germane to my archive in this chapter, what precisely constitutes the dematerialization of money? In his *Given Time*, for example, Derrida diagnoses the end of the gold standard as "a certain dematerialization of money and therefore all scenes that depend on it."[18] Sometimes called the expiration of commodity money or the realization of a purely fiduciary money, the end of the gold standard in the 1970s has been a benchmark for a new period and its aesthetic, whether labeled late capitalist, neo-liberal, or postmodern. The most familiar account comes from Derrida and Baudrillard and gets picked up and recirculated through Harvey, whereby it justifies all sorts of postmodern cultural logics.[19] Ultimately the common theoretical sense that has been inherited is that when the United States abandoned convertibility between the dollar and gold in the early 1970s, the relationship between value and its representation, between the economic and the aesthetic, was somehow correspondingly destabilized. I do not quarrel with this broad telling, but I do want to specify it in a manner more conducive to historical methodology and literary close reading. Categories such as the dematerialization of money, which are now employed as a way to understand and qualify economic abstraction, have become too abstract themselves to lend their qualifications any level of specificity.[20]

In this section, I want to "follow the money" as it was described and transformed and as it circulated through S&L institutions but also through literary theory. It seems likely that Jean Baudrillard himself visited one of these institutions and recorded the interaction in his *America*. The 1988 autobiographical, picaresque text is introduced by Baudrillard as a journey to see "how far we can go in the elimination of meaning," but by way of a car rather than semiology; Baudrillard drives through the southwestern United States in the mid 1980s.[21] Thus he, probably unknowingly, speeds through both the time and place of the nascent S&L crisis. In a text whose tone is impressionistic and whose structure is episodic, Baudrillard's experience with the place of the bank and the object of money appears idiosyncratic. The bank is presented as simultaneously ephemeral and monumental. Baudrillard describes it as an empty site, composed of "*really* no one" (italics in original) and claims that "there is no more modern institution." In an almost Kerouac-like language he presents an impassioned monetary moment of bank-induced "madness," one whose object is money:

> One day I tried to close my account, taking all the money out in cash. The teller would not let me go with such a sum on me: it was obscene, dangerous, immoral. Would I not at least take travelers' cheques? 'No, the whole lot in cash.' I was mad. In America, you are stark raving mad

if, instead of believing in money and its marvelous fluidity, you want to carry it around on you in banknotes....[22]

The tone of the text makes it difficult to understand its own level of irony. One could find it ironic that Jean Baudrillard—theorist of the simulacrum—does not believe in money and its marvelous fluidity. But one could also understand him as indicating that, at the level of the perceptual and quotidian, money is always somehow material and that dematerialization has its own irony. After all, whether one pays with cash, check, credit card, phone, text message, in kind, digital mark, and so on, some *thing* must manifest materially in an exchange.

Baudriallard's ambivalent description indicates that abstractions and thus generalizations such as the "dematerialization of money," no matter how hegemonic and organizing they become, remain contests. It is absolutely true that the abandonment of the gold standard and the consequent introduction of floating exchange rates induced more volatility, fluctuation, and volume into the circulation of global capital in the 1970s. And some of that money arrived in the United States, where S&Ls were—as a result of Reagan's emancipation proclamation—free to attract it by offering higher interest rates. Indeed, for a variety of reasons unimportant to this chapter, S&L's were well positioned to become key nodal points of capital circulation. But S&Ls also placed a limit on that movement toward dematerialization. They induced money out of the sphere of pure circulation and back into the much more prosaic world of fixed capital: residential subdivisions, golf courses, corporate headquarters, and often combinations of all three. The history of S&Ls, then, both provides an account of money becoming dematerialized as well as an account of how that process was circumscribed. And because S&Ls represent as much an interruption of dematerialization as an example of it, they ask us, as critics, to reconsider what was (and is) stabilized through the homological argument in which money is liberated from its earthly strictures, just as aesthetics turns toward the fragmentary and abstract.

The S&Ls' relationship to money exemplifies an instance where content that might have been considered abstract quickly and forcefully returned to the concrete. Tracing how it did so reveals a specificity of money during these early moments of financialization. One of the first places liberated money went was to the pages of classified

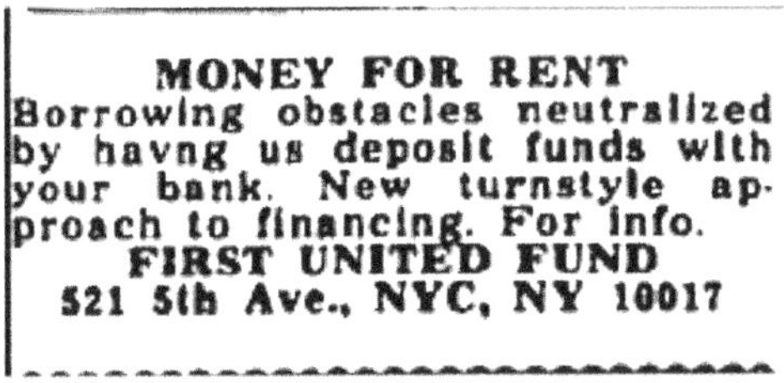

FIGURE 4.1 *June 16, 1980, The Wall Street Journal*

advertisements in financial print culture where there appeared advertisements for something called "money for rent" in *The Wall Street Journal* and the *New York Times,* among others. "Money for rent" is another term for a loan, whereas the idiomatic language of "turnstyle [*sic*]" finance does not possess an obvious correlation to formal economic terminology. A record of increased circulation, this advertisement may be read as an introduction to the vernacular of overaccumulated money capital.

The more common and expansive term, however, is "hot money," and it denotes a process of circulation that "money for rent" hints at.[23] "Hot money" may be understood as a kind of compromise formation between abstract and concrete value; it appears where money flees the scene of production and it looks to profit on short-term transactions.[24] "Hot money" or "money for rent," or what a literary character I introduce in the next section calls "too much money," are all variations on a style of money that roams the globe looking for quick profits and hopes to encounter few barriers. It moves in and out of countries, states, and banks for ever-shorter periods of time, seeking marginally ever-higher rates of return. It is money that has been decoupled from productive employment and now, in Arrighi's words, it takes "flight."[25] In the archives of financial print culture, hot money appears as a pejorative term in the *New York Times* where it is linked with drug money and other illicit forms.[26] *The Wall Street Journal* deploys "hot money" as a colloquial term, where it stands in for "brokered deposits." Indeed, *The Wall Street Journal* found it so notable that one bank refused to accept it—"[this savings and loan] just doesn't like 'hot money,' deposits that would move out as fast as they moved in"—that this refusal itself became noteworthy in an article called "Money Talks."[27] Finally, "hot money" abbreviates for various forms of capital flight in scholarly publications such as *The Review of Radical Political Economics.* Yet it remains to be excavated from the literary record, where it appears in financial fiction, or the "fi-fi," of the 1980s as well as in Dick Francis's 1988 eponymous novel, *Hot Money*.

Just as hot money attempts to elide state control, taxation, even accounting itself, it theoretically circumvents a Marxian derived framework of political economy and a Foucault-inspired framework of disciplinary and institutional apparatuses.[28] For Marxists, hot money does not distinguish itself as a form of money: It is still a universally convertible commodity and a material incarnation of a representation of abstract labor power. And while some hot money is criminal, the Marxist tradition, for its part, has avoided the rubric of financial crime to advance the more encompassing notion that the system of capital is more criminal than specific infractions against its legal superstructure. Hot money does not search for a Rosa Luxembourg–like spatial outside; rather it searches for an inside, a site to double-down without labor or risk.[29] Hot money, then, would seem more suitable to a Foucauldian critique, the kind that emerged in the humanities in the 1980s at the very moment hot money itself reemerged.[30] That critique directs its attention toward the boundedness of concepts, their ability to be rendered articulable and visible in institutions, documents, statements, and, crucially, toward their institutionalization, on the one hand, and deviance from it in the form of criminality on the other. But while the latter may seem the more intuitive approach, hot money has one defining quality that distinguishes it from Foucauldian and other poststructuralist approaches to value: hot money never ceases its drive to accumulate more money, and poststructuralism does not allow for accumulation for the sake of accumulation.

I understand hot money as both a symptom and an object of financialization, itself a structural answer to the problem of having too much money for it to be employed profitably in any given present.[31] I position it as a mediating ground between money sitting idle and money being routed into the future through financial devices. One way in which hot money becomes visible is through the savings and loan crisis and, conversely, savings and loans institutions become "money-making machines" through capturing hot money. It is hot money that allows S&Ls to make more money when there is already too much of it. This is not a causal relationship; the overaccumulation of money capital and the presence of hot money did not produce the S&L crisis.[32] But together they did produce claims such as this: "Developers didn't borrow in order to build, they built in order to

borrow, and borrow some more," and "money availability became
more a reason for a real estate development than economics."[33]
Correspondingly, the individual S&L failures that comprise my archive may be understood as a kind of narrative device that delimits
overaccumulation and its idioms and processes. The S&L crisis allows
access to a different vernacular of finance than that introduced through
the logics of high finance in chapter 2 and personal banking in chapters
1 and 3, and it demonstrates how central modes of temporality, including narration and retrospection, and spatiality, including movement between different discourses, are to the production of certain
financial values.

That said, the S&L crisis is an unfamiliar financial event for the
same reasons that make it an interesting one and, I want to suggest, a
particularly literary one: It has a unique style of representation that
relies on retrospection for its understanding and ultimately its valor-
ization. To hold the literary and financial in tension, I suggest that the
time/space of these transactions transpire within what I label "the descriptive imperative" of finance. This is the productive contradiction
that structures this archive and the tendency of finance most compel-
lingly exemplified throughout the S&L crisis. The descriptive imperative reveals the need for finance to be recorded, even to produce
indexical forms of representation (thus the ruins of the chapter we
will soon see: holes in the ground, razed subdivisions, etc.) while
simultaneously remaining unable to be recorded realistically in the
moment of its execution because, if it were, the transaction in question
would cease. Thus the descriptive imperative designates how financial transactions organize a lack of coherency in different idioms
during different timeframes. Yet the descriptive imperative also
reveals moments of overlap and simultaneity, when and where money
is made.

A specific transaction will introduce how the descriptive imperative functions within the S&L archive. Called the Acquisition,
Development and Construction Loan (ADC loan), this is an anti-
septic name given to a transaction that is anything but. The ADC loan
establishes a horizontal space for the fictional, journalistic, and criminological texts I use throughout this chapter. Specifically, in the ADC
loan we can see most clearly how a transaction proceeds from a description. If there was an immediate "cause" of the S&L crisis, it may
be located in the seemingly unremarkable transformation of accounting rules that rendered suddenly opaque the basic microeconomic

distinction between a "loan" and an "investment." A loan contributes to an already existing stock of capital; an investment creates the ground for capital itself. S&Ls would harness hot money, *a*cquire land, *d*evelop it, and then *c*onstruct something. That was the idea, anyway. More often S&L bankers sold land back and forth to each other, repeatedly raised the price, and took out loans for real estate developments they never intended to build. As these loans were repeated in S&L institutions throughout the country, and as they repeatedly "failed," ADC loan transactions helped to constitute the S&L crisis. They made the S&L crisis possible, and they made money.[34]

In the event that a loan fails, the loaning institution has collateral. Furthermore, a loan from an S&L institution was federally insured up to $100,000.[35] By contrast, when an investment fails, the investing institution assumes the loss: There is no collateral and there is no recompense. Because "loan" and "investment" each marshal separate institutional and discursive apparatuses and contain different relationships to futurity, it seems as though it would be important to understand which kind of advancing of capital S&Ls engaged in. And yet, throughout the savings and loan crisis, no one did. "For accountants, the real question is whether the ADC loan is a loan or a direct real estate investment by the savings institution," explains one of the most in-depth journalistic accounts of the crisis; the question remains unanswered in the article.[36] Such initial confusion over basic typology begins a long process of indeterminacy as hot money circulates in S&L transactions where it is governed by a need for documentation and an incredible architecture of obfuscation. The more successfully such indeterminacy can be prolonged, the more money can be made. Thus, at the midpoint of the crisis, one newspaper reports: "And while the causes of the disaster are still being examined, its losses continue to accumulate each day." This claim may be interpreted as suggesting "losses" were enabled by lack of consistent representation. Indeed, lack of representation itself becomes a strategy of profit. And just as I have used the idioms of the business and real estate development community to intercede into 1980s literary and critical theoretical discourse, that community itself borrowed an emergent literary terminology to begin to note the effects of overaccumulation. In the pages of financial print culture, the results of this speculative activity—namely an overproduction of space—were themselves conceived of as postmodern and explained in *Barron's* as: "Post-modernism for $20 a foot, with a year's free rent!" and while cities, particularly in the South and Southwest, were reported to be "cluttered with post-modernism."[37]

For S&Ls, then, it became more profitable, and perhaps more postmodern, never to complete the construction and development aspects of the ADC loan—why risk the outlay of capital?—but rather to leave space only cosmetically commodified. Because of what seemed like impending development, the price of land increased; but because, in many cases, the development was in fact not impending at all, the price of land increased even more as those involved could represent the loan, take the fees and abandon the transaction. And because it was a loan, the transaction was guaranteed by the federal government. The entire ADC Loan package would then be sold from one bank to another. Again the vernacular is instructive: ADC Loans were often referred to as "rolling loans" and, as the phrase went, "a rolling loan gathers no loss."[38] These loan-based projects that gathered no losses included an 8-story-deep hole in Dallas Texas, once the future site of an oddly imagined health club, hospital, apartment complex, and golf course that would become "the nation's indoor county club," and a place called Costa Mesa, itself the barely begun site of a new subdivision in rural Arizona that contained, at the time of its bankruptcy, only concrete building foundations.[39]

In the historical literature on the S&L crisis, these indexical representations of capital function as revelatory as they narrate the disappearance of money from circulation. Here is Edwin Gray, chairman of the Federal Home Loan Bank Board, describing a video of the emerging crisis:

> The camera panned slowly from side to side, catching in sickening detail the carrion of dead savings and loan deals: thousands of condominium units financed by Empire Savings and Loan of Mesquite, Texas. The condominiums stretched as far as the camera could see, in two- and three-floor clusters, maybe 1.5 units per building. They were separated by stretches of arid, flat land. Many were only half-finished shells. Most were abandoned, left to the ravages of the hot Texas sun. . . .[40]

In Gray's explanation, however, we note that the indexical representation is mediated by the activity of viewing itself: The camera pans and sees for itself, and the viewer then receives its images secondhand. As such, there is still some distance from the direct representation, a style of writing that will be carried over into journalistic work through the figurative lens of "the auditor."

The first sign of fraud in the archive of ADC loans is betrayed by the awkwardness of some of their physical designs and the rapidity of their abandonment. Furthermore, the fact that, as loans, they were insured, and that included as part of the loans were the fees that the S&L operators paid themselves, meant that a failure could be as profitable as a success. Fraud will become a singularly important trope for representing the S&L crisis, but before I engage it, I want to provide a sampling of this archive out of which fraud will emerge to answer the questions: "What happened?" "How did it happen?" and "How did it happen so many times and so consistently?" I do not want to presuppose the concept of fraud in answering these questions because to do so would be to remove this investigation from the realm of the economic. Indeed, in the navigation of this uncertain space between the economic and the fraudulent, profit became possible.

These early evaluations that enable the narrative of fraud to emerge are located in financial print culture. Financial journalism begins to attempt to capture these unfolding bank failures and, in doing so, attempts to narrate these transactions. One of the central qualities of narrative representation is the maintenance of some categorical stability in the face of temporal change. Thus one of the challenges of representing financial transactions is to maintain the identity of money as it moves through multiple times, spaces, and discourses. Indeed, for money to function as money, it is necessary that "money must have a single, time-bound identity."[41] In the case of S&Ls, money was being "made" by individuals at banks which reported consistently less and less of it on their books, indeed at banks that were becoming insolvent. Under such circumstances, the identity of money itself must be questioned. The challenge of studying the S&L crisis is that to narrate financial transactions may impose an identity and consistency on money where there is none. But to decline to narrate these events may be to forgo the identification of a new value form and its realization.

To track and tease out this tension, I will focus on two particularly in-depth articles that each attempted to account for a single S&L bankruptcy as metonymic of what was emerging as "The Savings and Loan Scandals." The first article is entitled, "Showdown at 'Gunbelt' Savings" and the second, "The Lapses by Lincoln's Auditors."[42] I introduce them here to place this particular archive within the general ambit of 1980s financial print culture that I have borrowed from and analyzed throughout my study, and to discern a common logic at work in each text.[43] Some linkages are easily ascertained. For example, the first article employs interpersonal violence in its title: "Gunbelt" is in fact a reference to an institution called "Sunbelt Savings and Loan." In its own institutional vernacular it called itself Gunbelt for the supposed quickness of its transactions and the sense of competitive edge its employees believed it had over its competitors. As elsewhere in financial journalism, violence against women and hatred of the poor function as rhetorical markers of institutional prowess. Prostitutes appear regularly, as does a catalogue of profligate spending, including a Christmas party with "a live bear and wait-staff dressed as Russian peasants," a "live elephant and a jungle theme," and so on. While less colorful, "The Lapses by Lincoln's Auditors" seeks to explicate what was, during the scandals themselves, the most canonical of S&L-oriented events: the bankruptcy of Lincoln Savings and Loan under the directorship of Charles Keating.

My argument is that the movement between the operative discourses of economy, criminology, and complexity should be read as a certain kind of financial transaction, one that realizes value. The identity of money within each of these discourses is different enough that the transitions between them would not seem capable of sustaining narrative consistency. I will locate how economic discourse is gradually disavowed in favor of the discourses of criminality and complexity, and show how money is ultimately made through this disavowal. To discern their operative logics, these articles must be read twice, as it were, both as description and, crucially, as part of the transaction the article seeks to explain.[44] As description, they continue the masculine theatrics of writing about finance seen throughout my study. More importantly, they introduce a new vocabulary for rendering finance that continues until today, and that complements Tom Wolfe's project as seen in chapter 2: the idea that financial transactions are complex and therefore difficult to understand and represent. As transactions, they initiate the process of rendering the money "lost" as opposed to "made." They provide a new discourse in which money can be understood and maintain its value, namely that of white-collar crime.

At the same time, however, there exists a real difficulty with "reading" these articles as transactions. They do offer a historically crucial but theoretically ambiguous example of the kind of writing about finance that itself is a form of financialization: the moment when all representation can create value, what in my reading of *Wall Street* I described as "realist subsumption," or the moment when all content can function as information. But mine is also a potentially problematic claim because it risks valorizing financial objects and dissociating them from the social conditions necessary for financial transactions to occur in the first place. Fredric Jameson himself offers an example of this danger when he claims that: "[Finance] needs neither production nor consumption (as money does), [it can].... supremely, like cyberspace, live on its own internal metabolism without any reference to an older type of content."[45] LiPuma and Lee's work on derivatives fits here, too: "There seems to be no way to characterize the real effects of speculative capital," they write in their *Derivatives and the Globalization of Risk.*[46] In Jameson's account, financial value becomes semiotic and autonomous; it is based on an internal nonidentity, is self-realizing, and ultimately beyond representation itself. In Li Puma and Lee's account, it is outside the scope of the real altogether.

One might respond to such explanations of financial value by criticizing their lack of labor, materiality, and agency.[47] I am going to proffer a different account. By moving between the discourses of criminality, microeconomics and journalism, I locate the moment that value is produced and obfuscated, that is, when it can no longer be represented and thus begins to appear as self-realizing. While my focus will not be on the labor process and its phenomenology, the language being used here does derive from a kind of intellectual labor so common to late twentieth-century capitalist organizations, namely white-collar work. In literary criticism, white-collar logics and aesthetics have begun to shed their veneer as staid and predictable, routine and professional, in favor of something more aesthetic, periodizing, and even canonical.[48] Nonetheless, one of the most interesting, and profitable, manifestations of white-collar organizations has received less attention. In my archive, white-collar labor goes by a different name: that of white-collar crime. What white-collar labor and white-collar crime have in common is that they are conducted, for the most part, by white people. Meanwhile, drug-money narratives of African-Americans and Latinos and mafia conspiracies of ethnic Italians have arguably become the stock narratives of neoliberalism because the form of money remains invisible while the ethnically and racially marked body itself becomes a site of circulation.[49] The representation of financial crime in general and the S&L crisis in particular, is distinguished by the fact that it does not transpire through a racially marked body or a laboring body. These qualities are part of the disappearing act of the S&L crisis, a disappearance that transpires on the way to abstraction.

"Gunbelt" and "Lapses" explain how each respective S&L institution was bankrupted through a series of ever more speculative and fabulous ADC Loans. How, each article asks, could not only bankers and real estate developers but professional auditors have let this all transpire? Then as now, white collar-crime is mitigated by enough technical language that no business journalist can simply claim "funds were expropriated" or "money was stolen."[50] Rather money, in these stories, is "lost." That is, the identity of money is destabilized to the point that money loses its ability to be represented as money. Indeed, the subtitle of the "Lapses" article is "Losing 2 Billion: An Accounting Quagmire, a Special Report." The locution "lost money," however, presumes that it has changed locations or owners. Money does not evaporate, even it changes form and fluctuates in value. R. T. Naylor may be correct that much of this money wound up in pensions and that "the process of converting corporate into private property [is] what financial capitalism is all about," but in these articles, the destination of lost money is never revealed.[51]

Rather, a series of frauds is suggested as the answer to the question: What happened to the money? But fraud, like hot money, has its own representational difficulties. In the larger discourse of value that organizes business journalism, that of microeconomics, "value is measured by the price of the last market sale, except in cases of fraud."[52] Much as the difference between a loan and an investment was ambiguous during the S&L crisis, fraud is almost impossible to represent in microeconomics. The impossibility of representing fraud in fact derives from neoclassical economics where value is represented by arm's length sale price—unless the sale is fraudulent.[53] But unless everyone making similar transactions knows of the fraud, even the representation of fraud is value-producing because the fraudulent sale will effect other similar sales. After all, price, which is represented individually, is in fact a measure of the ability of something to not be individual, but to be jointly recognized and represented as such. "Fraud is extremely difficult for auditors to find," explains the "Gunbelt" article. Even when transactions were called, in the vernacular, "cash for trash," or "rolling loans," or "fast finance," the fact is that "something as simple as an employee's hand in petty cash is fairly easy to ferret out; but a sophisticated scheme with many parties and false documents is very hard to uncover" ("Gunbelt," 12). At the seemingly crucial points of profit, representation becomes difficult if not impossible.

This failure of representation in cases of fraud results from the fact that a hand in petty cash is a momentary occurrence whereas the epistemology that organizes fraudulent transactions is bound by the stasis of microeconomic temporality and its tautological sense of causality. Theft is representable in a manner that fraud is not. In explaining that there is no singular moment in which a fraud emerges, one auditor claims, "That's the way the banking business is: It's always a good asset until it's not," ("Gunbelt"). "The Lapses of Lincoln's Auditors" renders a similar atemporal dynamic: "Assets don't become bad until they become bad." This transmutation from good to bad asset can be discerned by an auditor, but only in retrospect: "Examination is by nature after the fact," explains the "Gunbelt" article. Afterward, however, is already too late: once a fraudulent transaction has occurred, any sale price established therein may circulate as a form of evaluation and be used as a basis for further transactions. It is both a necessary and impossible task to examine a bounded transaction for fraud because fraud is an individual act, but value is a social relation.

This is why Marx claims that, falsely individuated from their social context, such transactions exist in the "eternal virginity of bourgeois economics." And it is why Fredric Jameson has said that all of *Capital* can be read as against the notion of the static equation as such.[54] The S&L transactions occur in and exploit this space of tautology. It is within that atemporality, that eternal virginity, that S&L's money can circulate as value and that particular S&L transactions may be read as an allegory of microeconomics itself. During the transaction, money takes on a momentarily lateral and directionless freedom, whereby it can metabolize a timeframe to which it is not subject. To narrate this at all is, in some sense, to miss the point because it imposes a narrative coherence that circumscribes profitable difference (or *différance*). But not to narrate it is to miss the point, too. Thus the difficulty for journalists in communicating precisely what transpired, a difficulty that is faced by many contemporary cultural critics of finance.

Indeed, we would seem to need an account of nonnarrative financial effectivity to manage this particular problem. Such a project has recently been initiated by Donald MacKenzie and the "social studies of finance" school in which his work is grouped.[55] MacKenzie has argued that in producing financial models that supposedly represent financial transactions, financial economists instead produce a financial world that resembles their models. What MacKenzie has called his "performativity of finance" argument claims that "financial economics did more than analyze markets, it altered them; [financial economics was] an engine...not a camera." More specifically, MacKenzie explains that "in the case of the use of an economic model, for example, one possibility is that economic processes or their outcomes are altered so that they better correspond to the model." Thus, he claims, "the use of a model makes it [the model] more true."[56] The definition of a model that grounds MacKenzie's analysis is that of a "verbal or mathematical representation of an economic process."[57] MacKenzie recounts how the once-marginal field of finance began the ultimately successful process of establishing itself as hegemonic in economic institutions, including both economics departments in universities and investment organizations such as various forms of banks.

The distance between the representation of a process and the process itself is what interests me about MacKenzie's discussion of models and what I think the S&L crisis complicates. This chapter is not simply about how the S&L crisis was represented. It is about how representation figured within the economic transactions themselves. Despite the fact that "everyone seemed to be buying or starting" a savings and loan institution, there were no economic models to represent this process. This was not for lack of information or informal models, however. Indeed, the foregoing quotation is from a corporate seminar, and there were many such events throughout the decade. Here we have the preliminary representational work involved in producing a model of a process whose distinctive mode of value production required that an official model never be completed. MacKenzie's historiographic and ethnographic account of financial model production is useful in thinking through the representational work that must happen for an economic model to be produced—or not.

What MacKenzie's account suggests, although he does not draw this conclusion himself, is that an economic model might be a literal example of what Marx called "the expenses of representation," literally the kind of representational space that must be purchased for certain transactions to proceed. McKenzie relays, for example, that one of the most central institutions of financial-model production, located at the University of Chicago, was underwritten by an investment bank. He explains that "Merrill Lynch's $50,000 grant was the initial foundation of the University of Chicago's Center for Research in Security Prices."[58] Thus the models produced at the University of Chicago were "sponsored" by Merrill Lynch, the institution that would ultimately make money off them. But they were developed at a non-profit educational institution that did not "make" money. In cases such as this, modeling becomes a site of mediation between knowledge that can be represented in a certain fashion and money that can be made as a result of that representation.

Insofar as a model is a verbal or mathematical representation of an economic process that exists independently of the activity of modeling itself, then a model could be considered indifferent and independent of its object. Such is the case, for example, with a model of a DNA molecule. Economic models, however, are of a different sort. Economic processes by their very nature involve verbal and mathematical description. To describe the economic world is always implicitly to describe a manner of making money, losing money, or maintaining money's value in that world. As such, economic models are always also strategies, as MacKenzie appreciates. But the division between academic economics, which does the work of modeling, and commercial banking and financial activities, which constitute the economic processes to be represented, obscures the strategic nature of economic models and lends them an aura of independence—the value of which has not gone unnoticed by the likes of Merrill Lynch.[59] What becomes especially clear in reading these skeletal accounts of the S&L crisis is that the representation of its economic process before it was able to be modeled was crucial to the efficacy of that process. Whether a representation comes in the form of an economic model out of the University of Chicago or a verbal or mathematical description in the pages of financial print culture, we must attend to the way that representation enables or inhibits the process of money making itself. And where a model is lacking and description is wanting, as is the case with the S&L crisis, we need to ask why, indeed whether, the absence of representation belongs to the moneymaking process.

By archives' end, when the money has been lost, two discrete epistemologies have become available for understanding this collection of bank failures. Together they reveal why the S&L crisis has become a financial nonevent and why it has been so difficult to narrate or locate models within or derive models from. First, there is the view that the operative structure of accumulation is too complex to be described or understood—a now familiar claim about financial activities more

generally. And second, the activities of the S&Ls are granted the structure of a criminological action that violates the microeconomic definition of value—price based on last arm's-length sale except in cases
of fraud—which then removes these activities from the economic domain altogether. In the second case, the epistemological question
becomes not how accumulation is possible, but why certain people
become criminals. But to concede to either of these epistemologies
the authority to give a comprehensive account of the crisis would be
to overlook the way that these events reveal a general feature of economic processes, namely, the way that economic processes take
account of the expenses of representation.

If we go with the first understanding, it's complex. As S&L-related
bank failures increased throughout the 1980s so did the repetition of
a series of phrases: "complex financial deal" or "complex financial transaction," or "complicated financial deal" or some variation thereof. If a
single term unites these discourses and allows precisely for their repetition it is the term: "complex deal," a term with so much surplus
meaning and money attached to it that the descriptive imperative is
almost reducible to it. The words designate the need for some writing,
but allow that the writing produced need not contain specific semantic content. Complex, in this archive, is a performative term
in that it is invoked to suspend the potential for further description.
To return to "Gunbelt" we see that: "While what Sunbelt [Savings and
Loan] did in principle was simple, in practice the deals were exceed-
ingly complex." Crucially, the story never explains what was complex,
a tension present throughout the archive.

The *Dallas Morning News*, really the local newspaper of the S&L
crisis, offered a similar explanation for "Gunbelt": It was bankrupted
in "a complicated scheme of land flips" through "shell corporations
and fictitious financial statements," activities that were "complex and
contradictory." In the face of this object, the article itself claimed to
offer a "complex portrait" of an institution "enmeshed in complex
financial transactions," in which auditors failed to "analyze complex
business transactions" that included "complex loans."[60] *Newsweek*
employed the term "complicated" to similar effect and claimed that
white-collar criminal transactions are rarely prosecuted because they
are "so complicated...and so routine."[61] This pairing of complicated
and routine hints at how complexity may become value producing and,
indeed, how we might locate a model within the pages of financial
print culture.

If we go with the second understanding, it's immoral. In academic discourse, the S&L crisis has been an object of criminological study rather than of neoliberal conceptions of money, credit, debt, or value. For example, William K. Black, whose work I will return to in the next section, advances the thesis that the S&L crisis produced a new instance of white-collar crime that he terms the "control fraud" and defines as a "wave of frauds led by the men who control large corporations [that] caused the massive losses from property crimes."[62] The discourse of "complexity" refuses narration but the discourse of white-collar crime requires an odd navigation of it. Unlike, for example, the crime of pocket-picking, white-collar crime relies on the continual description and periodizing of employed instruments and techniques for its definition. While the technologies of pockets change (zippered, buttoned, front, back, etc.) the crime remains the same because the identity of money does not change when the money changes hands. Not so with bank fraud. If banking is being conducted in a new period, then it requires new regulations, or lack thereof. Actions such as ADC loaning and its accounting had to be described anew before a crime against them was possible. A fraud requires an established norm to mimic and from which to deviate. As finance is here subject to the descriptive imperative, so white-collar crime is a crime of description: Once the agents describe the techniques of their actions anew, the law must be updated or a crime will not have occurred. What we might call white-collar criminological time is crucial to both economic representation and economic effectivity.

And there is infinite latitude for redescription of financial devices. Indeed, some scholars have asked the perfectly legitimate question of whether any financial device warrants an understanding as "new." John Kenneth Galbraith, who described the S&L crisis as "the ultimate scandal," has also claimed that: "The world of finance hails the invention of the wheel over and over again [but] all financial innovation involves, in one form or another, the creation of debt secured in greater or lesser adequacy by real assets."[63] It was the same language of historical break that made the transactions possible—the ADC used to be an investment, now it was a loan (and thus government insured)—that also made them understandable as white-collar crime.

In addition to these two dominant epistemologies, two much less common discourses are present in this archive, and I mention them here as they will be important in the next section on novelistic representation. The first is that of fiction itself, which some of these transactions require in addition to that of fraud. The difference between the two is that fiction makes no claims to legitimacy. "The development that was never built," "paper empires," "Monopoly money," "skyscrapers in the sand," each of these was used to described how a failed transaction relied on a fictional space.[64] This discourse of fiction is quite different from what *Forbes* explained, in 2011, is the basic content necessary for a financial economy. "Without trust, the necessary fictions of finance cannot function," the magazine declared.[65] In the context of the S&Ls, however, the turn to fiction is a way to cement the site of "loss," rather than to make reference to an ill-defined status quo. In the case of the S&Ls, the discourse of fiction confirms that not only can the money never be recovered, but that its foundation never existed in the first place.

Finally, during the crisis itself, the only analyst to produce a comprehensive account, to refuse the discourse of complexity and the separation between the criminal and the economic and not turn to a language of fiction, was a Texas-based journalist named Pete Brewton, whose monograph's argument is in fact reducible to its title: *The Mafia, CIA & George Bush: the Untold Story of America's Greatest Financial Debacle*.[66] Brewton's claim is that there existed "evidence suggesting a possible link between the Central Intelligence Agency and organized crime in the failure of at least 22 [S&Ls]." His argument was that key mob figures repeatedly looted S&Ls and some of this money was covertly used to fund CIA operations abroad. Brewton's narrative is both local and particular. He avoids both the language of obfuscation and of moralization. Brewton, rather, uses another narrative device for understanding the crisis: the mafia, a shadowy conspiracy of businessmen who are both legitimate and illegitimate, and who are most often narrated fictitiously and ethnically as white. One can almost be sympathetic to Brewton's turn toward the mafia as a narrative device; how else was he to tell the story? But the results were predictable: since the mafia is a popular fictional construction, the story was branded a fabulous one; indeed Brewton himself was marked as fabulous because under capitalism economic coherency intimates conspiracy theory. In its forceful and reaching conclusion, Brewton's text approximates the problem of historical narration itself as conceived of by Hayden White: "condemned because it consists of nothing but plot; its story elements exist as nothing but manifestations ... it intimates rather than invites imaginative identification."[67]

As different as these discourses are, they all attempt to address the same questions: How do we account for similar kinds of bank failures, repeated over time? What kind of money was made? How should these processes be represented?[68] The advantage of a model's abstraction is that it can explain repetition without narrative which has a tendency toward conspiracy. Indeed, we can discern the faint outlines of a model in the pages of financial journalism. It qualifies MacKenzie's definition because there is quite simply no space between the verbal or mathematical representation of the economic process and the process itself. Here we see that the "model"—in the more general sense of a plan to be followed—involves the self-presentation of complexity and the careful navigation of the boundaries between legitimate and illegitimate means of making money as well as the temporal and descriptive registers that demarcate each. The economic processes at work in the S&L crisis resist verbal and mathematical description precisely by being shrouded in a discourse of incomprehensibility. But that discourse is also constitutive of the model because it is the crucial feature that must be repeated in order to make money. The representation belongs to the economic process.

Before I move on, I want to reconsider where this section began, namely with the concomitant appearance of S&Ls as newly desirable for their money-making capacity, with an increase in the amount of stateless and interstate money in circulation coupled with its inability to be productively employed, and with a contention in critical theory that money had become a dematerialized, a kind of fictitious capital in David Harvey's words. By tracking the money as it was routed through S&Ls and as it became a site of scandal and ultimately crisis, I have attempted to locate a bifurcation in how this money was represented. In critical theory, it became reduced to its sign, underwent a "semiotic shift" according to Rotman, and lost some essential representational stability. In journalism, it became too complex to track, as it spiraled from one transaction to another, from one discourse to another. In criminology, it was neither complex nor groundless but it was also outside of the bounds of economics. To arrive at this conclusion methodologically requires the historical isolation of "money" itself and the act of doing so leads to the myriad forms of its representation. One of the kinds of representation that was available was the assertion that no representation was possible. Indeed, its lack of representation, part of which I have grouped under the logic of the descriptive imperative, became a reliably profitable fixture of these transactions. Writing about housing, writing about loans, writing about loss, all writing in this scheme, could become more. It could become value.

Unreal Estate

In this section, I read the S&L crisis as aspects of it were transformed into fictional representation. I use this transposition to think through the question at the center of literary and cultural criticism about finance, beginning with Jameson's 1997 inauguration of literary studies of finance capital and continuing until today: How should transactions like the foregoing, with their strange negotiation of materiality and discursive slippage, be represented? On the one hand, the bank failures that collectively constituted the savings and loans crisis were dependent on forms of representation, including both the journalism that explained what happened as well as indexical representations at building sites that made the appearance of real estate construction, and therefore the transfer of money via loans, possible. On the other hand, these transactions and the bank failures that they occasioned were not represented generically or cumulatively as an economic event because they did not rely on the stock narratives that we find in stock markets, with their easily quantifiable indexes of daily fluctuation, and, more importantly, because to represent them during their execution would have been to end the very transactions that were the object of the representation. The S&L crisis as a collection of individual transactions and a noneventful financial event is crucial to the realization of financial value in the 1980s because it disavows narrative in its present representation only to demand it in retrospect; it manages multiple discourses and idioms and as it moves from fraud to fiction, from complexity to aporia. Consequently, its representation becomes a site to explore the very concept of narrativized economic representation as such: when it functions as efficacious, when it functions as critical, and when it is simply not possible.

A film such as J.C. Chandor's 2011 *Margin Call* or Oliver Stone's *Wall Street* (I or II), for example, could not be, and has not been, made about the S&L crisis. Rather there are now book-length journalist accounts and academic criminological studies. Likewise, there are no quotidian objects that can metonymically represent the S&L crisis such as the proliferation of automated teller machines represents personal banking in both financial print culture and in postmodern fiction, including in two of our most canonical postmodern texts. The reason for that impossibility is that the specific bank failure in question is not prosaic or quotidian; the specific transaction has no ready connection to technological or historical objects of the 1980s—think of the bulky white cell phone or boxy Walkman that Mary Harron used to periodize her film adaption of *American Psycho*. Smiley's novel *Good Faith* gestures toward the limits of economic periodization without technology or branded products when, for example, its two main characters stand in the lobby of a shuttered bank and appreciate the "grandeur" of "the old teller windows and how they harken back to a time when "people stayed close to their money" (149). But even as steady and forceful of a referent as an old bank standing in for the changing nature of banking itself in a book about the collapse of a savings and loan institution fails to secure an easy association to the S&L crisis. This extraordinary lack of connection is because the S&L crisis itself was dependent on modes and styles of description and obfuscation for its execution, what I have referred to as "the descriptive imperative."

None of this means that the transactions were not or cannot be represented because of their essentially abstract character or because the form of money they used was dematerialized or credit based.[69] Yet a clear component of the event itself was its lack of narrative representation and its ability to be legible as a model. As critics, then, we must be clear whether we are completing the transactions by describing them (as did the financial journalism) or criticizing the event in a new idiom that possesses its own immanent logic, as we would be if we settled on the problematic as one of abstraction. While one could certainly conjecture that the S&L crisis was "too abstract to represent," it could be rejoined that not representing the crisis directly was part of its efficacy. In MacKenzie's argument, the writing of economic models transforms the real world of economic practice. In the case of the S&L crisis, one has to take a step back and locate the real world of economic practice in the writing since the writing was the site of "modeling" and money making.

Published in 2003, *Good Faith* begins with the periodizing claim that, "This would be '82." The conditional mood of the sentence sets the opening for a conjectural history that the book tells, a history that extends from 1982 until what the narrator himself calls, "The Resolution-Trust period," a reference to the Congressionally created agency responsible for liquidating and dissolving the hundreds of

S&L institutions that had failed throughout the 1980s. *Good Faith* takes
the S&L crisis as its historical setting, and the ADC loan, in particular,
as its structuring plot device. The novel is told from the retrospective
longing of a real estate agent, Joe Stratford, some time after the two-
year period during which he came under the sway of Marcus Burns,
the man who taught him to "live on borrowed money" and to live such
that he would "never pay taxes again." Immediately recognizable as a
kind of modern-day confidence man in the best tradition of Melville,
Marcus is an arriviste in Joe's small northeastern town who ultimately
relieves Joe of his savings and flees to the Bahamas with his current,
and Joe's former (and married) lover.[70] He leaves several ruined sexual
and business partnerships in his wake, and he leaves Joe himself to
perseverate endlessly on the questions that structure Joe's retrospective investigation and thus the novel's narrative: when did Marcus
know what he was doing, how did he plan to abscond with Joe's former
lover and Joe's money, and what were his motivations—was his
white-collar crime opportunistic or premeditated? Had he ever been
committed to his S&L-funded real estate venture with Joe, or was it
always a fraudulent enterprise, a form of "unreal estate" in Marcus's
own vocabulary? Because the novel's financial plot will turn out to
have been an elaborate fraud and because within its diegesis the novel
requires a simultaneous heterosexual plot for its support, *Good Faith*
may contain a literal version of what Lee Edelman has called "the
ponzi scheme of reproductive futurism." In such a scheme, the hoped-
for windfall of normative sexuality is not possible for all. To that
scheme the novel adds what the criminologists Kitty Calavita et al.
have called an "ADC Ponzi" or a "hot deal," in which a bank is looted
through a construction loan.[71]

There could be no better narrator for a novel suspended between
Edelman's and Calavita's respective ponzis than someone fixated on
a white-collar crime and perhaps desiring of the white-collar criminal.
"I couldn't move on . . . not knowing from his own lips what [Marcus's]
story was," explains Joe, at the novel's conclusion (416). Unlike the
detective, so famously transformed into a literary perspective by Walter
Benjamin, or the "social detective" as suggested by Fredric Jameson,
Joe assumes the role of the white-collar criminologist in his narrative
retelling.[72] The detective attempts to locate and identify the perpetrator
of a known action: There was a burglary; items are missing; *who* stole
them? The white-collar criminologist's approach is different. It focuses
not on personal identity but on the legal and social categories of the

criminal's actions: Mr. X suddenly has a lot of money; he manages a bank that just declared bankruptcy; *how* did he become wealthy and were his appropriations legal, or were they inventive enough to be outside the scope of criminal legibility? Both the reader and Joe know by the novel's end that Marcus has fled to an offshore tax haven, taking with him the eight-hundred and sixty-thousand dollars that had been intended for his and Joe's real estate development. But what neither the reader nor Joe knows is *how* Marcus accomplished this: what were his accounting tools, his organizational logics, his own understanding of his actions? As we saw in the previous section, before such actions are described and codified, they cannot be criminal; but once they become criminal, they cease to be economic. This transitional space between categories is precisely the content of Joe's narration.

In contrast to both the realist works of chapter 2 and the economic events that occasioned them, *Good Faith* has not been considered canonical by critics and it records a financial event that remains uneventful to economists and historians.[73] Nor does the novel contain such realist trappings as an omniscient narrator with its ability to transition between times and space, between different story lines. In this novel, the person authoring the economic process and recording it is one. Smiley does not possess the cache, or the masculinity, to make front-page pronouncements in financial print culture about the importance of her work, her choice of aesthetic mode, or the necessity of her prose to the representation of a new economic era. In an interview, Smiley periodized the moment of *Good Faith*, the early 1980s, in terms that are less aesthetic or global than they are civic and national:

> I think only intelligent people think of the 80s as a grim decade. I think too many people think of the 80s as lots of fun, or as a time when there was "a new dawn for America." I think of the 80s as the beginning of a tragic civic decline that resulted in the stolen election of 2000 and the national chaos and uneasiness that we have today. The 80s were when the government gave the corporations permission to do whatever they wanted, including not paying taxes, not following health and safety regulations, shamelessly exploiting the environment, not contributing in any way to the public good.[74]

Just as her economic object, the savings and loans crisis, was not represented eventfully, neither was her choice to write about it. Rather the fact of a *lack* of eventfulness as regards her economic object becomes part of the foil within her text even as it denies her access to a space in financial print culture to represent herself. Fittingly, there is no "scandal" per se: not within the novel's story-world, as there is in Wolfe's novel, and not external to it, as with the circulation of Ellis's text. Rather, like the archives of articles in financial print culture that I have introduced to understand the Savings and Loan crisis, *Good Faith* presents a single, detailed example of an ADC loan gone bad that we assume must be similar to those which came before and will come after. *Good Faith*, then, is generic.

Thus it is not set in New York City with its singular financial infra-structure. Rather it is set in a fictitious town, one carefully suspended between the local and the national. Joe gives expression to this com-promise as he considers: "the nationwide quality of Marcus Burns's ideas and the sheer localness of Plymouth Township" (207). The text is seldom marked with proprietary signifiers, with the odd exception of Donald Trump, while the circulation of hot money, the fact of overaccumulation, and the expansion of commodified space as place-holder for such accumulation, are each indirectly made reference to without being presumed as a causal agent for the events that unfold. Indeed, the novel remains ambivalent about whether greed or access "caused" its own particular bank failure. "We're not going after wid-ows' pensions…that's a game of the S and Ls;" utters one business partner. "It looks to me like they're going to let S and L's do pretty much anything they want," predicts Marcus (177); "The tax code is transforming before your very eyes" (109), claims the local S and L chairman. Such specific historical statements make reference to a time period of excess circulation and deregulation that the S&L crisis does not yet represent because of its defined lack of narrative struc-ture and dearth of iconic signs. Conversely, the S&L crisis may come to represent this historical moment through the success and dissemi-nation of a text such as Smiley's novel were it to be (or have been) broadly disseminated in financial print culture. That the novel did not circulate as such may suggest that financial masculinity is as much an authorial position as a discursive construction.

Good Faith is realist because of its verisimilitude to the interplay of sexual, financial, and criminological discourse structured through retrospection; the writing is similar to the writing of the S & L archive and the transaction described is almost identical. Indeed, it is capi-talist realist in that the structure of financial accumulation it describes

ultimately subsumes the novel into its own form. *Good Faith* is generic, however, because the specificity of character and setting are
missing and because the denouement is not only predictable but predicted throughout.[75] The characters' names hint at this: Felicity maintains her felicitousness, Marcus Burns ends up "burning" Joe, and so
on. Its lack of surprise is part of its pleasure, and Smiley herself seems
to enjoy the challenge of rewriting across genres: first *King Lear* in her
novel *1,000 Acres* and now, as the *Dallas Morning News* named one
report on the savings and loan crisis, "Chronology of a Bank Fraud,"
in *Good Faith*. This is the story of a confidence man who swindles
those around him and whose authorial, moral disapprobation is distributed through tropes of sexuality. Those who swindle and get
swindled are also those who have extramarital affairs. Yet the text
does have the ability to become genre delimiting because it portrays a
genre of value (ADC loan stories) that we didn't know was one until
its various texts across media were collected and compared, a process
similar to *American Psycho*'s approach to the financial autobiography.
The process of collecting and comparing is central to the logic of
genre itself, but here it takes on a heightened reflexivity as it is required to understand the very transaction around which the genre
is structured.[76]

One aspect of its generic dimension is found in the fact that *Good
Faith* offers itself as a national allegory of the S&L crisis. The novel
could easily be read from a position of national interest through the
subject of the collective "we," or the referent of the "taxpayer," who
was presumed in financial print culture—once the crisis began to
wane, that is—to have been adversely affected by S&L failures. As a
national allegory, the novel addresses collectively questions including:
"How did we let this happen?" and "How much will we have to pay?"
and "Where does our tax money go?"[77] In supposing a national collective with both a literal and figurative investment in the smooth
functioning of commercial real estate and banking, Smiley produces
a rather conventional demand: Let market transactions be fair!
Likewise, almost every page of the novel contains some flippant and
frequently humorous phrase about the nature of money, a "personal
theory of value," or a repetition of "deal" that resituates the language
of real estate and banking into the stuff of romantic comedy. The novel's humor renders its finance easily digestible and comprehensible so
that the question Is finance too abstract to represent? seems inappro-
priate to this text. Marcus Burns, for example, explains quite fluidly

why real estate development is a good business in 1982: "Here's the key. More people mean scarcer recourses, scarcer resources mean inflation, and inflation means property and interest-bearing capital have a higher value and work has a lower value. It's as simple as that" (147). It may be incorrect, but it is simple.

I locate the force of the novel's critique in the fact that it contains stock characters and predigested narratives of an event that was said to have neither and thus could not be represented. It is the presence of the tension between the generic (this is genre fiction) and the specific (it's also one of the clearest portrayals of the transaction whose repetition coalesced into the S&L crisis) that makes *Good Faith* an important text in my archive. The novel represents realistically the constitutive, discursive gaps that structure these financial transactions as well as the retrospection that reveals such a space and renders it value-producing. Then, like the genre of which it is a part, the ADC loan story, the novel disappears value as such. In its place it offers a resolution in which new constellations of heterosexual pairing and white-collar criminality are devices to conclude its narrative. *Good Faith*'s intervention is that it ultimately refuses the discourse of complexity and gives the reader, in its place, the discourse of discourses. By the novel's end, when Marcus and the money have disappeared, Joe receives this advice from a former business partner: "Don't speculate. Every motive you attribute to [Marcus], every story you make up, it compromises you. And I don't just mean legally" (411). The resolution of a bank fraud, then, is the moment one ceases to represent it.

Because we are familiar with the ADC Loan as an economic device turned narrative device, the structure of *Good Faith* will be immediately familiar, as the foregoing is here reversed: Now the ADC loan is the novel's narrative device that extends to capture and index the economic. With the death of an old town patriarch, a huge swath of land becomes available for purchase. Formerly small-time realtors take advantage of an S&L institution that is suddenly flush with money capital—"this one little S and L, they're rolling in it!"—Portsmouth Savings and Loan, to transform the land into a 400-unit, high-end subdivision, complete with a shopping center, a golf course, and a branch of said savings and loan institution (219). Money is everywhere available in the novel: for the acquisition of the land, for the development of the property, and for the construction of units. "I've never heard of a deal like that," comments Joe. To which Marcus replies that money these days has become "like cockroaches. For every dollar you see, there are a hundred more in hiding. And it's looking for a home!" (179). Marcus's explanation reveals the double nature of money's relationship to space in the text: It seeks for a place to invest in order to cease its circulation (a home), but one of the most common of those places is literally "a home," as in a residential development.

Smiley's period-specific choice of references provides an easy continuity with the archive already established in my study. "They know Donald Trump," explains one business partner about two perspective investors. Indeed, "Trumpish" somewhat anachronistically functions as an adjective in the text while Real Estate Investment Trusts—the new investment tools of real estate that Trump himself recounts being introduced and becoming highly profitable in *The Art of the Deal*— are here used as a reason investors with "too much money" might be interested in Joe and Marcus's development, Salt Key Farm. *Good Faith's* most notable interruption of my study's archive is its refusal to link its own financial masculinity with an idiom of either social or interpersonal violence. "Big money is like the army or the priesthood or the Senate. It's about being a guy among guys" (289), Marcus explains. Yet there is no aggressive tone or reference to "making a killing," to a deal as a form of "war," "conquest," "battle," or so on. There does exist masculine homoeroticism among business partners. Joe clearly says, "I was turned on by the revelation of Marcus having an affair" and his colleague notes "the bank has me by the balls." But in *Good Faith* such homoeroticism threatens no one character to the point of him needing to marshal a defense against it. It may be true, as Marcus claims to Joe, that "men are better off married" and that "you don't want to look like you're queer" since "investors don't like it" (287). But it is also true that the only two investors in the text to make a legal profit are its gay couple who, "scavenge and improve and add value…and are exotic all the same time."

The "Davids," as they are called, are a couple whose same gender, same name, and ability to negotiate multiple sites of value production simultanously hint that there may be something profitable about tautology and repetition in this text. These are different structures, but since they occupy a similar place in the novel I will cluster them together. Perhaps this tendency to value tautology will manifest as the novel's version of business journalism's tautology: "A good asset's good until it's not," at which point the asset is not worth less but rather is worthless. David John and David Pollock become known as one name in plural much as their gender is repetitive rather than different. And indeed Marcus's sister, Jane—who arrives midstory to assist with the real estate development, who has experience evaluating third-world loans, and with whom Marcus will profitably flee the scene by the story's end—herself expresses the tautological desire to have a "tangible asset on my hands" (281). Tangible already suggests "in hand," and "on my hands" clearly implies tangible. Yet it is Marcus, of course, who takes this repetition to its extreme: "There's money everywhere. Money Money Money!" (179). The stress on repetition in the presentation of moneymaking characters segues into a larger realization of how repetition and tautology unite value in ADC loan stories and in Smiley's text.

Indeed, the relationship between tautology/repetition and difference/narration organizes both the novel and the event of the savings and loan crisis on multiple levels. During the crisis, it was lack of narrativization and enforcement of tautology that created the possibility for the frauds to proceed undiscovered. Once narration was possible, those involved in the transactions and those charged with analyzing them could conclude that the money had been "lost." For *Good Faith* to locate the realization of value in characters associated with tautology/repetition might highlight this element of the transaction. Yet while genre fiction requires elements of repetition from other stories, its own narrative structure also requires emplotted change. Particularly in narrative fiction, something must happen. The tension between generic realism's steady narrative accumulation—Will the affair be revealed? Will the loan be approved? Will an impoverishing or enriching event occur to reorient the time/space of the text?—seems at odds with the text's conception of value as tautological and repetitive. The text must find a strategy to manage both, and it does so through the deployment of difference and repetition in multiple idioms in which one can only locate sites of contiguity in retrospect. But, as in the transactions themselves, in retrospect is too late and the narrator and reader are forced into the position of either white-collar criminologist or fool.

In *Good Faith*, foundational nodal points of value are omitted from the narration. At its outset, for example, the novel chooses not to represent certain elements of financial transactions and financial knowledge that will structure the text's narrative. Here Marcus explains to Joe how he made his transition from IRS agent to real estate developer. "'I went around the country, just reconnoitering. I went to LA and SF, Denver... interviewing for investment jobs but mostly listening rather than talking, and I'm telling you'—he shook his head in amazement—'Gordon and I have talked about this'" (72). The quotation ends there. "Telling me what?" might be an interlocutor's, not to mention an investor's, response. But the text is silent, and Joe accepts the lacuna in Marcus's explanation. There is no telling, only a pause and then a reference to another conversation. But there is no other conversation to which the reader herself is privy. *Good Faith's* decision to omit these processes does not, however, structure narrative tension because the novel never returns to the process itself; there are no completed transactions in this text, only transitions between idioms and discourses. This is a story of criminological retrospection that loses its own object, namely, the money. Instead, it constructs a narrative whose narrator, Joe, claims: "I didn't have the heart to follow the money, wherever it had gone" (407). In place of the money, his "heart" is reunited with its own love object, his now-single affair partner, Felicity, who, after two affairs and a divorce is still felicitous. In following the money as far as he can, the object that he is following is reconfigured. That reconfiguration both follows and critiques the "lost" money of the transactions as they appeared in financial print culture.

Joe as a first-person narrator styles his retrospection as unified but self-conscious and as carefully constructed through two sets of antimonies: legitimate and illegitimate financial transactions, and legitimate and illegitimate sexual relations. His techniques of retrospection and periodization suspend between the matrimonial and the historical so that the time of the novel's beginning, "this would be '82," is quickly and more personally periodized as a time when "my marriage was finished and [my colleague's] hadn't started" (3). Joe soon finds himself in an illegitimate sexual relationship with a married woman and (what will turn out to be) an illegitimate business relationship with Marcus Burns. A Greimasian square could easily represent the transmutation between legitimate and illegitimate financial value and between legitimate and illegitimate forms of sexuality and conjugality. Those in faithful, state-sponsored heterosexual marriages have the least access to hot money, which makes for the quickest and most profitable returns; those having heterosexual affairs can access hot money but not profit from it; those in socially condemned sexual relationships such as homosexual and (implied not actual) incestuous ones are, at the narrative's conclusion, in possession of more money than they were at its beginning.

My critical concern remains less with the legitimate or illegitimate money—after all it's still money and 1982 is not only the year of the novel's opening but also the year in which "money laundering" is first used as a legal term as a way to signify this distinction—than with the relationship between retrospection and value. In the representation of the crisis in financial print culture, retrospection became value-producing and the designation of a transaction as "fictional" was the signal point of its completion. In the novel, we are present in a fictional story world inscribed by precisely such a transaction. Joe may "look back" to complete the transaction that ruined him or he may "look back" to disavow it. Ultimately, he does both. In the previous section, I commented that we might think of the temporality produced and occupied by these transactions as existing in "white-collar criminological time." Such time is available for profit in the moment, but representable only in retrospect. In the discourse of white-collar crime, this time is produced by the ceaseless updating of financial devices and terminology, and the requirement that with every new instrument, the legal code must be written anew. In the novel, this is the time of narrative action because it is intimately connected to both Marcus's transactions and with Joe's narration.

"Looking back," Joe explains, "I would have to say that's the eighties began…when modest housing in our rust-belt state got decked out with Italian tile" (71). Joe relies on a stock characterization of "the eighties" as a moment of excess; Marcus, however, understands the decade as a moment of changing properties of money itself. "You know," Marcus explains, "you can invest in anything now. It's like everything in the world all of a sudden turned into money, and whatever it is you just pass it back and forth and it's all the same" (145). That money is a general equivalent is a long known fact of economic knowledge. In fact, what Marcus refers to is not simply money but to monetization, or the manner in which future revenue streams transform access to actually existing space.[78] Money creates the open ground for many differences to come together; monetization means that same spatial ground can become a temporal one. The real estate that Joe and Marcus work to develop unites space and time through a language of "futurity." Meanwhile, what propels the plot of the novel is that, as Joe explains, "every real estate deal includes incentives to go through with it" (121). Once a deal is set in motion, it is more difficult to disrupt than to complete. Once Marcus and Joe set their deal in motion, Joe's affair recedes and the financial deal grounds and orients the plot to its own demands.

Joe operates in retrospect; his role as a narrator demands it. Marcus, however, operates in future perfect, particularly when it comes to real estate. "Don't waste your time building future teardowns," he suggests to Joe (75). A future teardown is defined as a house not yet built that will need to be torn down. To which Joe responds, "You have previous real estate experience?" (75). "None whatsoever!" Marcus replies. When Marcus then mentions a "time-share," Joe responds, "Is that related to a teardown?" The negotiation between these two characters transpires between their tenses and allotments of time. And this future perfect of finance functions in parallel capacity as a future perfect of heterosexuality. Marcus instructs Joe that he needs to be married for other businessmen to take him seriously, but that he must be wary and conservative about his choice of a new wife. Marcus predicts that if Joe does marry his current girlfriend, "She will not turn out to be what you will have or would have wanted" (273). Marcus's knowledge exists in future-perfect form, and his claims about the fundamental newness of the present such that "the old rules don't apply anymore" rely on a suppressed but already known future.

What Marcus really has, then, is knowledge about the future itself and frequently this knowledge is revealed through references to "reading." Indeed, the text repeatedly draws a connection between reading and value. Marcus claims that "Tax returns are like reading the book of the future" (much as the reader is reading the book of the past), and he does, throughout the novel, read the tax returns of his business partners. His advice on how to file a tax return is to make it as long and convoluted as possible since the more complicated it is, the less likely that it will actually be "read" by the IRS. Of course this is also the novel's hint at dramatic irony as Joe, in fact, has read Marcus's tax returns. Indeed, Joe read them before he ever met Marcus and he was aware of their fraudulent claims. Marcus lies on tax returns and tax returns are the book of the future, thus it is rather unsurprising that Marcus turns out to be a dishonest business partner by the novel's end. The experience of their real estate business venture is, in the contemporary of the text, controlled by Marcus, and it is he who is oriented toward reading and writing: "Marcus himself was keeping the books" (145), explains Joe. But now "the books" are being renarrativized by Joe in his own novel, as the two vie for control of the story's organizing temporality. Other sites of narrative capital are denoted throughout the text in similar fashion. "There's some books I'd like to get my hands on" (110–11), Marcus fantasizes about a local S&L branch;

"if they'd just ask me, I could tell you in an hour or two what was up with the books" (304), he explains of yet another local bank. And finally, the text offers a glimpse into a future yet to come. Joe reveals that: "Marcus told me that after the billion comes in [when their deal is complete], he's going to quit business and write books" (310). The deal, however, is never completed, and the billion is never realized. Instead Marcus flees with what capital their business had and Joe writes a book, but not before explaining that certain elements of the story will never be known because "Marcus took our books with him [when he vanished]" (407).

Unsurprisingly, Marcus's own financial philosophy is readerly and future-oriented. He describes knowing before the attending physician that his wife would need a caesarian section and claims the conclusion was "as simple as reading a book" (168). He lives on "borrowed money" and does this so that he can avoid paying taxes. He explains that his is the "simplest legal way that takes no cheating and no creative bookkeeping and passes every audit." By avoiding taxes, one avoids accounting for past labors; by living on borrowed money, one is always, in some sense, living in the future. The moral question that animates *Good Faith* is: Whose future is one living in when one is living "on borrowed money?" The immediate answer within the novel's diegesis is that one is living on Portsmouth Savings and Loan's future, at the behest of its new president, the novel's minor character, Jim Crosbie. Crosbie, however, lives on T-Bill (treasury bill) futures, which are, of course, US Government debt. Crosby and his cabal of vice-presidents, not to mention those to whom he makes loans such as Marcus and Joe, are living in a collective, national future which has the structure of a Ponzi-scheme: not all who pay in can retrieve their money.

Indeed, there is so much transitioning between future and past, and so much of it indicated in terms of reading and bookkeeping that it becomes necessary to mark carefully the novel's present since that sets the condition of possibility that money can be made and that bookkeeping can be value-producing. Much as the hot money of the ADC transaction that structures the novel must find sites of lateral, directionless movement where it can metabolize time that it is not subject to and therein make money, so must the novel's narrative. The text marks that present in sexual terms, but only on the condition that the sex is outside the bounds of state control, much as hot money itself. Indeed, illicit sex is the novel's hot money. For example, during his affair with his married lover, Felicity, Joe is informed that "It's okay for us to have no future. Two people having a future is more or less a habit, when you think about it" (141). With their affair "there's no precedent" and its sexuality is possible because it is such "a pleasure to have no future" (143). The profitable and legitimate gay investors, the Davids, possess a different temporality of the present, too: "We always buy on impulse. We drive down a road or a street and we say, "Time to buy and that's the one" (53). Joe too has his moments of intense, present feeling: "Maybe because it was such an unexpected idea, inserted into my brain without any preparation on my part, it rather blossomed there for a moment. I saw myself driving around the countryside, everything paid for, in some sense everything free" (249), but for him, the actualization of those moments remains a longed-for fantasy. At one point, the text's need for a present manifests in Joe declaring that his assignment was to "keep everyone's mind off the future" (357).

While Joe alternatively anticipates his riches and struggles with the anxious worry that they may not arrive, Marcus uses his white-collar criminological present to accumulate the very objects of Joe's desire including, eventually, his former lover in addition to his money. And therein lies the narrative crux. Joe is forced to retrospect in order to locate the exact nature of Marcus's accumulation, but in the genre of the ADC loan story, it is the retrospecting itself that ultimately completes the transaction in that it consigns money to the status of being truly "lost." "No one was interested in our particular events as long as I was" (416), Joe explains, and with nothing else to do, he does what narrators always do and he tells his story. Yet Joe never divulges the longed-for content of what process Marcus meant to designate by the pause, "I'm telling you," in the line, "Gordon and I have talked about this—he shook his head—and I'm telling you. . . ." Marcus repeatedly makes reference to a new style of accumulation without explaining what constitutes it despite his circumlocution through his impressive economic vocabulary. Finally, when the explanation is due, both he and the accumulated money have vanished. Or rather, the explanation is due because he and the money have vanished.

If Joe is a white-collar criminologist narrator who has identified his suspect but is not quite sure what the suspect did, then Marcus is an extension of the descriptive imperative itself. Joe describes him obsessively, completely, and accurately but none of these local modes provide knowledge of how money was made or lost under Marcus's direction. Marcus instantiates the descriptive imperative in that he organizes the need to record and obfuscate financial transactions simultaneously. He produces enough narrative content to assure that something is described, namely a vast housing development. The model of the development that Marcus asks to be brought before the town planning commission hardly needs to be "accurate." "We should have a model [maybe] 3-D," Marcus suggests but "some sketches will do" (205). Yet this model, however rough, does manage to represent what ultimately will constitute Marcus's moneymaking operation.

The "model" presented for the development of Salt Key Farm does become moneymaking, although it does not rely on the relationship between model and effect that other characters in the novel assumed it would, that is, the selling of real estate. Marcus's model for a housing development using an ADC loan is an "engine not a camera," but for a process that no one—not the reader and not the other characters—is privy to. MacKenzie reports that economic models do not need to be identical to their objects nor do they need to be accurate in order to be repeatable and profitable. Indeed, to dismantle any one of Marcus's particular claims is to realize, as Joe does, that he's "full of shit" (178). If one claim is dismantled, another one, many other ones, are available to take its place. For example Marcus suggests that even if his predictions of population boom and inflation are inaccurate and the housing development fails, there are millions to be made in the bottling and selling of spring water on an adjacent property. That particular possibility clearly articulates Marcus's imbrication in the most basic financial form. He pays people to "gather information" and believes that "some fact might turn up" that could be transformed into something more. The reader or narrator will never be privy to what constitutes that something, but Marcus does end the novel with more money than he began it with.

Marcus's model, as well as the description of the content and affect that compose his character, have little to do with real estate. Rather Marcus operates in a world of transactions that he designates as "unreal estate." Joe finds a land deed for a farm worth some 800,000 dollars left on the office photocopier. He realizes the deed is tied to Marcus's family and is being used as collateral for the S&L loan on which their property development depends and on which both his and Marcus's name appear. When he asks Marcus about this land he first receives the answer "oh that." Pressed further, Marcus explains that "There's real estate and then there's unreal estate, as they say" (305). With no further discussion, this odd term is lodged into the text without clear designation. In fact it will become clear that what sutures together literary mode and value form as historical critique in this text is "unreal estate."

Joe does not locate what happened to the money, but he does move the ultimate discourse of how it disappeared outside the bounds of the economic. He betrays an unprofessional, perhaps even sexual, fascination with his object in order to do so. "But he was my best friend," Joe repeats. "Why did he take *my* money?" he asks of Marcus (italics in original). By not revealing this content, the novel enables a certain secret of criminality to remain consecrated. This process follows the familiar logic of amplification that structures any divide between legitimate and illegitimate, in which opposing terms function not only as mutually definitional but as continually reciprocal. Criminologist William K. Black explains the problem. "If everyone thought like white-collar criminals," which is what Black says is required to catch them, "then there would be more supervisors who could catch them." But if everyone thought like white-collar criminals there would be "more white collar criminals," too. If Joe understood what Marcus was doing or had done, he might very well do it himself. But if Joe failed to understand what Marcus was doing or had done, he would be unable to stop him, report him, or, ultimately, to represent him. In his criminological study, Black resolves this in an unsatisfactory manner: "Fortunately most people do not think like white collar criminals," he concludes.[79]

Both financial journalism and criminology provide a crucial efficacy in ending these transactions. And Joe's narrative, too, must play a role in finalizing the transactions he narrates. When Joe "looks back," his narration is a completion of the transfer of value, a way to consecrate it to Marcus with a sense of finality. Simultaneously, his narration functions as an attempt to avoid such a process by replacing what was lost with his sexual object rather than his money, as the latter is recoverable. When, journalists realized how "full of shit" S&L operators were, fraud was not forceful enough a claim. Rather they resorted to a discourse of fiction. Fraud denotes that some recognized and codified object or practice has undergone a perversion. But fiction moves beyond fraud and takes us into a different ontological space. In this archive, both novelistic and journalistic, fiction seems the ultimate site of loss, the point from which the money cannot be recovered. Of course the fact of *Good Faith*'s novel-form means that now the discourse of fiction cannot function with the same critical force that it did in journalism. Conversely, the novel will be freer to "lose" the money without sacrificing narrative coherency or obfuscating economic processes.

In place of the rhetoric of fiction, the novel turns first to the rhetoric of literary mode and then to the representation of financial print culture. Consider the larger economic processes that Joe and Marcus each organize. Joe is a "real estate" agent; Marcus trucks in "unreal estate." Joe, then, could be said to sell "realism" and Marcus to sell "unrealism." Similar to Patrick Bateman's odd discussion of the ontological status of an ad in the *New York Times* with the "real estate agent" Mrs. Wolfe in *American Psycho*, in *Good Faith* realism encounters unrealism and unrealism emerges as the more profitable organization of value. In the case of the former, I argued that *American Psycho*'s subsumption of Wolfe's text demonstrated that it was the more critical and capacious, perhaps even realistic, rendering of finance. *Good Faith*'s contest between real and unreal estate participates in a similar process. It is in unreal estate that money is to be made. Unreal estate insists that writing about, imaging, modeling, and predicting value may, at some point, become a value-producing transaction. Ironically, it is in the domain of unreal estate that *Good Faith* locates its verisimilitude and that is most accurately depicts the kind of transactions of which the savings and loan crisis was composed. To be "realistic" about this archive would be to collect, track, and manage the dissociations, disavowals, and the representations of the representations. As if to underscore the fact that the real of finance is as discursive as it is material, the novel solicits the presence of financial print culture.[80] *Good Faith* uses the representation of newsprint, here the local newspaper's account of the bankruptcy of Portsmouth Savings and Loan, to structure its conclusion and to take the reader, momentarily, outside of the narrative's central story world. The account provided by Joe leaves the immanence of his own experience and turns to the representation of the scandal in the *Portsmouth Herald*. In the novel's penultimate conclusion, Joe relates how he came to know certain details of the collapse of the S&L that had bankrolled his and Marcus's development. He simply says: "I read about it in the paper" (417).

The ultimate conclusion then follows and jettisons the economic per se. The novel evokes the kind of sentimental melodramatic turn that concluded *The Bonfire of the Vanities*. After he has accepted the loss of his money and of Marcus, Joe suddenly and unexpectedly encounters Felicity, the woman with whom he had "no future." "Oh Joey, it's you at last," she exclaims when the two greet on a ski slope. This encounter is the "last" interaction that the text considers. For the reader, of course, the encounter is neither sudden nor unexpected. When Marcus emerges with all his confidence and bluster, Felicity recedes in Joe's imagination. When Marcus disappears, she reemerges (having now slept with Marcus, no less) and transitions the force of the claim "I didn't have the heart to follow the money" from "money" to "heart." Together, they reminisce about the future they both thought Marcus Burns would deliver them. "We're all poor now. Don't you ever think about that? This is what it's like not having to pay taxes ever again," laughs Felicity (416). She is correct: To have no money is to pay no taxes. But to have illegitimate money, to have "hot money," to have money that has been lost, is to pay no taxes, too.

Conclusion

In his famous section on method from the *Grundrisse*, Marx argues that, "even the most abstract categories, despite their validity—precisely because of their abstractness—for all epochs, are nevertheless, in the specific character of this abstraction, themselves likewise a produce of historical relations."[81] Marx suggests that for abstraction to remain critical and elucidate the processes under which we live and are governed it must also be historical and contested. For Marx, capital possesses both an abstract and a concrete dimension, and labor, money, thought itself, are instantiated in both. In our moment, however, finance has become, perhaps more than any other logic, exemplary of the problem of abstraction and what happens to its critical capacity when its specific dimensions are not historicized.

In this chapter, I have tracked the particular path of a certain financial transaction to demonstrate how it eventually became too complex to explain, and I have suggested that this process is similar to the critical process of rendering finance too abstract to represent. I have also argued methodologically that particular transactions should be not simply be resituated and explained in the field of representation, but should themselves be subject to the kind of reading strategies and modes of critical analysis we usually reserve for literary texts. Such an approach was the signature method of the new historicism, and I endorse it provided one crucial caveat: namely that the transition between documents, discourses and disciplines be considered a value-producing one.

This process would then mitigate what might be termed the excess abstraction by translating financial language into one that literary scholars are more able to criticize. After all, it should be our readings that determine what precisely constitutes the transaction; the transactions themselves cannot come to us preformed. Only when we, as critics, re-present the object can we determine whether and how it can or cannot be represented. The risk is that such methodology is unwieldy and that to locate what, precisely, one is criticizing requires an amount of research that takes one far afield from the literary itself. Yet the risk of not doing so is hardly more rewarding, and it allows for the coherency and continuance of financial transactions that are anything but.

Smiley's realism in its genre-fiction variety is one aesthetic response to the problem of financial complexity as it transpired within the savings and loan crisis and consequently it is also a response *avant la lettre* to the problem of financial abstraction. And it is to *Good Faith*'s credit that it refuses such a discourse. As *Wall Street*'s genre-realism managed to critique information even as that realism collapsed into melodrama, Smiley's realism provides a similar critique of how writing about finance becomes finance. Kant said of the aesthetic that its signature pleasure was one of purposefulness without purpose. Fiction critical of transactions must do something similar and deliver the process of evaluation without the increase in value. Smiley's text demonstrates that realism can accomplish such a feat, provided that it remains firmly grounded in unreal estate.

Coda

In his 2010, postcredit-crisis documentary, *Capitalism, A Love Story*, Michael Moore converses with an unsuspecting "Ivy League–educated" derivatives trader in a park in lower Manhattan. In the wake of the 2007–8 credit crisis, derivatives had been widely profiled in the American media as causal agents in the economy's undoing. The nation's avuncular liberal billionaire, Warren Buffet, went so far as to assail these financial instruments as "weapons of mass destruction." Thus Moore's turn to them in his film is unsurprising. Moore advances the idea that derivatives exist as a singularly powerful object of contemporary capitalism and that some of their power comes from the fact that no one knows how they operate. Moore asks the derivatives trader, "What are these things?" The man stutters, looks askance, laughs, interrupts himself, and then says he cannot actually explain derivatives, even as they are the object of his training and employment. The scene is then repeated with a professor from Harvard who displays a similar inability to either represent or explain them. Like turbines from the great industrial scapes of films such as *Metropolis*, aspects of the contemporary financial economy are both the desire of and impediment to economic representation. Perhaps the lesson to be learned from the historicization of a financial form is that when a particular economic form becomes metonymic of the economy as such, it is endowed with so much representational capital that it can only be figured as excessively complex, abstract, somehow a challenge to figuration.

Political economy has periodized finance and categorized it as unique among many competing forms of value in that it has achieved contemporary dominance. Sociological works on finance present it as so many expansions of technique and instrumentality, able to be mastered, able to be executed. While both approaches have the advantage of providing a great deal of information about the structure and function of finance and financial markets, they too often displace the possibility of mediation and, particularly, of mediation through representation. Li Puma and Lee may be taken as exemplary in this regard: "There seems to be no way to characterize the real effects of speculative capital," they write in their *Derivatives and the Globalization of Risk*.[1] But this is where we must remember that finance capital is not a process without a subject, and it is in the space of representation and culture that its effects are amplified, contested, and, indeed, made efficacious. Those effects may well participate in what Alfred Sohn-Rethel has, following Marx, called the "real abstraction" of all commodity exchange, but they must be understood outside of our contemporary discourse of abstraction that, like Michael Moore's presentation of the derivative, leaves certain content and function unrepresented.

Since the time that I began the current work, this lacuna in literary and cultural critiques of finance has begun to change, and I hope this book will be received as part of a conversation that has already been initiated at conferences and in working groups. My specific contribution to critical studies of finance, as I have recently heard it called, transpires in the voluminous, bidirectional traffic between the literary and the economic. I suspect that any scholar of literature or culture would be unsurprised that the 1980s financialization of the American economy had aesthetic ramifications. What I do continue to find surprising, however, is the depth and presence of financial idioms, objects, and processes—what I have grouped under the construction "financial form"—in some of our most canonical and period-defining texts. Indeed, it is their financial form that provides them with their distinguishing claims. Of course, there is a real risk of tautology in my argument. What I have designated as now-canonical texts I have also argued became canonical in a financial period. And what I have argued constitutes a financial period, I have delimited primarily through archival work on the proliferation of such texts, which then bear the trace of their financial times as indicated by social and historical data. That tautology is one that I am unable to overcome and that is indeed endemic to the problem of periodization itself. I do hope, however, that it is also one that I have demonstrated is deeply and structurally mediated and refined in the field of representation itself.

In much current literary scholarship, finance is either postmodern, in which it destabilizes narrative; or it is narrative and therefore cannot be subsumed into postmodernism (or poststructuralism, even). What I have attempted to demonstrate in my study is that finance and its transactions contain and critique elements of both construc- tions. Finance is uniquely temporal but that hardly means that it is teleological or narrative. What it does mean is that finance necessarily navigates and reconfigures these organizations of time and, for literary scholars, what I have argued is that this understanding provides a new site for the historicization of literary mode.

That argument about the identificatory work of finance in contem- porary literary modes could be expanded and updated to encompass our own present. From Jonathan Franzen, both in his earlier incarna- tion as a metaficitonalist in *The Twenty-Seventh City*, in which the protagonist explains that "you know real estate speculation is a for- malism," to his later incarnation as a realist in *The Corrections*, in which stock price forms the nexus of the novel, one could trace the organizational work that finance accomplishes across modes.[2] Such a project could be further extended to David Foster Wallace's unfin- ished *The Pale King*, a novel set in the Internal Revenue Service amid its charts, papers, and rules, whose exacting epigraph from Frank Bidart about the relationship between financial and literary form deserves full quotation: "We fill pre-existing forms and when we fill them we change them and are changed."[3] The branded science fic- tion of William Gibson's *Pattern Recognition* and capitalist magical realism of Karen Tei Yamashita's *Tropic of Orange*, as well as the whole new compendium of works released since the onset of the Great Recession such as Paul Auster's *Sunset Park* would be likely candidates as well.[4]

An even more expansive cultural and institutional history of what I have covered here would take seriously the dictates of finance cap- ital in the publishing industry, film industry, and even in the world of academic publishing of literary and cultural criticism. In that case one might also include Jay McInerney's *Brightness Falls*, a novel in which it is book editors themselves who become involved in a finan- cially-driven corporate restructuring of their own organization. But that more expansive work would also appreciate the prescience of many of these texts, and the ability for the very transactions we now see across a deracinated global financial space to be depicted and critiqued in financial print culture. Outside of fiction, the represen- tation of financialization before financialization anticipates many of the theoretical developments that have had a rejuvenating effect on economically oriented cultural criticism, particularly those of "linguistic capital" offered by Christian Marazzi as well as theories of affective labor and its relationship to the production of value as offered by the autonomist tradition. I have tried to make this second argument more subtly, in the footnotes and introduction primarily, although it motivates my literary readings and therefore is present throughout the foregoing. I can hardly think of a more prescient take on the contradictions of our current moment than the one offered by *Forbes* in 1989: "The Way to Wealth Is Debt," the magazine declared.[5]

{ NOTES }

Introduction

1. *Good Faith*, Jane Smiley (New York: Random House, 2002), 172, 145.

2. Stephen Marglin claims that "if the recession of the 1980s imposed significant costs on the people of the United States... the results have been nothing short of disastrous in the poor countries of the Third World.... For the first time in living memory, perhaps for the first time since the era of the *conquistadores*, net capital flows from the First to the Third World [were] negative: they [were]·aiding us!" Stephen A. Marglin and Juliet B. Schor, *The Golden Age of Capitalism: Reinterpreting the Postwar Experience* (New York: Oxford University Press, 1992), 35–6.

3. See Calavita, Kitty, Henry N. Pontell, and Robert Tillman. *Big Money Crime* (Berkeley: University of California Press, 1999), 12.

4. My definition of finance will necessarily evolve throughout this project. For two very basic definitions to support this claim, however, see Greta R. Krippner, "The Financialization of the American Economy," *Socio-Economic Review* 3, no. 2 (May 1, 2005): 173–208, doi:10.1093/SER/mwi00. Krippner claims that "finance refers to demarcations of manifest, structured time and that its operations refer to activities relating to the provision (or transfer) of liquid capital in expectation of future interest, dividends, or capital gains." See also the work Robert Guttman, who claims that the temporal possibilities of financial practices are used to bridge "the real temporal disjuncture between intention, production and consumption" and make the credit-based "time aspect crucial to economic activity." Robert Guttman, *How Credit Money Shapes the Economy* (Armonk, NY: M.E. Sharpe Press, 1994), 12.

5. There are many sources that relate the effects of overaccumulation. Ernest Mandel, for example, claims that: Whatever tendencies of capitalism the significant economic changes in the 1970s demonstrated, that the postwar "international credit expansion based on the use of the paper dollar as a world currency could collapse like a house of cards," was surely one of them. Ernest Mandel, *Late Capitalism* (New York: Verso, 1975), 464; see also Krippner, op.cit. Arrighi's chapter 3 is particularly important for its argument about the transition from overaccumulation to financialization, a term I will specify and refine throughout. Since the publication of Arrighi's book in 1994, the most consistent articulation of the relationship between overaccumulation and financialization has come from *The Monthly Review* crowd, particularly Robert W. McChesney and John Bellamy Foster. See their "The Endless Crisis" in *The Monthly Review* 64, no.1 (May 2012): 1–29. For an argument against financialization as a result of overaccumulation, see Andrew Kliman, *The Failure of Capitalist Production: Underlying Causes of the Great Recession* (London: Pluto Press, 2011).

6. *New York Times*, October 5, 2009, "Study Says Reporting on Economy Was Narrow."

7. These terms are now being used in conferences and working groups, primarily. Financialization is an economic order. This book is about financialization, but here, in the introduction, I need to situate financialization in a larger, political, historical context that many

critics refer to as neoliberalism. I like Michael Hardt's definition of neoliberalism as one in which the market controls the state; classical liberalism reverses the roles. Hardt, Michael. "Militant Life." *New Left Review* 64, July-August 2010. See also, Leo Panitch and Martijn Konigns "Myths of Neoliberal Deregulation" *New Left Review* 57 (May-June 2009): 67–83, for a definition that rejects the commonly held view that neoliberalism is an effect of deregulation. In the broader field of representation, for the cultural logics of neoliberalism see, for example, *Everybody's Family Romance: Reading Incest in Neoliberal America* by Gillian Harkins (Minneapolis: Minnesota University Press, 2009).

8. This definition should be seen to complement Randy Martin's idea of financialization as "integrating markets that [were] separate" and "asking people to accept risk into their homes," in R. Martin, *The Financialization of Everyday Life* (Philadelphia: Temple University Press, 2002), 12.

9. The logic derived from such representation has been made possible through events such as transformation of the daily movement of the Dow Jones Industrial Average from an indexical measure of thirty companies into an almost hegemonic economic heuristic that daily "speaks" for "the market" on a variety of topics; as well as the imbrication of a whole new population in financial operations through the development of the 401k retirement account. For a wonderful history of the financialization of pensions and retirement accounts, see Robin Blackburn, *Banking On Death* (New York: Verso, 2003).

10. For example, the liberal economist Dean Baker has argued that the daily representations of the stock market, the seeming hegemonic pleasure at its upward movement, are indications of nondesirable social situations such as the privatization of social services. For the argument as it applies to social security, see http://deanbaker.net/books/social-security-the-phony-crisis.htm; the whole website is of interest.

11. Fredric Jameson, *The Cultural Turn: Selected Writings on the Postmodern, 1983–1998* (New York: Verso, 1998), 149.

12. The quotation is from William Greider, *Secrets of the Temple: How the Federal Reserve Runs the Country* (New York: Simon & Schuster, 1989), 88. See also David Harvey's *The New Imperialism* (New York: Oxford University Press, 2003) for the Volcker Shock in tandem with other major demarcations of a neoliberal era.

13. "The Financialization of the American Economy," Greta R. Krippner, *Socio-Economic Review* 3, no. 2 (May 2005): 173–208 and 174. This article has been subsequently turned into the book, *Capitalizing on Crisis: The Political Origins of the Rise of Finance* (Cambridge, MA: Harvard University Press, 2012).

14. For a wonderful history of corporate takeovers of media companies and their effect on film production throughout the decade see, Stephen Prince, *A New Pot of Gold: Hollywood Under the Electronic Rainbow, 1980–1989* (Berkeley: University of California Press, 2002). For Boesky in particular, see http://www.nytimes.com/1989/06/15/business/mulheren-indicted-on-42-counts.html?pagewanted=all&src=pm (accessed September 3, 2012).

15. See *The Diners' Club Magazine*, published from 1962 to 1965, which, at its peak, had a circulation in excess of three million. It has not been archived well, but selected issues are available at the New York Public Library.

16. See Jack Banks, *Monopoly Television* (Boulder, CO: Westview Press, 1996) for a history; see also E. Anne Kaplan, *Rocking Around the Clock* (New York: Routledge, 1987) for early cultural critiques of MTV. American Express copartnered with Time in this venture.

17. For an in-depth consideration of postmodern narrative form and its relationship to temporality, see Ursula K. Heise, *Chronoschisms: Time, Narrative, and Postmodernism*

(Cambridge: Cambridge University Press, 1997). See also Teresa Heffernan, *Post-Apocalyptic Culture* (Toronto: University of Toronto Press, 2008).

18. Jameson's already-cited argument that "finance capital underpins and sustains post-modernity as such," has motivated me to think through the relationship between the two on a more discrete level.

19. Ian Baucom suggests something similar. See Ian Baucom, *Specters of the Atlantic: Finance Capital, Slavery, and the Philosophy of History* (Durham, NC: Duke University Press, 2005). Mary Poovey's recent work could also be read in support of this claim. See Mary Poovey, *Genres of the Credit Economy: Mediating Value in Eighteenth- and Nineteenth-century Britain* (Chicago: University of Chicago Press, 2008).

20. Mark McGurl, *The Program Era: Postwar Fiction and the Rise of Creative Writing* (Cambridge, MA: Harvard University Press, 2009).

21. See Matthew J. Packer, "'At the Dead Center of Things' in Don DeLillo's *White Noise*: Mimesis, Violence, and Religious Awe," in *Modern Fiction Studies* 51 no. 3 (Fall 2005): 648–666, 1n.

22. Tom Wolfe, "Stalking the Billion Footed Beast" in *Harper's Magazine,* November 1989, 56.

23. Amy Kaplan, *The Social Construction of American Realism* (Chicago: University of Chicago Press, 1988), 8. Kaplan claimed that "successive generations of literary critics have asserted that realism fails in it claims to represent society" at the same time she sought a new purchase on what it is that realism could accomplish.

24. *The Wall Street Journal*, B1, May 6, 1982. For a wonderful history of the relationship between the rise of the service economy in the United States in the latter part of the twentieth century and corresponding transformations in masculinity see Bethany Moreton's *To Serve God and Wal-Mart* (Cambridge, MA: Harvard University Press, 2011), 102–112.

25. My use of the term is quite independent of Mark Fisher's work so I use it with a bit of hesitation. Yet it does seem like the necessary term for what I am attempting to delimit: the moment when realism succumbs to the processes it aims to record, a quite postmodern logic. Yet these texts insist they are realist. See my coauthored introduction to collection of essays, *Reading Capitalist Realism*, with Alison Shonkwiler (Iowa City: University of Iowa Press, 2014).

26. See Doug Henwood's text for a wonderful glossary of such terms, here Special Investment Vehicle and Leveraged Buyout Offer; *Wall Street: How It Works and for Whom* (London: Verso, 1997).

27. See Peter Knight, "Cultures of the Market" (paper presentation, University of Manchester, September 10, 2010).

28. That the discursive complication of finance transpired during its "democratization," as more and more people were encouraged to engage in day trading, brokering, etc., is a historical irony that should be attended to. I do not pursue it here but do so in "The Rules of Abstraction: Methods and Discourses of Finance," in "Fictions of Finance," ed. Aaron Carico and Dara Orenstein, *Radical History Review* 2014, no. 118 (special issue, Winter 2014): 93–112.

29. For the classic account of print culture, what he calls "print capitalism," see Benedict Richard O'Gorman Anderson, *Imagined Communities: Reflections on the Origin and Spread of Nationalism* (London: Verso, 2006). While it may seem odd to not include Anderson's argument about nationalism here, the nation form is not necessary to the argument I make. My use of Anderson may seem anachronistic as well, yet to me his text is prescient to a description of value seen later with Jonathan Beller's "attention theory of value," which also

makes recourse to Anderson's claim. See Jonathan Beller, *The Cinematic Mode of Production* (Dartmouth, NH: New England Publishers, 2006).

30. *New York Times,* October 13, 1987.

31. See Michael M. Thomas's review essay in the *New York Times*, "Tough Times for the Fi-Fi Novel." New York, N.Y.: Oct 20, 1985. A.1; Thomas Novel Entwines Oil, Arabs, Stock Market.

32. *Barron's*, July 27, 1991, 10.

33. Jonathan Culler offers an interesting critique of Anderson's use of the novel form per se in his "Anderson and the Novel," *diacritics* 29 no. 4 (1999): 20–39. The whole issue is of interest.

34. Erika Beckman has recently attempted to locate precisely this kind of profitable but nonrepresentational economic space in her discussion of the relationship between South American literature and the Deepwater Horizon oil explosion in the Gulf of Mexico. Ericka Beckman, "An Oil Well Named Macondo: Latin American Literature in the Time of Global Capital," *PMLA* 127, no. 1 (January 2012): 145–151, doi:10.1632/pmla.2012.127.1.145.

35. See Dan Schiller *Digital Capitalism* (Cambridge, MA: MIT Press, 2000) for a wonderful history of this infrastructure, as well as Philip Mirowski for the specific relationship between finance and the rise and institutionalization of computers in *Machine Dreams*: *Economics Becomes a Cyborg Science* (Cambridge: Cambridge University Press, 2001).

36. Thanks to Lara Cohen for reminding me of Gitelman's argument in *Always Already New* (Cambridge, MA: MIT Press, 2006).

37. Now these companies, for example Dow Jones—which continues to publish *The Wall Street Journal*—are more often multimedia conglomerates and certainly the materiality of their newspapers is less important than it once was. Dow Jones is owned by Rupert Murdoch's News Corporation.

38. As Laura Kipness has commented: "Scandal is the realm of proto-knowledge about the social totality." Laura Kipness, "Adultery," *Critical Inquiry* 24, no. 2, Intimacy (Winter 1998): 289–327, 316.

39. Edward LiPuma and Benjamin Lee, *Derivatives and the Globalization of Risk* (Durham, NC: Duke University Press, 2004), 3.

40. Jameson, *The Cultural Turn*, 144. Richard Godden has mounted a similar critique against Jameson, and he too turns to the work of LiPuma and Lee as well as Moishe Postone. I am largely in agreement with his critique of Jameson, but I use different sources to accomplish it and do not place the importance on metaphor that Godden does. See R. Godden, "Labor, Language, and Finance Capital," *PMLA* 126, no. 2 (2011): 412–21.

41. The kind of abstraction that Moishe Postone, for example, has so carefully delimited in *Time, Labor, Social Domination*. Both Postone's and my versions of abstraction are quite different from Mary Poovey's conception of abstraction, "to generalize in order to construct a formal model" of which she provides one example of in her claim: "Substituting writing objects... constitutes a prime example of the *abstraction* to which all credit systems theoretically aspire and that... derivatives [take] to the logical extreme" (Poovey, *Genres of the Credit Economy*, 98, 51). Perhaps the most intuitive account of abstraction is to be found in William Cronon's *Nature's Metropolis* (New York: W. W. Norton, 2002), 132, in which units of grain become units of capital, deracinated and free-floating from their earthly referent.

42. As, for example, Alfred Sohn-Rethel and Alberto Toscano have sought to do in exfoliating Marx's concept of "real abstraction." See Alfred Sohn-Rethel, *Intellectual and Manual*

Labour: a Critique of Epistemology (Atlantic Highlands, NJ: Humanities Press, 1983); Alberto Toscano, "The Open Secret of Real Abstraction," *Rethinking Marxism* 20, no. 2 (2008): 273–87, doi:10.1080/08935690801917304. Conversely, Karen Ho questions whether finance is abstract at all in her *Liquidated: An Ethnography of Wall Street* (Durham, NC: Duke University Press, 2009), especially the introduction. See also my "The Rules of Abstraction: Methods and Discourses of Finance."

43. Anne McClintock, *Imperial Leather: Race, Gender, and Sexuality in the Colonial Contest* (New York: Routledge, 1995); Kristin Ross, *Fast Cars, Clean Bodies: Decolonization and the Reordering of French Culture* (Cambridge, MA: MIT Press, 1996).

44. There are many genealogies of this tension available. I nonetheless rehearse it here, as I see cultural studies and new historicism as more antagonistic than some Marxist critics, such as Jameson or Žižek, do. Whereas new historicism focused on exchange between similar systems, cultural studies more often turned to ideas of "consumption" and "consumption studies." For new historicism, see Catherine Gallagher and Stephen Greenblatt, *Practicing New Historicism* (Chicago: University of Chicago Press, 2001). For consumption specifically see, Rachel Bowlby, *Just Looking: Consumer Culture in Dreiser, Gissing, and Zola* (New York: Methuen, 1985). See also, *Consumption and the World of Goods,* John Brewer and Roy Porter, eds. (London: Routledge, 1993). Also prominent here are the cultural historians Richard Fox and Jackson Lears; see their *The Culture of Consumption* (New York: Pantheon, 1983). For a more contemporary read that attempts to bridge this gap in a rather different fashion, see Kevin Floyd's recent work, *The Reification of Desire: Toward a Queer Marxism* (Minneapolis: University of Minnesota Press, 2009).

45. For an exploration that routes the question of production through "real" and less real, linguistic, economies, see Joshua Clover, "Value Theory Crisis" *PMLA* 127, no. 1 (January 2012): 107–14. In a much broader scope, production had been a site of possibility for economically oriented criticism at least since Georg Lukács; other early avatars include A.A. Zhdanov and Georgi Plekhanov in the Soviet Marxist tradition. The Frankfurt School would follow in the productivist tradition through their adoption of Lukács's commodity form but with the added addition of Freudianism. For a good summary of the history itself, see Terry Eagleton's *Marxism and Literary Criticism* (Berkeley: University of California Press, 1976). For an entirely different approach, see Pierre Macherey, *A Theory of Literary Production* (London: Routledge, 1978), 75–83.

46. Jean Baudrillard, *The Mirror of Production* (St. Louis: Telos Press Publishing, 1975), 129.

47. Jacques Derrida, *Given Time*, op. cit., 129.

48. Laclau and Mouffe thus cite Althusserianism and its theorization of relative autonomy as the height of Marxist absurdity. Ernesto Laclau and Chantal Mouffe, *Hegemony and Socialist Strategy* (London: Verso, 1985), viii; E.P. Thompon, a noted anti-Althusserian, makes a similar claim in his *The Poverty of Theory* (New York: Monthly Review Press, 1980). In retrospect, one could also read Althusserianism as the most successful attempt to combine a proto post-structural analysis with a Marxist framework. Indeed, newer combinations of poststructuralism and Marxism have relied on Althusser. See, for example, Roderick A. Ferguson, *Aberrations in Black: Toward a Queer of Color Critique* (Minneapolis: University of Minnesota Press, 2004).

49. Chris Nealon has a wonderful rejoinder to this in his *The Matter of Capital*: "as though it were the critic who tried to name the totalizing work of capital, rather than capital,

who was failing to do justice to particulars, or to aesthetic experience." Christopher Shaun Nealon, *The Matter of Capital: Poetry and Crisis in the American Century* (Cambridge, MA: Harvard University Press, 2011), 10.

50. *The Order of Things*, 263.

51. Douglas Kellner, ed., *Jameson Postmodernism Critique* (Washington, DC: Maisonneuve, 1989), 59. The interview is from 1986.

52. In order to theorize finance, which he only hints at in his "Postmodernism" essay, Jameson will have to wait for Giovanni Arrighi's 1994 *The Long Twentieth Century* and, retrospectively, David Harvey's 1982 *The Limits to Capital*.

53. See Michael Tratner's "Derrida's Debt to Milton Friedman" for a fascinating, homologous approach to monetarism and deconstruction (*New Literary History* 34, no. 4, Multicultural Essays [Autumn 2003]): 791–806.

54. Marc Shell, *Money, Language, and Thought: Literary and Philosophic Economies from the Medieval to the Modern Era* (Baltimore: Johns Hopkins University Press, 1993); Walter Benn Michaels, *The Gold Standard and the Logic of Naturalism: American Literature at the Turn of the Century* (Berkeley: University of California Press, 1987); Jean Joseph Goux, *Symbolic Economies* (Ithaca, NY: Cornell University Press, 1991).

55. The quote is from Osteen and Woodmansee, and they, too, cite the 1980s as a key moment in their reasons for the advent of a new economic criticism: "The political economy of the 1980s thrust economics and its discussions of interest rates, stock market speculation, takeovers, leveraged buyouts, and so on, into the public attention as never before"; however this orientation never raises to the level of formal critique. Martha Woodmansee and Mark Osteen, *The New Economic Criticism: Studies at the Intersection of Literature and Economics* (New York: Routledge, 1999), 12 and 2, respectively.

56. See Brian Rotman, *Signifying Nothing, The Semiotics of Zero* (New York: St. Martin's Press, 1987). This does not mean that money has no value, but rather it has gone through a process of deixis, or loss of index, to become what he calls "xenomoney." Rotman's work is interesting and certainly on the poststructuralist side of the divide, but more grounded in economic history than the other work cited here. He too relies on the metaphor of scandal: "Xenomoney, by making no promise to deliver anything, avoids such double dealing. Its scandal, if such exists, is the fact that it is a sign which creates itself out of the future" (91).

57. The quotation is not given a precise author nor dated in R. T. Naylor's 1987 *Hot Money and the Politics of Debt* (New York: Simon and Schuster, 1987), 72.

58. See his *Carbon Democracy* (London: Verso, 2012), especially chap. 5.

59. Marx himself still provides the best historical definition of political economy available: "Let me point out once and for all that by classical political economy I mean all the economists who, since the time of W. Petty, have investigated the real internal framework of bourgeois relations of production, as opposed to the vulgar economists who only flounder around within the apparent framework of those relations…for the domestic purposes of the bourgeoisie" (*Capital*, v. I [New York: Penguin, 1971], 174, 34n). In terms of contemporary political economy, I use it to refer to those theorists who self-define as political economists, from Giovanni Arrighi to R. T. Naylor to those who publish in the *International Journal of Political Economy* and the *Review of Radical Political Economics*.

60. Marx, *Capital* v. I, 283.

61. Obviously, the most common form of such analysis is through the lens of the commodity form and its binary relationship between forms of value and forms of appearance.

"Any analysis of capital necessarily includes the obstacles to that analysis. "Marx structures his investigation of money as a dialectical unfolding in the course of which he logically derives both the social form of money, leading to his analysis of capital, as well as the forms of appearance that veil that social form" (Moishe Postone, *Time, Labor, and Social Domination* [Cambridge: Cambridge University Press, 1993], 264).

62. Kliman, *The Failure of Capitalist Production.*

63. *Late Capitalism*, 191.

64. Ernest Mandel defines the organic composition of capital as "the technical or physical relationship between the mass of machinery, raw materials and labour necessary to produce commodities at a given level of productivity, and the *value* relationship between constant and variable capital determined by these physical proportions" (ibid., 595).

65. David Harvey, *The Limits to Capital*, 281.

66. The whole archive of the *Monthly Review* in the 1980s is of great interest, particularly the later part of the decade as the S&L scandals and the 1987 Dow Jones crash began to reveal obvious instability.

67. Arrighi, *The Long Twentieth Century*, 1.

68. Ibid., 299.

69. Ibid., 180.

70. *The Arcades Project* is, of course, the example par excellence of this approach.

71. Arrighi does make one little-cited aesthetic argument. He hints that it was the financial expansion of the fifteenth century that made possible the Italian Renaissance. "The expansion of trade had been an intellectual stimulus; but when the point comes that it no longer absorbs the same energy, art can be pursued for art's sake, and learning for the sake of learning," Arrighi, *The Long Twentieth Century*, 95.

72. See Jameson, "Culture and Finance Capital."

73. Alex Preda, *Framing Finance: The Boundaries of Markets and Modern Capitalism* (Chicago: University of Chicago Press, 2009).

74. See Donald MacKenzie, *An Engine Not a Camera* (Cambridge, MA: MIT Press, 2006).

75. Gayatri Chakravorty Spivak, *In Other Worlds: Essays in Cultural Politics* (New York: Routledge, 2006).

76. The question of whether value is one of many discursive techniques or whether it is a unique substance is central to this debate and cannot, of course, be resolved. Rather I am interested in the sinews of the arguments that allow for the claims on either side of the question. For one particularly trenchant collection on the question of historicist methodology, see *The Limits of Literary Historicism,* ed. Allen Dunn and Thomas Haddox (Knoxville: University of Tennessee Press, 2012).

77. This new field includes the work of Michel Callon, Donald MacKenzie, and Alex Preda. Its organizing rubric is one of "performativity." Appropriately, Judith Butler herself has joined this conversation and engaged this notion of economic performativity. See Judith Butler, "Performative Agency," *The Journal of Cultural Economy* 3 no. 2 (2010): 147–61.

78. Michael Tratner, *Deficits and Desires: Economics and Sexuality in Twentieth-Century Literature* (Stanford: Stanford University Press, 2001), 1.

79. James Chandler, *England in 1819: The Politics of Literary Culture and the Case of Romantic Historicism* (Chicago: University of Chicago Press, 1999).

80. Richard Godden, *William Faulkner: An Economy of Complex Words* (Princeton, NJ: Princeton University Press, 2012), 1. His forthcoming *Fictions of Finance Capital* will treat

some of the texts I do here, including *American Psycho*. Godden, "Labor, Language, and Finance Capital," *PMLA* 126, no. 2 (March 2011): 412–21.

81. Michael W. Clune, *American Literature and the Free Market, 1945–2000* (Cambridge: Cambridge University Press, 2010), 2 and 22.

82. Nealon, op. cit. Joshua Clover, "Autumn of the System: Poetry and Financial Capital," *Journal of Narrative Theory* 41, no. 1 (2011): 34–52, doi:10.1353/jnt.2011.0090. Both Nealon and Clover attempt to expand these theoretical interventions in *PMLA* 127, no. 1 (January 2012): 101–06 and 107–15, respectively, and, importantly, both Clover and Nealon criticize poetry not narrative.

83. See McGurl, op. cit. and Andrew Hoberek, *The Twilight of the Middle Class: Post–World War II American Fiction and White-Collar Work* (Princeton, NJ: Princeton University Press, 2005).

84. Stephen, *Fantasies of the New Class: Ideologies of Professionalism in Post–World War II American Fiction*, (New York: Columbia University Press, 2011).

85. Anna Kornbluh, *Realizing Capital* (New York: Fordham University Press, 2014).

86. To do so, Beller relies on an archive that I largely avoid, that of affective labor and immaterial labor as developed in the Italian tradition, particularly through the work of Antonio Negri (and sometimes Michael Hardt) as well as through the early French post-structuralist work of Jean Baudrillard and Guy Debord.

87. David Graeber, *Debt: The First 5,000 Years* (Brooklyn: Melville House, 2011), 391.

88. Guttman, *How Credit-Money Shapes the Economy: The United States in a Global System* (New York: M.E. Sharpe, 1994).

89. Graeber, *Debt*.

90. Narrative is probably one of the most difficult terms in literary studies to define. I think this attempt, from Barthes via Hayden White, does a good job of delimiting a process I rely on and showing as well how I diverge: "Arising, as Barthes says, between our experience of the world and our efforts to describe that experience in language, narrative 'ceaselessly substitutes meaning for the straightforward copy of the events recounted.' And it would follow, on this view, that the absence of narrative capacity or a refusal of narrative indicates an absence or refusal of meaning itself." While I agree with the first part of the claim, about the recounting of meaning, I do not subscribe to the claim that a refusal of narrative is a refusal of meaning. See "The Value of Narrativity in the Representation of Reality," Hayden White, *Critical Inquiry* 7, no. 1, On Narrative (Autumn, 1980): 5–27, 8.

91. I have used many sources to delimit this claim and many of these sources offer similar claims. Mine is different, however, in its focus on narrative. See Marx himself, of course, *Capital* v. I and III; David Harvey, *The Limits to Capital* (London: Verso, 2006); Robert Guttmann, *How Credit-Money Shapes the Economy: The United States in a Global System* (New York: M.E. Sharpe, 1994); in literature see Clover "Autumn of the System: Poetry and Financial Capital," and Godden, *William Faulkner, An Economy of Complex Words*; see my "Reading Finance Capital" for a longer reading of the Arrighi, Harvey, and Guttman texts in Robert J. Balfour, *Culture, Capital and Representation* (London: Palgrave Macmillan, 2010), 116–32.

92. For a contemporary understanding of this problem at a social level, see Richard Dienst's *The Bonds of Debt* (London: Verso, 2011).

93. This perspicacious quote is from *Capital* v. I but is not cited in Paul Baran and Paul Sweezy's *Monopoly Capital* (New York: Monthly Review Press, 1966), 43.

94. For a classic Marxist conception of value with some amount of variation, see Diane Elson (ed.) *Value: The Representation of Labor in Capitalism* (London: CSE Books, 1979). For a classic poststructuralist account, see Jacques Derrida, *Specters of Marx: The State of the Debt, The Work of Mourning & the New International* (New York, Routledge, 2006). A text like Michael Hardt and Antonio Negri's *Empire* or their more recent work on affective labor does seem to me to be a genuine mediation between these two traditions and I attempt to contribute to that kind of project, only I proceed at the level of the text.

95. Marx does not use the term finance. Sometimes he describes interest-bearing capital; other times he describes fictitious capital.

96. Marx, *Capital* v. III (New York: Penguin, 1981).

97. As Max Haiven explains in his own attempt to define finance: "Dubious investments through a sublimely complex process…[lose] almost any reference to original, real-world commodity referents." But that caveat, "almost any reference," is important because some reference always remains. Max Haiven, "Finance as Capital's Imagination? Reimagining Value and Culture in an Age of Fictitious Capital and Crisis," *Social Text* 29, no. 3 108 (2011): 93–124, doi:10.1215/01642472-1299983.

98. Marx, *Capital* v. III (New York: Penguin, 1981), 515–6, emphasis in original.

99. *The Limits to Capital*, 396–7.

100. Robert Meister, lecture at NYU, April, 17 2012, cited with permission. See also his "Debt and Taxes: Can the Financial Industry Save Public Universities?" Bob Meister *Representations* 116, no. 1, The Humanities and the Crisis of The Public University (Fall 2011): 128–55.

101. Schiller, *How to Think about Information*, 8.

102. Dick Bryan, Randy Martin, and Mike Rafferty, "Financialization and Marx: Giving Labor and Capital a Financial Makeover," *Review of Radical Political Economics* 41, no. 4 (December 1, 2009): 458–72, doi:10.1177/0486613409341368.

103. *Capital* v. I, 92.

104. Marx's example is from the sale of state debt is longer and more elaborate account of the production of a national future through the deployment of financial mechanisms, here the alienation of state debt (*Capital* v. I, 921.)

105. Fredric Jameson has returned to this theme of temporality again and with more specificity than ever in his *Representing Value: A Reading of Volume I* (New York: Verso, 2011).

106. The best explication of the relationship between biopower and commodification is to be found in Silvia Federici's *Caliban and the Witch* (Brooklyn: Autonomedia, 2004).

107. Michel Foucault, *The Order of Things: An Archaeology of the Human Sciences* (New York: Routledge, 2002), 190.

108. The most famous example of this logic is found in Foucault's critique of psychoanalysis in *The History of Sexuality, Vol. I: An Introduction*, trans. Robert Hurley (New York: Vintage, 1990). Correspondingly, it actually seems more germane to me than Foucault's own engagements with neoliberalism in his lectures and his suggestion that a market economy has the properties of a Kantian regulative idea: structuring and orienting but unable to be experienced or witnessed directly.

109. For the classic work on index, icon, and symbol, see Charles Sanders Peirce. For index and the relationship between literature and capital, see Richard Godden, *William Faulkner, An Economy of Complex Words*, 1–8.

110. James C. Scott, *Seeing Like a State: How Certain Schemes to Improve the Human Condition Have Failed* (New Haven, CT: Yale University Press, 1998), 91.

111. Graeber, *Debt*. He, indeed, cites Marc Shell on the link between language and money.

112. Christian Marazzi, *Capital and Language: From the New Economy to the War Economy* (Cambridge, MA: Semiotext(e), 2008), 77.

113. Joshua Clover, "Autumn of the System," 231. Clover is additionally interesting in this conversation for his argument that narrative is an overvalued site of financial representation.

Chapter 1

1. I'll use the term consumer society in this chapter to be faithful to the literature and to distinguish "information society" from *information*, which is one of the key theoretical terms of this chapter.

2. Dana Phillips, "Don DeLillo's Postmodern Pastoral," in *Reading the Earth: New Directions in the Study of Literature and Environment*, edited by Michael P. Branch, Rochelle Johnson, Daniel Patterson, and Scott Slovic (Boise: University of Idaho Press, 1998), 235–46.

3. Frank Lentricchia, *New Essays on White Noise* (Cambridge: Cambridge University Press, 1991).

4. See Jennifer Szalai, "After the Fall: Don DeLillo without His Towers," *Harper's* (July, 2007), 91–96 (94).

5. The quote is from DeLillo in Lentricchia but is uncited, p. 7.

6. Lauren Berlant, *The Female Complaint: The Unfinished Business of Sentimentality in American Culture* (Durham, NC: Duke University Press, 2008).

7. I refer to what Bethany Moreton in her excellent book on the history of Wal-Mart has called "the threat of the service economy to masculinity itself." Bethany Moreton, *To Serve God and Wal-Mart: The Making of Christian Free Enterprise* (Cambridge, MA: Harvard University Press, 2010), 51.

8. Randy Martin, *The Financialization of Everyday Life* (Philadelphia, PA: Temple University Press, 2002).

9. For a good definition of depersonalization see Jean Laplanche and Jean-Bertrand Pontalis, *The Language of Psycho-Analysis* (New York: W. W. Norton & Company, 1974).

10. Andrew Hoberek, "Introduction: After Postmodernism," *Twentieth Century Literature* 53, no. 3 (October 1, 2007): 233–47. See also, Rachel Adams, "The Ends of America, the Ends of Postmodernism," *Twentieth Century Literature* 53, no. 3 (October 1, 2007): 248–72.

11. See my introduction, where I covered this in depth. See also Fredric Jameson, *The Cultural Turn: Selected Writings on the Postmodern, 1983–1998* (New York: Verso, 1998).

12. Abstract, etymologically, signifies a process of "drawing away from," according to the *Oxford English Dictionary*. In this chapter, I have a particular concern with the idea of abstraction as a denominator of either an aesthetic style in which it indicates nonfigurative media or as a conceptual heuristic that indicates something not fully realizable by a particular. These two orientations share a particular direction, to be sure; but they are marked by a divergence of aims, too, which makes the use of abstraction as an axis of translation problematic. In aesthetics, the abstract highlights a perception; a certain immediate figuration is lost so that other properties of the medium may be brought into relief. In history, abstraction indicates a metonymic reach: the incomplete representation stands in for something larger that cannot be represented.

13. By proliferation of theories of the postmodern in the mid 1980s, I refer to Fredric Jameson's essay 1984 "Postmodernism, or, The Cultural Logic of Late Capitalism," reprinted in the book of the same name (Durham, NC: Duke University Press, 1991) and the subsequent discourse on Jameson, for example the special issue of *Diacritics* (1986) devoted to Jameson's essay. See also *Jameson Postmodernism Critique*, Douglas Kellner, ed. (Washington, DC: Maisonneuve, 1989). For more general themes see Hal Foster, ed., *The Anti-Aesthetic* (New York: New Press, 1987) and J.F. Lyotard, *The Postmodern Condition* (Minneapolis: University of Minnesota Press, 1984); for a more retrospective look, see Andrew Ross, ed., *Universal Abandon? The Politics of Postmodernism* (Minneapolis: University of Minnesota Press, 1989), especially pp. 1–27.

14. Bryan Burrough and John Helyar, *Barbarians at the Gate: The Fall of RJR Nabisco* (New York: Harper Paperbacks, 2003).

15. In personal conversation with the author at the New School lecture entitled "Digging in the Shadows of Master Categories." March 21, 2007, New York City.

16. Saskia Sassen, *Globalization and Its Discontents: Essays on the New Mobility of People and Money* (New York: The New Press, 1999).

17. For the changes in personal banking and credit see Robert D. Manning, *Credit Card Nation: The Consequences of America's Addiction to Credit.* (New York: Basic Books, 2000). See also Joseph Nocera, *A Piece of the Action: How the Middle Class Joined the Moneyed Class* (New York: Simon and Schuster, 1994).

18. It is first recorded in *American Banker* in 1982; the much older term, personal finance, has been in circulation since at least the 1920s.

19. See Nocera, *A Piece of the Action,* 143. Nocera now writes a personal finance column for the *New York Times,* exactly the type of column that was so helpful in propagating and popularizing the automated teller.

20. *The Wall Street Journal,* May 6, 1982, B1.

21. See Foster and Magdoff for an instructive genealogy of the terms financialization, globalization, and neoliberalism. John Bellamy Foster and Fred Magdoff, *The Great Financial Crisis: Causes and Consequences* (New York: Monthly Review Press, 2009) p. 77.

22. See Thomas Peyser, "Globalization in America: The Case of Don DeLillo's' White Noise," for a reading of DeLillo's novel in relationship to early discourses of globalization.

23. See Teresa A. Sullivan, Elizabeth Warren, Jay Westbrook, *The Fragile Middle Class: Americans in Debt* (New Haven, CT: Yale University Press, 2000), 17.

24. Concerns addressed included the cultural status of the automated teller machine: Was it a form of progress and convenience, or was it the end of the banking services that some customers had come to expect? Was it for personal banking only, or should it be used for noncommercial monetary distribution, like disbursements of welfare payments, as the state of Michigan suggested? What or who, precisely, was the customer, or welfare recipient, interacting with when she was doing her own banking?

25. *Boston Globe,* June 29, 1981, A1.

26. See, for example, a host of personal financial advice columns and business trend reports I cite herein. But with those newfound freedoms came risks. Newspapers also frequently reported on personal crimes committed at, or in the vicinity of, the automated teller.

27. See Nocera, *A Piece of the Action: How the Middle Class Joined the Moneyed Class* (New York: Simon and Schuster, 1994).

28. Paolo Savoia makes a very clear distinction between these two categories and I have found his work useful to think through these categories. "There are two meanings of the word' 'subject': subject to someone else by control and dependence, and tied to his own identity by a conscience or self-knowledge» («Il y a deux sens au mot "sujet": sujet soumis à l'autre par le contrôle et la dépendance, et sujet attaché à sa propre identité par laconscience ou la connaissance de soi»: Foucault 2001, 1046)." The first explanation constitutes subjection, the second subjectivation. "Subjection and Subjectivation. Foucault on the Making and Remaking of the Self." Unpublished paper, cited with permission.

29. *Boston Globe*, June 29, 1981, A1.

30. Ivan Kreilkamp, "A Voice Without a Body: The Phonographic Logic of 'Heart of Darkness,'" *Victorian Studies* 40, no. 2 (January 1, 1997): 211–44.

31. Of course the phonograph could be configured through its global political economy, but Kreilkamp does not explore this dimension.

32. All references to *White Noise* are to the 1985 Penguin Edition.

33. See Manning, *Credit Card Nation*.

34. The equivalent to ATM brands would be the system of networks that connect ATMs such as PLUS or NYCE. But they do not function as branded as such—rather they follow the brands of the banks themselves.

35. See Edward Bellamy, *Looking Backward* (Mineola, NY: Dover Publications, 1996), as well as Frank Tashlin's film, *The Man from the Diners' Club*.

36. All etymology is from the *Oxford English Dictionary*.

37. Andrew Hoberek, *The Twilight of the Middle Class: Post–World War II American Fiction and White-Collar Work* (Princeton, NJ: Princeton University Press, 2005), 116.

38. Dan Schiller, *How to Think About Information* (Champaign: University of Illinois Press, 2006), 8.

39. Wallace's footnotes are of a different sort, for example, than T.S. Eliot's in *The Waste Land*—which do seem to me part of the poem. Compare to *Infinite Jest* in which one must read the notes to comprehend the plot.

40. Dorrit Cohn, *The Distinction of Fiction* (Baltimore, MD: The Johns Hopkins University Press, 2000).

41. The anxious memory of being incorporated with Janet Savory is also in contrast to Jack's shooting of Mink toward the novel's end. Jack shoots the man only to decide to rescue him and take him to a hospital. After the shooting, Jack decides, "I felt I did honor to both of us, to all of us, by merging our fortunes…." (*WN*, 314–15).

42. *The Wall Street Journal*, 1979, A13, April 12, 1984.

43. Robin Blackburn, "Finance and the Fourth Dimension," *New Left Review*, May/June 2006, accessed online March, 2007.

44. On the gendering of production and consumption in relation to the postmodern leveling of high and mass cultures, see Andreas Huyssen, "Mapping the Postmodern," in *After the Great Divide: Modernism, Mass Culture, Postmodernism* (Bloomington: Indiana University Press, 1986), 178–221. On the feminization of service, see Moreton's claim that "During the 1970s and 1980s the eclipse of production by the service economy heightened Christian fears that the wellsprings of American virility were drying up" (*To Serve God and Wal-Mart*), 102.

45. See N. Katherine Hayles, "Postmodern Parataxis: Embodied Texts, Weightless Information," *American Literary History*, vol. 2, no. 3. (Autumn, 1990): 394–421, 398.

46. Georg Lukacs, *Writer and Critic, and Other Essays* (London: Merlin Press, 2006).

47. Richardson explains adopts the term from David Hayman and then modifies it to consider denarration, when the text undermines itself. Brian Richardson, *Unnatural Voices: Extreme Narration in Modern and Contempory Literature* (Columbus: Ohio State University Press, 2006), 82.

48. See Lentricchia, 105.

49. Ibid., 102.

50. A term of 1970s sociology, "information society" migrated into literary studies in the 1980s and may be understood to mark early designations of postindustrialism and be seen as prefiguration of "knowledge economy." The term seems to be little in use as of this writing.

51. See Rodrigo Alves Teixeira and Tomas Nielsen Rotta "Valueless Knowledge-Commodities and Financialization: Productive and Financial Dimensions of Capital Autonomization," *Review of Radical Political Economics* 44, no. 4 (February 3, 2012): 448–67.

52. For an interesting article on the limitations of representation such a state of affairs produces, see Martha Buskirk, "Commodification as Censor: Copyrights and Fair Use," *October* 60 (April 1, 1992): 83–109.

53. From the *Oxford English Dictionary*: brand, *v.trans. Marketing.* To apply a trade mark or brand to (a product); to promote (a product or service) on the basis of a brand name or design. *v.* 2. 1909 *Times* 2 Oct. 16/6 The Government had introduced the "Rune" brand for Swedish butter…Only the really best butter would be branded. 1912 *Q. Jrnl. Econ.* 26 715 The textile manufacturers who are beginning to brand their goods seek to increase their sales by building up a demand for their product as against the product of other manufacturers. 1994 *Independent on Sunday* 20 Nov. (Rev. section) 32/3 Most BBC "junctions" (telly-speak for breaks) show trailers bookended by the "1," "2," wobbly jellies and hatching eggs that brand the channels. 1985 *Chicago Tribune* (Nexis) 3 Jan. 9B, "The chicken industry has been successful with branding their products."

54. Naomi Klein, *No Logo: No Space, No Choice, No Jobs* (New York: Picador, 2002), p.80.

55. Lentricchia, p. 103.

56. *The Wall Street Journal*, A1, Dec 13, 1984.

57. Trish Hall, "Brand-Name Produce Hits Stores—But Will It Really Taste Better?," *The Wall Street Journal* 65, September 23, 1985, 1.

58. Jonathan Beller, *The Cinematic Mode of Production: Attention Economy and the Society of the Spectacle* (Dartmouth, NH: Dartmouth College Press, 2006). Beller's term is most appropriate, as all attention does become a site of value-production.

59. See Anne McClintock, *Imperial Leather* (New York: Routledge, 1995), chap. 5, "Soft Soaping Empire."

60. Berlant, *The Female Complaint*, particularly the introduction.

61. Lee Konstantinou, "The Brand as Cognitive Map in William Gibson's *Pattern Recognition*," *Boundary 2* 36, no. 2 (June 20, 2009): 67–97, 87.

62. David Foster Wallace attempted to reproduce a branded logic in *Infinite Jest* by transforming the chapter/temporal structural of the novel into branded time periods, for example, *Year of the Depend Adult Undergarment* or *Year of the Whopper*, etc. Later in the novel we learn that corporations have acquired branding rights to time.

63. Haruki Murakami, *Sputnik Sweetheart: A Novel*, trans. Philip Gabriel (Vintage, 2002). The difference between *White Noise*'s representation of brands and *Sputnik Sweetheart*'s might be categorized as the difference between criticism, in the former, and product placement

in the later. Morgan Spurlock's *The Greatest Movie Ever Sold* (2011) does execute a critical representation of brands.

64. The gun is a Zumwalt, but this is not a recognizable brand to either Jack or the reader and it has no narrative function within the text.

65. See Tim Engles for a good reading of Mink as "the other" to Jack's sense of white self.

66. George Lipsitz, *Possessive Investment in Whiteness* (Philadelphia: Temple University Press, 1998).

67. Tim. Engles, "'Who Are You, Literally?': Fantasies of the White Self in White Noise," *MFS Modern Fiction Studies* 45, no. 3 (1999): 755–787.

Chapter 2

1. For a good history of the Volcker shock as an orienting event of neoliberalism see the introduction to David Harvey, *The New Imperialism* (New York: Oxford University Press, 2005).

2. A more economic definition of financialization can be found in the wonderful article by Bryan, et al. They define it as simply: "The increasing role of financial motives, financial markets, financial actors and financial institutions" in a given, economic present. See Dick Bryan, Randy Martin and Mike Rafferty, "Financialization and Marx: Giving Labor and Capital a Financial Makeover," *Review of Radical Political Economics* 41 (September 30, 2009): 458.

3. The New York Stock Exchange conducts a census of stock ownership and has been doing so since 1983. See http://www.investopedia.com/articles/stocks/09/stocks-1950s-1970s. asp#axzz263u4kZeN (accessed September, 2012).

4. Two columns are of interest here. Anwar A. Shaikh, "The Crisis Underneath," *New York Times* (Late Edition [East Coast]), Nov. 1, 1987, A.15; see also Harry Magdoff, "A Free-Market Failure," *New York Times* (Late Edition [East Coast]), Nov. 1, 1987, A.12.

5. I am using class here in its familiar sense to describe an institutional, economic power bloc within the United States and those who have access to it.

6. See Leigh Claire La Berge, "Capitalist Realism and Serial Form: The Fifth Season of *The Wire*" in "The Wire," *Criticism* 52 nos. 3–4 (Special issue, Summer/Fall 2010): 547–67. When capitalist realism succeeds, as it did in *The Wire*, it is critical. When it fails, by contrast, it lacks self-consciousness of its own ambition and it presents rather a kind of commodified realism without understanding, or theorizing, its own commodification.

7. Mark Fisher, *Capitalist Realism: Is There No Alternative?* (London: Zero Books, 2009), 4.

8. Real subsumption is differentiated from formal subsumption, in which there are still spaces "outside" of capital logic. Both Steven Shaviro and Hardt and Negri provide helpful explanations of the dichotomy between the two. See Steven Shaviro, *Post Cinematic Affect* (London: Zero Books, 2010), 48 and 163.

9. Unlike Marx's dire predicament in which real subsumption is symptomatic of a total capital logic, I favor Hardt and Negri's theorization of it in which periods of real and formal subsumption alternate and metabolize each other.

10. Mine then is a more expansive and perhaps even metaphorical use of paratext than we classically understand. For the received articulation, see Gérard Genette and Marie Maclean, "Introduction to the Paratext," *New Literary History* 22, no. 2 (April 1, 1991): 261–72. doi:10.2307/469037.

11. "Let's be realistic" probably more often means "Let us accept the limits of this situation" (limits meaning hard facts, often of power or money in their existing and established forms) than "Let us look at the whole truth of this situation (which can allow that an existing reality is changeable or is changing)." Raymond Williams, *Keywords* (London: Oxford University Press, 1985), 259.

12. See Linda Williams "Melodrama Revisited" in Nick Brown, ed., *Reconfiguring American Film Genres* (Berkeley: University of California Press, 1998), 42–88.

13. This is precisely the critique of capitalist realism offered by *American Psycho*, which I explore in the next chapter.

14. From Claude Levi-Strauss via Fredric Jameson.

15. See Wolfe's interview with the *New York Times* Oct 13, 1987, C13, where he explains his decision to change his protagonist from a writer (as he was in *Rolling Stone*'s serialized version) to a bond trader. On the serial nature of Wolfe's text see, Michael Lund, "The Nineteenth-Century Periodical Novel Continued," in *American Periodicals: A Journal of History Criticism and Bibliography* 3 (1993): 51–61.

16. *New York Times,* Oct. 22 1987, B1.

17. Joanne Lipman, *Wall Street Journal* (Eastern Edition), Oct 28, 1987, 1.

18. Interview with Stone on the DVD of *Wall Street*, released 2000, MGM Pictures.

19. On the fundamental tautology of using certain concepts to define a period and on then arguing a period is that which is noted for its particular concepts see James Chandler, *England in 1819* (Chicago: University of Chicago Press, 1998), especially chaps. 1 and 2. I deal with this problem in my introduction.

20. *The Wall Street Journal*, October 29, 1987, A30.

21. Wolfe, November 1989, 56.

22. *New York Times*, October 13, 1987, C13, emphasis in original.

23. See http://forums.criterionforum.org/forum/viewtopic.php?f=7&t=11663.

24. For a reading of the text's racial logic outside of the specifically financial concerns that I present here, see James Kyung-Jin Lee, *Urban Triage: Race And The Fictions Of Multiculturalism* (Minneapolis: University Of Minnesota Press, 2004). Additionally, Wolfe's depiction of race has led Liam Kennedy to call *Bonfire* an "imperialistic and voyeuristic text." See Liam Kennedy, " 'It's the Third World Down There!': Urban Decline and (Post) National Mythologies in *Bonfire of the Vanities*," *MFS Modern Fiction Studies* 43, no. 1 (1997): 93–111.

25. All citations are to the 1987 Farrar, Straus and Giroux edition.

26. *New York Times*, October 13, 1987, C13.

27. Hoberek makes a similar point in Andrew Hoberek, "Introduction: After Postmodernism," *Twentieth Century Literature* 53, no. 3 (October 1, 2007): 233–47.

28. *Rolling Stone*, table of contents, May 18, 1984.

29. For a reading of Dreiser in the pit, see Wayne Westbrook *Wall Street and the American Novel* (New York: NYU Press, 1980), 111–14.

30. Michael Lewis *Liar's Poker* (New York: Penguin, 1989), 69–75.

31. It is notable, then, that Baucom is not concerned with the fact that what makes slaves' bodies bearers of value is, in the first instance, that they will be brought to work. This must be one reason for his attraction to Arrighi, who provides a Marxist narrative without the central protagonist, the labor commodity itself. Essentially, Baucom claims that slaves' bodies underwent something like a process of securitization.

32. Ian Baucom, *Specters of the Atlantic: Finance Capital, Slavery, and the Philosophy of History* (Durham, NC: Duke University Press, 2005), 17.

33. The best take on risk as a financial mode is to be found in Randy Martin's work. See Randy Martin, *An Empire of Indifference: American War and the Financial Logic of Risk Management,* annotated ed. (Durham, NC: Duke University Press, 2007).

34. This claim also, then, challenges Fredric Jameson's contention that finance dwells beyond the scope of narrative and is fundamentally an abstract form. See his "Culture and Finance Capital," in *The Cultural Turn* (London: Verso, 1998).

35. For Marx, these are forms of interest bearing capital, not "finance" per se, but I believe the translation is justified by what falls under the rubric of each.

36. From the *Oxford English Dictionary*, 1615 *Body of Man* 84, "Able to distinguish between natural and fictitious precious Stones."

37. *Radical History Review*, for example, published the recent special issue *The Fictions of Finance* (*Radical History Review* 2014, no. 118, [Winter 2014]).

38. We need a Michel Aglietta-derived, finance-specific regulation theory of literature where buyer and seller are arranged and calibrated so as to manage risk. I do not provide that here but I do hint at it. Some other scholars have tried as well. See, for example, Richard Ohmann, "The Shaping of a Canon: U.S. Fiction, 1960–1975," *Critical Inquiry* 10, no. 1 (September 1, 1983): 199–223.

39. See *Capital* v. III, 513.

40. Michael Hudson, *Critique*, 4.

41. David Graeber, *Debt: The First 5,000 Years* (Brooklyn: Melville House, 2011), 381.

42. The International Monetary Fund insists that "Overall, there has been a transfer of financial risk over a number of years, away from the banking sector to nonbanking sectors.... This dispersion of risk has made the financial system more resilient, not the least because the household sector is acting more as a "shock absorber of last resort." IMF working paper: http://www.un.org/en/development/desa/policy/wess/wess_bg_papers/bp_wess2007_jdarista.pdf.

43. Richard Godden's recent conception of finance as somehow not part of a "real" economy unlike productive activities is an example of one such critical trend. See R. Godden, "Labor, Language, and Finance Capital," *PMLA* 126, no. 2 (2011): 412–21.

44. John Bellamy Foster and Fred Magdoff, *The Great Financial Crisis: Causes and Consequences* (New York: Monthly Review Press, 2009).

45. Although that event has now been renarrated in economic discourses to revolve around a technical "glitch," in other words, as unable to represent a structural tendency or concern. Federal Reserve Working Paper, http://www.federalreserve.gov/pubs/feds/2013/201348/201348pap.pdf.

46. Actually, Farrar, Straus and Giroux was, at the time of *Bonfire*'s publication, one of the least corporate of publishers. That changed in 1994 when it was sold to a European media conglomerate. Wolfe left them in the mid-2000s. For details of the publishing industry in 1980s, see Albert N. Greco, *The Book Publishing Industry, Second Edition* (Mahwah, NJ: LEA, 2009). See also Albert Greco, Clara Rodriguez, and Robert Wharton, *The Culture and Commerce of Publishing in the 21st Century* (Stanford: Stanford Business Books, 2006). The story is an unsurprising one as it is a cultural logic familiar from the worlds of sports, academia, film, etc., namely the decision to elevate a few to the status of "star"—or "bestseller" in this case.

47. For the relationship between realism and typicality, I refer to Lukacs's "Art and Objective Truth" essay in *Writer and Critic, and Other Essays* (London: Merlin Press, 2006).

48. I attend to the satirical aspects of *Bonfire* in the next chapter.

49. *National Review*, June 24, 1991.

50. Tom Wolfe, "Stalking the Billion Footed Beast," 51.

51. Ibid., 52.

52. *New York Times*, December 21, 1990, http://www.nytimes.com/movie/review?res=9 C0CE7D8153FF932A15751C1A966958260, accessed June 20, 2006.

53. See my "Reading Finance Capital: The Case of Theodore Dreiser" in *Culture, Capital and Representation*.

54. Norris, *The Pit*, 1958, 237.

55. A fact well documented by Liam Kennedy in "It's the Third World Down There!"

56. Many of the most interesting studies of the representation of finance underplay time as finance's most important narrative structure. See for example: Mary Poovey, "Writing About Finance in Victorian England" in *Victorian Studies* 45.1 (2002) 17–41; Walter Benn Michaels "The Man of Business as the Man of Letters" in *The Gold Standard and the Logic of American Naturalism* (Berkeley: University of California Press, 1986); Renata R. Mautner Wasserman, "Financial Fictions: Émile Zola's *L'argent,* Frank Norris' *The Pit,* and Alfredo de Taunay's *O encilhamento*" in *Comparative Literature Studies* 38 no. 3 (2001): 193–214.

57. In a most basic sense, as Rudolf Hilferding colloquially explained a century ago in his *Finance Capital*, in a financial transaction, "everyone can't bet on the same horse." The Hilferding quote is found in Georg Lukács, *History and Class Consciousness* (Cambridge, MA: MIT Press, 1973), 103.

58. See *Charles Baudelaire, A Lyric Poet in an Era of High Capitalism* (London: Verso, 1982).

59. In an article on Asian immigration and anti-Asian racism and American Naturalism, Collen Lye suggests that "trust fighting" and "coolie fighting" can become sympathetic pursuits within this mode. In Wolfe's text, the problem is rather reversed: Through being exiled from the analogous world of "trusts," that of finance, Sherman can now return to a place of more whiteness and more masculinity. See Colleen Lye, "American Naturalism and Asiatic Racial Form: Frank Norris's The Octopus and Moran of the 'Lady Letty,'" *Representations* 84, no. 1 (November 1, 2003): 73–99.

60. The film was released in 2010.

61. Interview with Oliver Stone, DVD release.

62. Gilles Deleuze, *Cinema 2: The Time Image* (Minneapolis: University of Minnesota Press, 1977), 77.

63. And this is more than a Deleuzian problem. It was A.P. Giannini, founder and president of the Bank of America and the first financier to promote the credit card *en masse*, who understood that the nascent film industry presented an opportunity for financial operations. In the 1920s, Giannini was more concerned with the turnover time of fixed capital than with any formal or ideological affinities between film and finance. He realized that as the filmmaking process became more technically advanced, as the cost of film production rose, film studios would invariably need quick access to capital. While other financial institutions thought the financing of film too risky, Giannini simply kept the negatives of the film in his bank's vault until the debts could be repaid. The more money studios had access to, the longer and more

complicated their films could be. Gianinni, the man who would introduce such world-changing financial devices as Visa and branch banking to the world, also financed Charlie Chaplin's first feature length film (*The Kid*). See David Putnam, *Money and Movies*, 92–96.

64. See Julie Salamon, *The Devil's Candy* (Boston: Houghton Mifflin, 1992), 296–98. The idea is that with less opportunity for employment in finance itself, financiers took to other industries. Their interests were not aesthetic; rather "they were only interested in the deal," Salamon says. The "deal" is essentially buying and selling media companies—in other words, mergers and acquisitions.

65. For a history of contemporary media consolidation see Ben. H. Bagdikian's *The Media Monopoly* (Boston: Beacon Press, 2000).

66. Indeed, in *Working Girl*, an independent radio network is acquired by a conglomerate just as Twentieth-Century Fox, the production company, in fact, had purchased a small network of Television stations two years before the film's release. For an expansion and methodology on corporate restructuring and corporate plots in film, see Jerome Christensen, *America's Corporate Art: The Studio Authorship of Hollywood Motion Pictures* (Stanford: Stanford University Press, 2012).

67. See notes 7 and 8.

68. For a good psychoanalytic rendering of goodness=me, badness=not me and how this forms a broader ethical axis, see Fredric Jameson, "Imaginary and Symbolic in Lacan," in *The Ideologies of Theory*, (Minneapolis: University of Minnesota Press, 1988), 87. Jameson provides a wonderful summary and analysis of this structure but his analysis does not address value forms. Why is production good and finance bad? Production is associated with the Keynesian order of high wages for skilled workers in developed countries. However the temptation to see this state of affairs as the result a certain economic organization and not an organization of value and labor should be rejected. Neither finance or production is good or bad, of course; both can be organized and reorganized to benefit different factions of society.

69. As Marieke De Goede explains in an article on Daniel Defoe's satirical personification, Lady Credit, "Lady Credit embodies all the irrational, inconstant and effeminate aspects that had to be purged from financial discourse before it was able to gain respectability as a rational, disinterested and scientific sphere of action. Lady Credit is not unlike [the] ancient goddess, Fortuna, who ruled capriciously over the affairs of men." See Marieke De Goede, "Mastering 'Lady Credit,'" *International Feminist Journal of Politics* 2, no. 1 (2000): 58–81. For a broader history of the appearance of Lady Credit, see J.G.A. Pocock, *Virtue, Commerce, and History: Essays on Political Thought and History, Chiefly in the Eighteenth Century* (Cambridge: Cambridge University Press, 1985), 103–25.

70. For an interesting history of debt as a moral problem in American history, see Bruce Mann, *Republic of Debtors* (Cambridge, MA: Harvard University Press, 2009).

71. The film was novelized by Ken Lipper, who was, some years later, indicted. Kenneth Lipper, *Wall Street* (New York: Berkley, 1987).

72. Alison Leigh Cowan, "Making Wall Street Look Like Wall Street": *New York Times* (Late Edition [East Coast]). Dec. 30, 1987, C16.

73. "People on Wall Street have been hit dramatically in their own pocketbooks," said Gary L. Wilson, the chief financial officer of Walt Disney Co. See Steve Swartz and Bryan Burrough: *Wall Street Journal* (Eastern edition), Dec. 29, 1987.

74. See *The Wall Street Journal*, "What now?"

75. "Ken Lipper's fall epitomizes a tumultuous chapter on Wall Street. He was a creature of the times—at home in the 'greed is good' precincts of Wall Street and comfortable running with a fast Hollywood and Manhattan crowd." Here was a man who "flitted, almost *Zelig*-like, through the worlds of investment banking, politics, money management, movie production, philanthropy, and book publishing. In the mid-'80s, he was Edward I. Koch's deputy mayor. In 1999, he even won an Academy Award..." Marcia Vickers, "The Fallen Financier," *Business Week*, 9 Dec 2002.

76. See Vincent Canby's review of Stone's film in the *New York Times* (December 11, 1987) for specific information about the relationship between Stone's film and the contemporary art scene as well as for information on Boesky.

77. Both "Narrate and Describe" and "The Storyteller" resonate more closely with the kind of representational theory of finance that I am attempting to develop than, for example, does Rudolf Hilferding's 1912 book, *Finance Capital*. Lukacs, op cit.; Walter Benjamin, *Illuminations* (London: Pimlico, 1999).

78. "The Storyteller," 89.

79. Geoffrey Nunberg, "Farewell to the Information Age," in *The Future of the Book*, ed. Geoffrey Nunberg (Berkeley: University of California Press, 1997), 103–38.

80. Of course Lukacs did not see that, but Foucault, in *The Order of Things*, did. Capital always requires more taxonomy.

81. Joseph Nocera, *A Piece of the Action: How the Middle Class Joined the Money Class* (New York: Touchstone), 1995.

82. Imagine an interlocutor's response: when you argue, "Look, here's the structure," they return "no, it's only an individual instance"; when you argue, "the problem is this individual," they return "but an individual is only an effect of the structure." The inability of the individual and structural to appear as one underscores the strength of Althusser's Lacan-influenced critique of ideology in which individual and structural become mediated by a third term, namely ideology itself which is defined as "an imaginary representation of the real conditions of existence." See Louis Althusser, *Lenin and Philosophy and Other Essays* (New York: Monthly Review Press, 2000), 124.

Chapter 3

1. Although as result of the 2007–8 credit crisis, more scholars are now discovering *American Psycho*. See Leigh Claire La Berge, "The Men Who Make the Killings: American Psycho, Financial Masculinity, and 1980s Financial Print Culture," *Studies in American Fiction* 37, no. 2 (2010): 273–96. See also R. Godden, "Labor, Language, and Finance Capital," *PMLA* 126, no. 2 (2011): 412–21. Walter Benn Michaels claims Ellis's is one of the few texts able to grasp our contemporary, capitalistic world. See his "Going Boom," *Bookforum.com*, n.d., http://www.bookforum.com/inprint/015_05/3274.

2. John Pizer, "History, Genre and "Ursprung" in Benjamin's Early Aesthetics." The German Quarterly Vol. 60, No. 1 (Winter, 1987), pp. 68–87.

3. The "brat-pack" was first labeled as such in a May 12, 1987 *Village Voice* article (accessed online June 20, 2006) and quickly became a kind of marketing device more than a literary term. Yet. see also the recent MLA Panel "Whatever Happened to Brat-Pack Fiction?" at the Modern Language Association meeting, Chicago, Dec. 28, 2007, for a reconsideration of this group as generic rather than consumer based.

4. See James Annesley, *Blank Fictions* (London: St. Martin's, 1998) for a review of 1980s' fiction, including *American Psycho*, and its link to consumerism.

5. Bret Easton Ellis, *American Psycho* (New York: Vintage, 1991), hereafter cited parenthetically as *AP*.

6. The novel was marketed as the text that would end the 1980s, however after its first publisher dropped the book only weeks before its scheduled release, its publication was delayed by several months.

7. Tom Wolfe, *The Bonfire of the Vanities* (New York: Farrar, Strauss and Giroux, 1987), hereafter cited parenthetically as *BV*; T. Boone Pickens, *Boone* (New York: Houghton Mifflin, 1987); Ivan Boesky, *Merger Mania* (New York: Holt, Rinehardt, and Winston 1985); Donald Trump, *The Art of the Deal* (New York: Ballantine Books, 1987).

8. From Time.com, accessed July 12, 2006.

9. The two novels been compared, but not in a systematic fashion. See, for example, Jules Murphet, *Bret Easton Ellis's American Psycho* (London: Continuum, 2003), 65–75.

10. In *The New York Review of Books*, May 12, 1988, accessed online June 17, 2006.

11. In Galbraith, 1.

12. Joseph Nocera's column now runs in the *New York Times*. His columns have been concerned with promoting a variety of financial devices and worldviews, from the automated teller machine to a vision of "shareholder democracy." In *The Wall Street Journal*, December 17, 1987, 28.

13. The difficulty of assessing precisely where the value of these text is located is similar to an observation by Marx. As he writes in one of his rare descriptions of capitalists and not capital: "The actual capital that someone possesses, or is taken to possess by public opinion, now becomes simply the basis for a superstructure of credit," *Capital* v. III, 570.

14. See "Metro Matters" column, *New York Times,* Oct. 22 1987, B1, and see chap. 2 in this volume ("Capitalist Realism").

15. In 1987, the Supreme Court ruled that a former *Wall Street Journal* reporter, R. Foster Winans, and two associates were guilty of mail and wire fraud for trading on names mentioned in upcoming editions of the newspaper's "Heard on the Street" columns.

16. Marx, *Capital* v. III (New York: Penguin, 1981), 515.

17. David Harvey, *The Limits to Capital* (Verso, 2006).

18. This is quite different from the type of financial anxiety that, for example, J.G.A. Pocock describes in the context of eighteenth-century British economic history. See J.G.A. Pocock, V*irtue, Commerce, and History: Essays on Political Thought and History, Chiefly in the Eighteenth Century* (Cambridge: Cambridge University Press, 1985), 103–25.

19. Louis Althusser and Étienne Balibar, *Reading Capital*, trans. Ben Brewster (London: Verso, 2009), especially chap. 9. See also Donald A. MacKenzie, *An Engine, Not a Camera: How Financial Models Shape Markets* (Cambridge, MA: MIT Press, 2006).

20. *New York Times Book Review*, p.1, May 12 1987.

21. Milken published a book on cruciferous cooking after his battle with prostate cancer, a disease that also shortened the prison sentence he received for his insider trading conviction after Boesky turned states' evidence against him. See Michael Milken, *The Taste for Living Cookbook: Michael Milken's Favorite Recipes for Fighting Cancer* (New York: Cap Cure, 1998).

22. See Michael Lewis, *Liar's Poker* (New York: Penguin, 1989), 69–75. See also Nancy Goldstone, *Trading Up* (New York: Dell, 1989).

23. When women enter the financial world, as in the case of the 1988 Mike Nichols' film, *Working Girl*, they too hew closely to the patterns of financial masculinity. Indeed, following Judith Halberstam, we might say that financial masculinity is available to women, see *Female Masculinity* (Durham, NC: Duke University Press, 1998).

24. "Sex, Power, Failure: Patterns Emerge" by Daniel Goldman in the *New York Times*, May 19, 1987, C1.

25. Connie Bruck, *The Predators' Ball: The Inside Story of Drexel Burnham and the Rise of the JunkBond Raiders* (New York: Penguin Books, 1989).

26. Christopher Lehmann-Haupt, "Books of The Times; Conquering the Financial World With Junk Bonds." *New York Times,* June 16, 1988, C6.

27. For an interesting take on the debacle, see "Historical Violence, Censorship and the Serial Killer: The Case of *American Psycho*," by Carla Freccero, *Diacritics* 27, no. 2 (1997): 44–58.

28. Ellis's text does contain some rather gruesome passages but, as Linda Williams has noted, the same year Simon and Schuster decided not to publish Ellis's novel they did publish the nonfiction *Women Who Love Men Who Kill*—a study of women's attraction to serial killers—a title which attracted no protest. See also Roger Rosenblatt's "Will Bret Easton Ellis Get Away With Murder?" in Dec. 16, 1990 the *New York Times*, accessed online June 12, 2006.

29. For a history of this Vintage Contemporaries and changes in the American publishing market see Stephanie Girard, "'Standing at the Corner of Walk and Don't Walk': Vintage Contemporaries, *Bright Lights, Big City*, and the Problems of Betweenness," *American Literature* 68, no. 1 (March 1, 1996): 161–185.

30. Leslie Wayne, "The Corporate Raiders." *New York Times* (Late Edition [East Coast]), July 18, 1982. p. A.18.

31. Photographic insert, not paginated, in *The Art of the Deal.*

32. See the Oxford English Dictionary. I have modified the spelling here. It was originally, "dethe is my fynance."

33. On the trope of the serial in *American Psycho* see "Serial Murder, Serial Consumption: Bret Easton Ellis's *American Psycho*" by Sonia Baelo Allue in *Miscelánea* 26 (2002): 71–90.

34. These are, then, two very different constructions of satire. Steven Weisenburger has argued that satire in the twentieth century takes a "degenerative" turn, one that he uses to trace the emergence of postmodern fiction. Weisenburger's distinction between generative satire and degenerative satire is helpful in understanding these two texts' relationship to each other and to their respective literary modes of realism and postmodernism. Generative satire in its nineteenth-century form, precisely what Wolfe's novel attempts to reproduce, is "corrective" and "normative"; it momentarily relaxes boundaries and conventions with an eye toward their ultimate recodification and regeneration. Degenerative satire "functions to subvert hierarchies of value and to reflect suspiciously on all ways of making meaning, including its own." See Steven Weisenburger, *Fables of Subversion: Satire and the American Novel: 1930–1980* (Athens: The University of Georgia Press, 1995), 12–19.

35. This comes from James B. Stewart, *Den of Thieves* (New York: Pocket Books, 1993). We are perhaps not far enough away from our own capitalist realist moment to have searchable databases for the images found in print-based advertisements. I have seen repeated references to these images, but have not been able to locate them myself.

36. David Graeber, "Manners, Deference, and Private Property in Early Modern Europe," *Comparative Studies in Society and History* 39, no. 04 (1997): 694–728.

37. Paul Ricoeur, "The Metaphorical Process as Cognition, Imagination, and Feeling," *Critical Inquiry* 5, no. 1 (October 1, 1978): 143–59.

38. Salamon, *The Devil's Candy*.

39. June 24, 1991, *National Review*, accessed online June 24, 2006, http://www.unz.org/Pub/NationalRev-1991jun24-00045.

40. Murphet, *Bret Easton Ellis's American Psycho*, 53–4.

41. This then is a quite different approach to the text than some of the most recent and trenchant ones, including that of Richard Godden. See Godden, "Labor, Language, and Finance Capital."

42. As presented at "Cultures of the Market," The University of Manchester, September 10, 2010.

43. Mark Seltzer, *Serial Killers: Death and Life in America's Wound Culture* (New York: Routledge, 1998).

44. Whether in Marx's work or within the larger political economic tradition, sociological work on finance, anthropological work on finance, or even in the pages of *The Wall Street Journal*, finance is defined through its relationship to time. Finance is dependent upon demarcations of manifest, structured time; its operations "refer to activities relating to the provision (or transfer) of liquid capital in expectation of future interest, dividends, or capital gains" (Greta Krippner, "The Financialization of the American Economy," *Socio-Economic Review* 3 no. 2 (2005): 173–208, 174). In a different register, Robert Guttman describes how financial practices are used to bridge "the real temporal disjuncture between intention, production and consumption" and make the credit-based "time aspect crucial to economic activity." Robert Guttman, *How Credit Money Shapes the Economy* (Armonk, NY: M.E. Sharpe Press, 1994), 12.

45. Frances Ferguson has offered her own reading of *American Psycho's* use of branded language and its necessary tautology and un-substitutability in her *Pornography, The Theory* (Chicago, 2004), 146–153. Whereas Ferguson presents the brand as homologous to the immediacy and lack of metaphoricity of pornography itself, my reading of the brand focuses on its instantation of narrative movement.

46. The inside information trader's sanction safeguards against the circulation of inside information.

47. I took this example from Levine's autobiography, but Boesky would no doubt dispute it.

48. On the lack of reporting on all white-collar crime, particularly its distinguishing feature of being hard to detect, see Kitty Calavita, Henry N. Pontell, and Robert H. Tillman, *Big Money Crime: Fraud and Politics in the Savings and Loan Crisis* (Berkeley: University of California Press, 1996), especially chaps. 1 and 2. For popular criticism, *Newsweek*, for example, claims: "Wall Street financial crime often went unpunished because it was so complicated—and in some cases so routine" (May 21, 1990, 32).

49. See Rachel Lowry, *Brands* (London: Routledge, 2004), 15.

50. For a critique of consumption in the 1980s see Walter Benn Michaels, *The Gold Standard and the Logic of American Naturalism* (Berkeley: University of California Press, 1986), 12–9. Consumption Studies was born during this time period with the work of social historians such as Richard Fox and Jackson Lears, and subsequently used by literary critics.

51. Naomi Klein, for example, has suggested that there is an increase in brands and an intensification of the processing of branding in a finance-based economy. See Naomi Klein, *No Logo* (London: Picador, 1999), 3–67.

52. Donald Trump, *The Art of the Deal* (New York: Harper Collins, 1987), 21.

53. Fredric Jameson, "Culture and Finance Capital" in *The Cultural Turn* (New York: Verso, 1998), 148.

Chapter 4

1. I introduce the chapter with the quotation from Cherry because it is the first recorded literary use of the term "savings and loan," here as metaphor. I suggest that the savings and loans crisis was already, in 1991, on its way to become a problem of representation.

2. *Newsweek*, May 27, 1985, 30.

3. For a thorough journalistic account of the S&L crisis in its entirety, see *Inside Job* by Stephen Pizzo, Mary Fricker, and Paul Muolo, (New York: McGraw Hill, 1989).

4. My own freedom of appellation is important, for it signals that there is no codified name for this event, which has been known as the S&L crises, the S&L debacle, the S&L scandal, the S&L scandals, and the S&L frauds. Indeed, there is no codified event to which any of these names necessarily refer—although many of them hint that it was a criminal one.

5. John Kenneth Galbraith, "The Ultimate Scandal," *New York Review of Books,* Jan 18, 1990, 1. Galbraith was wrong here, obviously. New, revisionist, and much more academic accounts of the crisis continue to be published. See the recent one by William K. Black, *The Best Way to Rob a Bank Is to Own One* (Austin: University of Texas Press, 2005). See also Kitty Calavita, Henry N. Pontell, and Robert Tillman, *Big Money Crime* (Berkeley: University of California Press, 1997).

6. When S&Ls were deregulated and allowed to take more risk, the amount of insurance the federal government provided increased from $40,000 to $100,000. Many criminologists cite this as the key ingredient of so much systematic fraud.

7. R. T. Naylor's book review, "Fraud Cops and Bank Robbers: The S and L Debacle Revisited" in *Crime, Law and Social Change* 45 (2006): 231–39, 235.

8. Mark Danner in *The New Yorker,* September 24, 1990, as accessed on April 24, 2012, http://www.markdanner.com/articles/show/88.

9. See the *Columbia Review of Journalism*'s critique of journalistic coverage of the S&L crisis. November/December 1990, "The Mob, The CIA, and the S&L Scandal" by Steve Weinberg.

10. Thus this may be an early example of the "ungovernability" of "the economy" because it is outside of representation, an argument made by critics as diverse as Hayek and Foucault. The suggestion is found James Scott, *Seeing Like a State* (New Haven, CT: Yale University Press, 1998), 105.

11. *Big Money Crime*, 12.

12. Hudson, *The Monster*, 20. There is no date cited, so it's impossible to say if this was after Reagan's claim, but it does seem likely.

13. Allen Pussey, "S&Ls: How They Self-Destructed," *The Dallas Morning News*, Nov. 8, 1987, 11.

14. This is not a strictly causal claim, however. For an interesting discussion of how the definition of money itself changed in this period, and the manner in which monetarist economics requires additional forms of money that it itself does not consider money, see R.T. Naylor, *Hot Money and the Politics of Debt* (New York: Linden Publishers, 1976), 72. Even if money changes at the level of buying power or relationship to government debt, however,

so many kinds of money are always so many kinds of representation of the same thing, namely value itself.

15. The genealogy as I'm thinking of it goes something like this: first Baudrillard, particularly his *The Mirror of Production*; then Derrida, with his *Given Time* and David Harvey with his *The Condition of Postmodernity* (New York: Wiley Blackwell, 1991), which makes (still) the clearest link between flexible accumulation and cultural form. In this chapter, I am drawing on sources that do not use the term financialization, so I use it less. As I make clear, both here and in the introduction, I understand neoliberalism to be the political order of financialization; postmodernism is the aesthetic order.

16. See David Harvey, *Brief History of Neoliberalism* (New York: Oxford, 2006) for a good overview of this argument.

17. Again, I draw on the institutional history of postmodernism, from Jameson et al. See also Marazzi, *Capital and Language*.

18. Derrida, *Given Time*, 129.

19. David Harvey defines postmodernity as "dominated by fiction, fantasy, the immaterial (particularly money), fictitious capital, images, ephemerality," *The Condition of Postmodernity* (New York: Wiley Blackwell, 1989), 339.

20. Michael Tratner has provided a great account of the rise of the theory itself in relation to a change in economics. See "Derrida's Debt to Milton Friedman," *New Literary History: A Journal of Theory and Interpretation* 34, no. 4 (2003 Autumn): 791–806. For my understanding of historical abstraction, see Marx, *Grundrisse*, first notebook, especially pp. 95–108.

21. Which, according to Michael Hudson in *The Monster*, really began in Orange Country.

22. Jean Baudrillard, *America* (New York: Verso, 1989), 61.

23. Brian Rotman's term "xenomoney" is similar to hot money but not identical; he does not use the term. Rotman defines xenomoney as that which "anonymises itself with respect to individuals and states," and has undergone a process of deixis, or loss of index while hot many requires indexes and banks. The difference may, however, be more a matter of scale and methodology. See *Signifying Nothing*, 90.

24. Hot money was given its first descriptive/theoretical elaboration in 1987 with Naylor's *Hot Money and the Politics of Debt,* which I have already cited several times.

25. When, for example, Arrighi describes "capital flight" over a time-space axis in *The Long Twentieth Century,* he is in fact describing "hot money."

26. See Peggy Lenoux, "The Seamy Side of Florida Banking" for example, in *The New York Times,* Feb. 5, 1984, section 3, p.1

27. Clare Anbserry, "Money Talks, But Not So Loudly as You Might Think at this S and L," *Wall Street Journal*, June 19, 1986, p. 33.

28. LiPuma and Lee, for example, mention it once where it is equated with speculative capital in *Derivatives and the Globalization of Risk*, 127.

29. See Rosa Luxembourg, *The Accumulation of Capital,* for her argument about capital's need for geographic expansion.

30. It had circulated intensely before Bretton Woods was instituted, and then increased again with the collapse of that agreement. Timothy Mitchell has claimed that the central concern of the Bretton Woods Accords was the prevention of financial speculation, in part constituted by the circulation of hot money. See all of chap. 6 in his *Carbon Democracy* (London: Verso, 2012).

31. See my introduction for the relationship between overaccumulation and financialization.

32. I do, however, agree with the claim that the system of capitalism produces recurrent crises of overaccumulation and that financialization itself is an answer to the question of what to do with excess money. I accept that logic as an organizing one without having any real interest in the sinews of arguments for and against this particular Marxist reading of capital's logic. My own thinking has been informed by Ernest Mandel, for example, and his claim that: "The thesis that Keynesianism will ultimately provoke a serious economic crisis by inflation, which [Hayek] has put forward with remarkable obstinacy for years seems to be unchallengeable in the long-run. The only point is that for Hayek this leads to the familiar alternative between the devil and the deep blue sea: to prevent a serious economic crisis in the long-run, [Hayek] has consistently advocated an economic policy which would have unleashed the same economic crisis in the short-run. A retrospective look at the world of 1945–50 is all that is needed to understand why the governments of the victorious imperialist powers could not have regarded such an alternative as realistic…Keynes' classic answer to his critics [was]: 'in the long-run we are all dead.' It was an outlook of a class condemned by history" (Mandel, 415n23).

33. *Big Money Crime*, 43.

34. My knowledge here comes from *Big Money Crime*. The fact that the "deregulation" of the S&L industry included an *increase* in government insurance calls into question what, exactly, deregulation means. For an excellent take on deregulation and neoliberalism, see Leo Panitch and Martijn Konigs, "Myths of Neoliberal Deregulation," *New Left Review* 57 (May–June 2009).

35. Obviously, this was much less exciting when S&Ls financed conservative home mortgages, but it was much more of a boon when an institution could rely on this insurance to finance speculative business loans.

36. From "Showdown at Gunbelt."

37. *Barron's* Jul. 22 1991, 10.

38. *Big Money Crime*, 46.

39. See "Arkansas Thrift, Now Failed, Left $190 Million Dallas Project in a Hole" in *The American Banker*, Dec. 16, 1985 (no author provided).

40. From *Inside Job*, 3. Quotation from Edwin Gray. "Edwin Gray, chairman of the Federal Home Loan Bank Board (FHLBB), discovered something had gone very wrong. On March 14, 1984, he received in the morning dispatch a classified report and videotape from the Dallas Federal Home Loan Bank."

41. Rotman, 93.

42. Leslie Wayne, "Showdown at 'Gunbelt' Savings," *New York Times*, Mar, 12, 1989, p. F1; Eric N. Berg, "The Lapses by Lincoln's Auditors," *New York Times*, Dec. 28, 1989, D1.

43. I have located many articles similar in structure, style, and conclusions to these two, which leads me to believe there was a rubric for these stories that was imitated by other business reports and that these stories circulated through wire reports.

44. The articles themselves acknowledge this twin posturing of describing and transacting by repeatedly including the presence of the S&Ls' professional auditors, whose mission it was to scrutinize transactions. Indeed the individual articles that constitute the archive are frequently structured around the problem of reading and comprehending transactions: "After a huge bailout, the U.S. points the finger at auditor Grant Thorton" (Gunbelt).

45. Jameson, *The Cultural Turn*, 161.

46. LiPuma and Lee, *Financial Derivatives and the Globalization of Risk*, 17.

47. See Annie McClanahan's "Investing in Late Capitalism's Future," *The Journal of Cultural Economy* 6, no. 1, (2013): 78–93. See also, Joshua Clover, "Value/Theory/Crisis," especially pp. 110–11.

48. See Hoberek, op. cit. and Stephen *Fantasies of the New Class* (New York: Columbia University Press, 2011).

49. Thus it is unsurprising that some of our most incisive critiques of contemporary capital, for example David Simon's *The Wire*, foreground the dividing line between "clean" an illicit money through people of color; one could make a similar case for David Chase *The Sopranos*. See my "Capitalist Realism and Serial Form: The Fifth Season of *The Wire*," in *Criticism,* ed. Paul Farber and Robert LeVertis Bell. For the argument about the money and ethnic embodiment in *The Sopranos*, see "Waddaya Lookin' at? Re-Reading the Gangster Genre through 'The Sopranos,'" in *Film Quarterly* 56, no. 2 (Winter, 2002–2003): 2–13.

50. John Kenneth Galbraith makes a different point in his *New York Review* essay of books about the S&L crisis: "Both government and the public give special deference to crime in the field of high finance" ("The Ultimate Scandal," 2).

51. "Cops and Robbers" (235).

52. *Big Money Crime*, but this is a standard conception.

53. The transition from value to price, which I gloss over here, has given rise to the famous "Transformation Problem" in Marxist economics. See the work of Pierro Sraffa, particularly, as well as that of Joan Robinson and Henryk Grossman.

54. Marx in Jameson, *The Representation of Labor*, 104; Marx cited *Capital* v. I, 733.

55. This new field includes the work of Michel Callon, Donald MacKenzie, and now also Alex Preda. Its organizing rubric is one of "performativity" and I consider this problem herein. Appropriately, Judith Butler herself has joined this conversation and engaged this notion of economic performativity. See Judith Butler, "Performative Agency" in, *The Journal of Cultural Economy* 3, no. 2 (2010): 147–61.

56. MacKenzie, *An Engine, Not a Camera*, 19.

57. Ibid.

58. Ibid.

59. A contemporary example of a similar problem is found in the LIBOR case. In July, 2012 an international scandal broke around LIBOR, or the London Inter-Bank Offered Rate. As David Harvey has suggested, the interest rate is "a representation of value." LIBOR is an interest rate, a representation of the cost of money calculated, no doubt, through an economic model. But, scandalously, it turns out that LIBOR was being used as a strategy, a way to make money through representation—a fact that is in no way an indictment of its efficacy. But see, for example, Dean Baker writing in *Al-Jazeera*, http://www.cepr.net/index. php/op-eds-&-columns/op-eds-&-columns/the-fed-ben-bernanke-and-the-rotten-libor. A scandal like LIBOR ends a model's performative service. But, as Judith Butler makes clear, performativity always includes failure. If the theory presumes efficacity, then it fails to see that breakdown is constitutive of performativity (performativity never fully achieves its effect, and so in this sense "fails" all the time; its failure is what necessitates its reiterative temporality, and we cannot think iterability without failure). Its moments of breakdown are also important for another version of "critique."

60. Anita Cramer, May 7, 1989, *Dallas Morning News*, A1.

61. *Newsweek* May 21, 1990, 31.

62. See his aptly titled study *The Best Way to Rob a Bank Is to Own One*.

63. John Kenneth Galbraith quoted in Engelen et al. 2010, 37.

64. From "Gunbelt"; "Lapses"; *Newsweek*; *Dallas Morning News*.

65. Quentin Hardy, "How Tech Killed Finance," *Forbes*, Nov 6, 2009, 14.

66. Pete Brewton, *The Mafia, CIA & George Bush: The Untold Story of America's Greatest Financial Debacle* (New York: Spi Books Trade 1992).

67. Hayden White, "The Value of Narrativity in the Representation of Reality," *Critical Inquiry* 7, no. 1, On Narrative (Autumn, 1980): 5–27, 24.

68. The *Corporate Crime Reporter* was founded in 1987 and began to track precisely this kind of "capital" crime.

69. See Rafferty for great rejection of this logic. He suggests that all money is credit based.

70. For a very different and very provocative reading of Melville, confidence, and forms of money and debt see Ngai, *Ugly Feelings*.

71. For Edelman, of course, reproductive futurism is like a Ponzi-scheme (*No Future,* 4); here the reverse would be true: A Ponzi scheme is like reproductive futurism.

72. See Fredric Jameson, *The Geopolitical Aesthetic: Cinema and Space in the World System* (Bloomington: Indiana University Press 1992), 39.

73. For a reading of *Good Faith* in relation to other financial fiction, see Alison Shonkwiler's Ph.D. thesis, *The Financial Imaginary*, Rutgers, the State University of New Jersey, 2007. mss3.libraries.rutgers.edu/dlr/outputds.php?pid=rutgers-lib.

74. See: http://www.bookbrowse.com/author_interviews/full/index.cfm/author_number/298/jane-smiley for the full interview. Accessed, March 21, 2012.

75. Shonkwiler locates key phrases that substantiate a claim about the genre-fiction nature of this text, for example Marcus "laughs heartily" repeatedly.

76. As with my reading of *American Psycho*, this is a very different conception of genre in that it's multimodal and economically oriented. Rather like Michael Clune's "economic novel" except it is not confined to the novel. See Black, *The Best Way to Rob a Bank Is to Own One*.

77. Indeed, in the journalism this is the precise subject position assumed.

78. Bryan et al explain the process of monetization well: "It involves the proposition that the processes of securitization and financial derivatives, both of which have been growing rapidly for over 20 years, involve the commodification of finance, converting monetary processes into commodity relations (Bryan and Rafferty 2006). This commodification serves to blur the distinction between money and capital, giving a range of monetary interactions, once considered simply processes of exchange, a new meaning," 459.

79. Black, *The Best Way to Rob a Bank Is to Own One,* 49.

80. This turn furthers its place as period fiction. In the 1980s and in its historical fiction, to represent finance is likely to represent financial print culture, even in film. Think of such films as *Trading Places* (1983) or *The Secret of My Success* (1987), both of which repeatedly turn to the daily gossip of *The Wall Street Journal* in addition to its daily commodity prices.

81. Marx, *Grundrisse*, 108.

Coda

1. Edward LiPuma and Benjamin Lee, *Financial Derivatives and the Globalization of Risk* (Durham, NC: Duke University Press, 2004), 17.

2. Jonathan Franzen, *The Twenty-Seventh City* (New York: Harper Collins, 2003), 76.

3. David Foster Wallace, *The Pale King* (Boston: Back Bay Books, 2012), reprint.

4. *Book Forum* has recently put out an issue on money and fiction devoted to tracking precisely the flourishing of new titles in a Great Recession, post–Occupy Wall Street world, in June/July/August 2012.

5. *Forbes*, Oct. 20, 1989.

{ INDEX }

Made in the USA
Las Vegas, NV
19 February 2021